Ensuring Quality in Professional Education
Volume II

Karen Trimmer
Tara Newman • Fernando F. Padró
Editors

Ensuring Quality in Professional Education Volume II

Engineering Pedagogy and International Knowledge Structures

palgrave
macmillan

Editors
Karen Trimmer
University of Southern Queensland
Toowoomba, QLD, Australia

Tara Newman
Texas State University
San Marcos, TX, USA

Fernando F. Padró
University of Southern Queensland
Toowoomba, QLD, Australia

ISBN 978-3-030-01083-6   ISBN 978-3-030-01084-3   (eBook)
https://doi.org/10.1007/978-3-030-01084-3

Library of Congress Control Number: 2018962369

© The Editor(s) (if applicable) and The Author(s), under exclusive licence to Springer Nature Switzerland AG 2019
This work is subject to copyright. All rights are solely and exclusively licensed by the Publisher, whether the whole or part of the material is concerned, specifically the rights of translation, reprinting, reuse of illustrations, recitation, broadcasting, reproduction on microfilms or in any other physical way, and transmission or information storage and retrieval, electronic adaptation, computer software, or by similar or dissimilar methodology now known or hereafter developed.
The use of general descriptive names, registered names, trademarks, service marks, etc. in this publication does not imply, even in the absence of a specific statement, that such names are exempt from the relevant protective laws and regulations and therefore free for general use.
The publisher, the authors and the editors are safe to assume that the advice and information in this book are believed to be true and accurate at the date of publication. Neither the publisher nor the authors or the editors give a warranty, express or implied, with respect to the material contained herein or for any errors or omissions that may have been made. The publisher remains neutral with regard to jurisdictional claims in published maps and institutional affiliations.

Cover illustration: © GLYPHstock / Getty

This Palgrave Macmillan imprint is published by the registered company Springer Nature Switzerland AG
The registered company address is: Gewerbestrasse 11, 6330 Cham, Switzerland

Acknowledgements

The editors are very grateful to the following individuals without whom this book would not have been published:

* Ms Eleanor Christie and the editorial team at Palgrave Macmillan for all their work in getting this publication to press
* Ms Katrina Wilson for her attention to detail and patience in copy-editing the manuscript and composing the index
* The chapter authors for their respective chapters and for engaging wholeheartedly with feedback from editors and peer reviewers
* The scholars who provided double blind peer reviews of one or more submitted chapters:

    – Associate Professor Lindy-Anne Abawi, University of Southern Queensland, Australia
    – Associate Professor Dorothy Andrews, University of Southern Queensland, Australia
    – Dr Peter Ayriss, University of Southern Queensland, Australia
    – Associate Professor Lyn Brodie, University of Southern Queensland, Australia
    – Dr Chris Browne, Australian National University, Canberra, Australia

- Associate Professor Joan Conway, University of Southern Queensland, Australia
- Matt Eliot, Central Queensland University, Australia
- Professor Joy Higgs, Charles Sturt University, Sydney, Australia
- Mrs Vicki Horner, University of Southern Queensland, Australia
- Professor Margaret Jollands, Associate Dean School of Engineering, RMIT University, Victoria, Australia
- Associate Professor Warren Midgley, University of Southern Queensland, Australia
- Professor Sid Nair, Executive Director, Tertiary Education Commission, Mauritius
- Sasha Nikolic, University of Wollongong, NSW, Australia
- Professor Shirley O'Neill, University of Southern Queensland, Australia
- Associate Professor Petrea Redmond, University of Southern Queensland, Australia
- Professor Cath Rogers, University of Southern Queensland, Australia
- Dr Cheryl Ross, University of Southern Queensland, Australia
- Dr Ashley Schmitt, Texas A&M University, USA
- Mr Jay Somasundarams, Central Queensland University, Australia
- Associate Professor Linda Sweet, Flinders University, South Australia
- Mr Mark Symes, University of Tasmania, Australia
- Robert Templeton, University of Southern Queensland, Toowoomba, Australia
- Dr Victoria Terry, University of Southern Queensland, Australia
- Professor James Trevelyan, The University of Western Australia
- Jaclyn Viera, Judson Independent School District, Texas, USA

* Our colleagues for their continuing encouragement and interest
* Our families and friends for their inexhaustible love and support.

Karen Trimmer, Tara Newman and Fernando F. Padró
Editors

Contents

1 How about Professionalism, Professions and Standards: The Creation of Acculturated Professionals   1
   Fernando F. Padró, Megan Y. C. A. Kek, Nona Press, Karen Trimmer, Jonathan H. Green, Michael Hawke, and Laurie Hawke

2 Evaluating the Student Experience: A Critical Review of the Use of Surveys to Enhance the Student Experience   29
   Rhona Sharpe

3 'Quality' in an Era of Austerity: Challenges for Irish Universities   47
   Marie Clarke

4 Accessing Expert Understanding: The Value of Visualising Knowledge Structures in Professional Education   71
   Ian M. Kinchin

5 Serving Ethically: A Developing Country Perspective on Quality Education for Professional Practice 91
Jeanette Baird

6 Interrogating the Value of Learning by Extension in Enhancing Professional Quality: The Case of Australian and Venezuelan Engineers 115
David Thorpe, Emilio A. Anteliz, and P. A. Danaher

7 Developing Engineering Knowledge and Skills: The Advanced Engineering Project Management Course at USQ 139
David Thorpe

8 Designing Quality Engineering Curricula to Produce Industry Ready Graduates: A Whole of Course Approach 161
Neal Lake and Julienne Holt

9 Incorporating Sustainable Engineering (SEng) Within a Course Featuring Social, Political and Economic Contexts 183
Ian Craig, David Thorpe, and Tara Newman

10 The Transformative Dimensions of Professional Curriculum Quality Enhancement 201
Sara Hammer

References 215

Index 291

List of Contributors

Emilio A. Anteliz Faculty of Engineering, Central University of Venezuela, Caracas, Venezuela

Jeanette Baird Divine Word University, Madang, Papua New Guinea

Marie Clarke University College Dublin, Dublin, Ireland

Ian Craig Civil Engineering and Surveying—Faculty of Health, Engineering and Sciences, University of Southern Queensland, Toowoomba, QLD, Australia

P. A. Danaher University of Southern Queensland, Toowoomba, QLD, Australia
Central Queensland University, Rockhampton, QLD, Australia
University of Helsinki, Helsinki, Finland

Jonathan H. Green University of Southern Queensland, Toowoomba, QLD, Australia

Sara Hammer Office for the Advancement of Learning and Teaching, University of Southern Queensland, Toowoomba, QLD, Australia

Laurie Hawke Tarleton State University, Stephenville, TX, USA

Michael Hawke Tarleton State University, Stephenville, TX, USA

Julienne Holt Centre of Teaching & Learning, Southern Cross University, Lismore, NSW, Australia

Megan Y. C. A. Kek University of Southern Queensland, Toowoomba, QLD, Australia

Ian M. Kinchin Department of Higher Education, University of Surrey, Guildford, UK

Neal Lake Centre of Teaching & Learning, Southern Cross University, Lismore, NSW, Australia

Tara Newman Department of Curriculum and Instruction, Texas State University, San Marcos, TX, USA

Fernando F. Padró University of Southern Queensland, Toowoomba, QLD, Australia

Nona Press Office for the Advancement of Learning and Teaching, University of Southern Queensland, Toowoomba, QLD, Australia

Rhona Sharpe Department of Technology Enhanced Learning, University of Surrey, Guildford, UK

David Thorpe University of Southern Queensland, Toowoomba, QLD, Australia

Karen Trimmer University of Southern Queensland, Toowoomba, QLD, Australia

List of Figures

Fig. 2.1	Aspects of the undergraduate student experience and typical UK indicators	32
Fig. 4.1	A concept map to emphasise the key features of excellent concept maps	74
Fig. 4.2	The semantic plane indicating the typical knowledge structures that are likely to populate the quadrants (modified from Kinchin, 2016)	78
Fig. 4.3	The expert clinician's complex network of understanding may contain all sorts of uncertainties that are not passed on to the patient—who is *left* with a simplified and 'certain' chain of practice (from Kinchin, Cabot, & Hay, 2008a)	82
Fig. 4.4	An expert's knowledge structure of the application of local anaesthesia (LA) in dentistry (after Clarke, 2011), indicating the chain of practice (to the *left*) that is informed by the network of understanding (to the *right*)	83
Fig. 6.1	Conceptual framework for chapter discussion	120
Fig. 8.1	Embedded competency development model	173
Fig. 9.1	Three overlapping circles illustrating sustainability, as it relates to engineering studies. The circles suggest 27 Sustainable Engineering (SEng) topics, for purposes of discussion across university engineering departments	185

Fig. 9.2 Useful summary of climate information for engineers, regarding scenarios for future atmospheric carbon dioxide concentration (ppm), depicting three possible strategies: (1) 'Resilience' i.e. minimal incorporation of renewables into the energy mix, business as usual, strengthen emergency services, sharpen disaster response procedures, could be expensive and cost more than ~20% of global GDP in the longer term, according to Stern (2006), (2) 'Adaptation' i.e. gradual incorporation of renewable energy, deployment of major drought, fire and flood mitigation civil engineering projects, profitable, achievable, would provide employment, aim to stabilize CO_2 concentration at somewhere below 500 ppm, might cost 1–2% global GDP initially, and (3) 'Mitigation' i.e. rapid move to 100% renewable energy, appropriate engineering technology deployed with the aim to actually start decreasing atmospheric CO_2 concentration after 2050—would require an investment of ~5% global GDP initially 191

List of Tables

Table 2.1   Oxford Brookes University undergraduate student surveys 2015/16   33
Table 2.2   Comparison of satisfaction and engagement style questions   36
Table 7.1   Evaluation of course against desired development objectives   153
Table 7.2   Learner responses to "My Opinion" survey for 2015 course delivery   155

1

How about Professionalism, Professions and Standards: The Creation of Acculturated Professionals

Fernando F. Padró, Megan Y. C. A. Kek, Nona Press, Karen Trimmer, Jonathan H. Green, Michael Hawke, and Laurie Hawke

Introduction

Pitsoe and Letseka (2018) recently pointed out that the discussion about quality—particularly quality management systems (QMS) or what is also known as total quality management (TQM)—lacks an analytical framework based on the ideology, ontological and ontological-epistemological problems it represents. Deming (1994) called for a system of profound knowledge (SPK) to act as a theoretical map to understand organisations; however, the literature on quality has focused on application rather than underlying principles. This limitation eventually creates challenges in looking at the deeper reciprocal influences shaping the meaning of quality by an individual, an organisation and a community.

F. F. Padró (✉) • M. Y. C. A. Kek • N. Press • K. Trimmer • J. H. Green
University of Southern Queensland, Toowoomba, QLD, Australia
e-mail: Fernando.Padro@usq.edu.au

M. Hawke • L. Hawke
Tarleton State University, Stephenville, TX, USA

© The Author(s) 2019
K. Trimmer et al. (eds.), *Ensuring Quality in Professional Education Volume II*,
https://doi.org/10.1007/978-3-030-01084-3_1

One area where the lack of an understanding of what quality represents in terms of ideology, ontology and epistemology is professional education. A discussion of quality in relation to preparing students to enter into professions is per force a conversation about the nexus between higher education institutions (HEIs), professional associations or organization, (oftentimes parallel) government regulatory or accrediting bodies and employers. Each has a different view, often tacitly shaped by ideology of what a profession is and what a professional should do to benefit society. Schumpeter (2003) said that a capitalistic culture, higher education increases the supply of professionals beyond "the point determined by cost-return considerations" (p. 152). Today the sentence is completed by placing the considerations on individual students as well, employers, governments and professional associations. Context and notions of quality differ between these entities based on expectations, intentions, needs and preferences related to the transformation of someone wanting to be a professional becoming a professional (Reeves & Bednar, 1994; Rogers, 2014; Taylor, 2009; Yielder, 2004).

Per Noordegraaf (2011), professional education "is a resource for producing content (knowledge, skills, norms, rituals, subjectivities, etc.) and an actor in professionalization processes (selection, credentials, operation of closure regimes, symbols, etc." – p. 470, italics in original). Thus, upon graduation, individuals reflect job values that are a composite of personal achievement goals and job values shaped by their educational experience (Bråten & Strømsø, 2008). The value of the credentials within professions is both an endogenous and exogenous motivator in the sense that personal values driving motivation often work alongside extrinsic factors such as status, employability and compensation. All told, this reflects the transformative effects from changing a frame of reference as suggested by Mezirow (1997). Quality is more than a managed set of processes based on pre-determined standards and performance indicators; it is a reflection of a moral level commitment to a profession and professional practice on the part of those teaching in the programs and program graduates (Cheng, 2016).

For the remainder of the chapter, the focus is on defining quality within professional education settings. First discussed is how curriculum reflects quality **FOR** purpose—the one concept typically discussed in the quality literature—and quality **OF** purpose driving the rationale for quality. Then discussed are intrinsic attributes of quality shaping how quality is defined and treated. Finally, there is an overview discussion of how the perception of quality is shaped in professional education programs.

Quality FOR Purpose and Quality OF Purpose in a Professional Education Context

Curricula in professional fields and their constituent bodies of knowledge are vehicles for the initiation of new recruits (Jarvis, 1999). Features in defining quality for professional education programs include:

* The demonstration of the effectiveness of the identification and clarification of how the transformation of professional practice into adequate curricular elements in a manner that facilitates the learner's ability to integrate into the profession (Dall'Alba, 2009; Westbroek, Klaassen, Bulte, & Pilot, 2010). The curriculum crafted by higher education institutions (HEIs) includes introductory, reinforcing and extending 'expertise' coursework to begin the transformative journey of becoming a professional.
* The changing of the learner's frame of reference in reference to meaning through the contextualizing information and knowledge into a personal theory of action characterizing individual practice once performing the duties of the professional (Mezirow, 1997). The four elements from 'Prospect Theory' established by Kahneman and Tversky (1979) and Tversky and Kahneman (1992) act as potential bounding elements in this transition as these help explain the ecosystem influences on learners as suggested by Bronfenbrenner's bioecological model of human development (Bronfenbrenner & Morris, 2006): reference dependence, loss aversion, diminishing sensitivity and probability weighting.
* The workforce implications relating to the preparation of professionals; namely, the degree of expertise and the benefits that expertise provides end-users (clients or employers), the overall addition to the

nation's intellectual capital and broader social contribution based on achievement (community service and taxes). Experiences and preferences defined by professional bodies and/or regulatory bodies (depending on the professional field) inform and influence curriculum content through their benchmarks, criteria or standards. These entities shape in-class and co-curricular practices as their input represent the ever-changing expectations resulting from changing socio-economic needs (e.g., personal qualities and dispositions, organisation of work and workplaces), new technologies and the dynamics of job churning (Askenazy & Galbis, 2007; Billett, 2010; Press & Padró, 2017). All of the identified players add to but are not solely responsible for identifying preferred and required professional craft knowledge (technical or 'hard" skills—Higgs & Titchen, 2001; Kemmis, 2005) and the 'soft' skills such as collaboration, creativity/innovation, emotional intelligence, ethics, and leadership potential. Nevertheless, the triadic relationship does not always achieve expected results automatically. As Ericsson (2008) noted, 'superior performance does not automatically develop from extensive experience, general education, and domain-related knowledge' (p. 993).

Ultimately, the principal underlying element in establishing the presence of quality is the notion of fitness. Juran and Gryna (1970) made the case that the notion of 'fitness for use' is the basic meaning of the term 'quality.' Juran and Godfrey (1999) later distinguished between 'fitness for use' and conformance to focus on two types of decision-making related to the product, that of meeting needs versus those of conformance to specifications. Harvey and Green's (1993) definition of quality for higher education identifies 'fitness for purpose' as one of the five elements that make up quality for HEIs and the broader tertiary and higher education sectors. "Fitness for purpose" under Harvey and Green (1993) again seems to combine the aspects of meeting customer needs and conformance; however, the note the difficulty is how to frame 'fitness for purpose' as a concept. They noted how the students, for the most part, do not specify the product. They also noted how student satisfaction affects the curriculum and program offerings; yet, control of the curriculum and programs is in the hands of the providers. It seems that the unique features of the tertiary and higher education sectors challenging how quality can be determined was the reason why Harvey and Green (1993) decided to combine conformance and satisfaction in their definition in contrast to the approach taken by Juran—one of the seminal figures in the field of Quality—and his colleagues.

Swan (1998) suggested that due to quality neither being a 'thing' or a unidimensional characteristic, quality for HEIs should be seen in terms of 'fitness of purpose' and 'fitness for purpose.' For him, 'fitness of purpose' is about HEIs doing the 'right thing', things like 'pursuing knowledge and truth, cultivating intellect, creating individuality, teaching effectively and provoking critical and creative thinking' (p. 273). The implication is regarding whether HEIs are doing what they should be doing rather than looking at performance from a process perspective. Implicit, yet, in keeping with the literature there is a sense of considering the link between HEI mission, its programs and stakeholders (e.g., Harvey & Green, 1993). This is in contrast to the guarantee- or warranty-based view of 'fitness for purpose' as meeting intention. Looking at the distinction between '**fitness FOR**' and "**fitness OF**" provides a broader basis of understanding as it potentially provides a prospective, transformative view similar to Biggs and Tang's (2007) conceptualization of quality enhancement (QE). The question now becomes whether this distinction enhances or mitigates the political aspects behind the interest in developing a definition of quality and demonstrating its presence.

The Nature of Quality: Attributes of Quality

Below is a list of attributes that shape notions of quality. These do not directly focus on the application of quality as a process. These are primarily ontological in nature, shaping the definition of quality, its manifestation and interpretation by all parties involved. Noticeable is how these flow from one to the other in many regards. These are not discrete, separate attributes. Rather, they build on each other, shaping how quality is ultimately determined.

Quality Is Throughput

Quality as currently conceived and enacted is a throughput proposition due to conformance or compliance, especially because quality—as an indicator—is a legitimizing proposition of existing processes (Bekkers & Edwards, 2007; Lieberherr, 2013; Padró, Hawke, & Hawke, 2016). While what there is of the literature does not directly provide this linkage and often see the two as parallel elements, the nexus between the two is easy to see and the relationship between the two suggests that quality better reflects what happens when an organisation performs its functions.

Throughput, for the purposes of this chapter is the intermediary dimension of organizational performance (cf. Lieberherr, 2013), referring to the transformation of available resources (the input) through reorganization via interlocking processes to achieve an output (Katz & Kahn, 1978)—in the case of HEIs, the education and achievement of a professional. Other definitions of throughput found in the literature to keep in the back of one's mind include:

- Use as a six-sigma metric (*roll throughput yield*) as the yield based on the probability of passing a unit defect free throughout the assembly process (e.g., Chaudhuri, Mukhopadhyay, & Ghosn, 2011).
- An orientation process (*throughput orientation*—TO) to manage constraints, manage cross-functional performance measures and set a mindset ensuring stability and growth through increased throughput (e.g., Sahi, Gupta, & Patel, 2017).
- A consideration to time (amount of work done during a specified time) and volume that, in higher education is based on the number of students passing through a course or a program over time (e.g., Hagström & Scheja, 2014; Lindberg, 2014).

Throughput processes are utility-based in the sense of allowing organisations to bring all of the necessary resources to bear to create a desired outcome or product. Throughput reflects and *ipso facto* legitimizes the resulting connectivity that allows the transformation of input to output. It is, therefore, an administrative task as it is one of governance specifying the quality of the processes involved in the transformation (Padró & Hawke, 2003; van Meerkerk, Edelenbos, & Klijn, 2015).

Miles and Snow (1978) suggested organisations perform have three distinct performance areas: entrepreneurial (environmental scanning translating into strategies, action plans and key indicators), administrative (reducing uncertainty by balancing internal interests and managing processes) and engineering (the operationalization of processes ensuring the creation of the output based on specifications). Throughput elements exist within the administrative and engineering areas of the organisation. Padró and Hawke (2003) used the term 'efficiency throughput' to identify how internal processes monitored performance to ensure (and assure) that external expectations were translated into internal indicators as part of the rationalization process identifying and bringing together resources to create the product/generate the outcome. Within the HEI environment, this 'efficiency throughput' refers to the institution-wide and program level administrative activities in place to create the environment allowing enrollees to become graduates. The processes in place here relate to the program-level quality control (QC) loops feeding into the broader quality assurance (QA) processes. In contrast, the term 'effectiveness throughput' describes the selection and use of measures to track conformance to ensure (and assure) that expectations and/or standards are met upon completion of the creation/transformation processes. Within the HEI context, 'effectiveness throughput' refers to the enactment of the designed curricular and co-curricular experiences leading to graduation and opportunity for employment in appropriate profession tracks. QE can occur here based on the operationalization of improvement-based follow-up activities identified.

Quality, particularly the QA aspect, in this model is a throughput activity that helps explain and understand the tensions between input elements and output results and their resolution (cf. Lieberherr, 2013). The impact is the HEIs ability to demonstrate organizational integrity through 'stability' (Padró & Hawke, 2003). "Stability" is not equilibrium, as Pascale (1999) pointed out, as that implies remaining in place without changing and thus improving. Instead, 'stability' reflects what Maturana and Varela (1980) termed an *autopoietic organisation*, an organisation that is autonomous, self-referring and self-constructing. 'Every observation [of and within the organisation] must hold to difference schemata that enable it to draw conclusions about what, in distinction to other things, functions as a unit' (Luhmann, 1995, p. 35). In this respect, both the concepts 'of purpose' and 'for purpose' are important elements in the determination of quality (presence) as they encompass self-reference ('of'), self-constructing ('for') and, hopefully, QE aspects of HEIs based on identifying and maintaining the right purpose and how internal systems meet intended purpose. QE plays a complementary role to QA, particularly in terms of learning and teaching given its deliberate and transformative character (Elassy, 2015; Lomas, 2004; Middlehurst, 1997 as cited in Wong, 2012).

Quality Is Intentional (It Is Purposed)

Quality in the broader sense is intentional from operational and aspirational perspectives for HEIs, learners and stakeholders. Harvey and Green's (1993) identifies transformation as one of the five elements of quality in higher education. Although Harvey and Green (1993) indicate the potential challenge to 'fitness for purpose' because of the quality movement's service-based approach, they also note context as a mediator between transformation and fitness. Sustainable and viable reproduction is the most fundamental aspect of any organisation in terms of its maintaining relevance and, thus, continuity. 'For purpose' is a reproduction element in that it ensures relevance, sustainability and viability from the perspective of desirability of the output. 'Of purpose' is also a reproduction element because of its attention to institutional/organisational aims to determine either drift from original purpose or the agility or lack thereof to change purpose to changing environmental contexts impacting on the demand and interest of the institution/organisation output.

There is a phenomenological perspective to quality predicated on the perceptual characteristics helping define its presence. However, the use of the word quality makes this a sometimes hard to follow discussion. The distinctions originally proposed by John Locke are referent to the object rather than the creating and assurance process that the field of Quality represents (Padró et al., 2016). Notwithstanding the conceptual challenges of intentionality as reflected in the arguments between Edmund Husserl and his former student Martin Heidegger, the idea that the ensuring-assurance process of design meeting needs is based on intention (as a form of compliance, specifically that of repetition). As Deming (1994) stated, 'A product or service possesses quality if it helps somebody and enjoys a good and sustainable market' (p. 2). Quality is about meeting certain conditions, especially when the product or service has become commonplace and expectations have changed from a 'like to have' to 'a must have' (cf. Feigenbaum, 1983). Variability—the avoidance thereof—comes into play. It is one element of Deming's (1994) *System of Profound Knowledge* (SPK). They crucial aspect of variability is making sure that every end user has access and receive the same benefits and/or satisfaction from the product, service or graduate coming out from the organisation.

Arguably, using Husserl's (1931) thinking, quality is an accessible perception of the thing to which you are alluding. As a the 'consciousness of something' (p. 120), '[intentionality] is a state of mind directing a person's attention (and therefore experience and action) toward a specific object (goal) or a path in order to achieve something (means)' (Bird, 1988, p. 442). For Husserl, intentionality provides reflexive, sense-giving to accomplishments vis a vis meaning (Steinbock, 2001) because intentionality is a contextualized state of mind and of emotions involved based on experience linked to intentionalities (Hindle, Klyver, & Jennings, 2009; Howard, 2015). Meaning thus reflects a calculus mirroring the self and the language (and grammar) used reflects the psychological mechanism behind the meaning (Wittgenstein, 1986). Psychology is another element of Deming's (1994) SPK as many aspects of quality are psychological in nature (Padró et al., 2016). Deming (1994) talked about motivation in terms of appreciation, rewards and concerns about the over-justification effect of rewards ('the shift in attribution from internal to external sources that performance-contingent rewards produce'— Cameron, Banko, & Pierce, 2001, p. 26); yet, his thrust is not to treat people as if they were the same. This is ironic given that in education the need to balance the interests of becoming competent and proficient with the individual capacity for learning that itself is influenced by different life-centred factors that shape what individuals actually learn

(Bronfenbrenner & Morris, 2006). Notwithstanding the irony, Deming's (1994) actual focus was for organisations to understand people and their interactions. This allows for a better understanding of the meaning behind the information found within organizational feedback loops, the degree of internal interest in producing the best possible output and external interest in the output.

Quality Is Immanent and Perceptual (Existing and Recognised within the Output, Organisations and Systems)

According to Husserl, intentional experiences are immanent in nature (Sheehan & Palmer, 1997). Quality, as an immanent proposition, is an embedded constituent within the outcomes achieved by universities. Quality is embodied or based on a subject, hence context-dependent, distinguishing between internal thought—that which serves as the underpinning as well as manifestation of perception—and the outward expression of the thought (Friedman, 1995; Robinson, 2010). Moreover, it is dependent on the interactions on the behaviour of the various elements within the system because, actions depend on how these elements want to engage (or not—Vanderstraeten, 2002). Evaluative judgement of the outcome is based on cognitive cues of what the outcome and its underlying processes represent based on expectation and actual experience.

As a functionalist conception, quality represents a becoming rather than the intrinsic values an object has (Deleuze & Guattari, 1987). The becoming or assembling aspect of generating is a part of the object that gives thought to the idea of quality (Peirce, 1958). Locke (1689/1952) saw quality as causal properties of an object as these allow individuals to have sensations or views pertaining to the object. As such, these sensations or views make up the consciousness regarding to the object or aspects of it (Husserl, 1931—see above). Peirce (1994) noted that qualities are concerned in facts, but they do not make up facts. Quality thus acts as a broad construction, a mnemonic representation of what the outcome stands for or, in other words as a perceptual chunk of what the outcome represents. "Perception is a source of knowledge and justification mainly by virtue of yielding beliefs that constitute knowledge or are justified" (Audi, 1988, p. 16). As such, perception is a key mechanism of human cognition, representing an efficient view of the outcome based on how an individual automatically grouped or organized the information into something that is familiar (Gobet et al., 2001; Larkin & Simon, 1987; Miller, 1956). Quality characterizes a correlational inference between the different aspects of the outcome even if the functional or technical attributes are not fully understood as the inference is based on a perceived resemblance to their cognitive prototype of the outcome (Alba & Hutchinson, 1987; Lee & Olshavsky, 1994; Roest & Rindfleisch, 2010). The concern is that perception is a definition of 'what is' based on interpretation (Heidegger, 2008/1962). It is only a representative knowledge of an object and not an understanding of the fundamental object itself, providing a "simple, formal, reflective perception" (p. 109) of the object.

Quality Represents Integrity (of Outputs, Organisations and Systems)

Benchmarks, criteria, guidelines and standards: these define the integrity of a program either in a suggestive normative perspective of recommendations or prescriptive requirements that have quasi- or fully legal implications. Integrity refers to fidelity and honesty in the performance of a duty (cf. The Law Dictionary, https://thelawdictionary.org/integrity/), thus aligning with and supporting notions of accountability, conformance and intention. Quality in this regard is the overall embodiment and representation of the outcome, providing a coherent approach toward valuing the output, organisation and whole systems. According to Dworkin (1986), integrity is purposive in legal deliberations. Integrity in the sense discussed in this narrative provides rules that are/should be adhered to and interpreted through obligations, duties of care and ethical practices defining outcomes and shaping functional expectations for the produced output. Paradoxically, obligations, duties of care and ethical practices are themselves influenced or directly shaped by external values and expectations (Padró & Hawke, 2003).

There is an instrumental element in integrity (Crowe, 2007) because it embodies an external shaping of boundaries of appropriateness based on meeting demands and/or expectations specific to the becoming and actual identity (characterization) of the outcome. First, it paves the way for consistency through fidelity to the fundamental goals of the profession and assurance of trust (Eriksen, 2015). Secondly, according to Dworkin (1986), integrity provides justification through a sense of personification with the community served and, as such, provides a means of countering skepticism of either substance (internal) or the classification of claims (external). It also defines boundaries based on conflict of interests and practices falling outside professional ethical practice and performance standards (Banks, 2010). It thus serves as a bounding element in and of practice based on "the capacity to deliberate and reflect usefully in the light of context, knowledge, experience, and information (that of self and others) on complex and conflicting factors bearing on action or potential action" (Edgar & Pattison, 2011, p. 94).

Temporality

Quality is time-bound in two respects: (1) relating to the formation process and (2) changing expectations, experience-based perceptions and values of the object over time. This suggests there is a time lag between current state of appropriateness and current value. The lag means that status (and reputation) is historical on one hand and developmental on the other. This change in quality, when quality is seen as a semi-structure with some prescribed or determined features, context changes need to be accounted for through rhythmic transition processes to avoid negative consequences of disruption to maintain the recognition of appropriateness for and of purpose (Brown & Eisenhardt, 1997).

Pitsoe and Letseka (2018) argued that quality has a symbiotic relationship with Heidegger's notion of temporality from an experienced perspective in which the present is a process of what was before. Quality, especially when framed from the perspective of improvement is a directional discussion of change. Conceptions of change are based on universalities rather than a specific, individual object (Dewey, 1887; James,

1890). Experience with the object over time changes its perceived quality (Karapanos, Zimmerman, Forlizzi, & Martens, 2009). The emphasis is on the dynamics behind the object's creation and valuation. It can then be a study into the change of preferences (needs and requirements) and how these influence the value and creation processes (cf. Büthe, 2002).

Stakeholder-Based and Outside-in Focused

In the field of education, when quality is viewed as a problem, it is the media, politicians and education bureaucrats saying so (Mockler, 2018). This is the negative side of the reality that quality is a perception driven by the outside world. It is an active manifestation of stakeholder impact on organisations and sectors. It is also a reflection of Deming's (1994) that an organisation cannot know itself unless it takes into account how the rest of the world looks and values it.

Stakeholders are external groups or individuals that can affect a business because they are the recipients of the value created by an organisation or sector (Freeman, Harrison, Wicks, Parmar, & de Colle, 2010). Stakeholders exist on the inside as well as out; yet, most attention is placed on external stakeholders. Stakeholder theory suggests that their interests comprise an essential component of organisational management. These interests have to be identified, listened to, interpreted, evaluated and acted upon to a determined extent. Stakeholders (external and internal)—and in some regards the extent to which their interests have to be accommodated—can be identified by (1) the power to influence an organisation or sector, (2) the legitimacy of the relationship between organisation or sector and (3) the urgency of a claim on the organisation or sector (Mitchell, Agle, & Wood, 1997).

Quality from an applications perspective—QMS or TQM—reflects the power and influence factors that stakeholders apply to the organisation and/or sector (Padró, 1988; Pitsoe & Letseka, 2018). The development and application as a regulatory object of benchmarks, criteria, guidelines and standards are predicated on power over organisations and sectors to comply with these formal or 'highly recommended' points of reference. Power is based on the ability of stakeholders mediating organisational behaviour through standards or equivalents based on a mutual dependency reflecting the degree of recognition and acceptance of the different needs and action between stakeholders and organisations (Dahl, 1957; Emerson, 1962; Freeman et al., 2010; Luhmann, 1995). Power is neither one-directional, although it may seem that way, and it is not always a zero-sum, win-lose proposition with one winner and one loser because there are different gradations nor types of power being exercised (French & Raven, 1959; Giddens, 1968; Parsons, 1963). Power, as a means of generating influence, is based on norm homogeneity that, as Hollander and Willis (1967) pointed out, represents compliance in a restrictive unidimensional manner. Another paradox surfaces as a result. Within quality, the relationship between professional associations, regulatory bodies and sectors in which these hold sway there is a paradoxical relationship resultant from the degree of equivocality that is possible (Weick, 1979). The paradox comes from standards or equivalents requiring compliance to ensure replication to meet user satisfaction in environments where freedom to improvise on outputs and products is necessary for success (Brown & Eisenhardt, 1997).

Quality Is Autopoietic

Deming (1994) stated that quality is grounded on systems thinking. The component parts of the system represent a composite unity, viewed by how the components relate to each other within the whole of the organisation (Maturana & Varela, 1980). Luhmann (1995) along with Maturana and Varela (1980) saw the purpose of systems to be self-determining (self steering) through self-reproduction (*autopoiesis*) to remain viable. "In order to 'survive' an autopoietic system constantly has to produce further elements" (Seidl, 2004, p. 4). Meaning is operationally-based and convergent. Convergence occurs in the present (Luhmann, 1995) in terms of continued appreciation of meaning, but as previously indicated there is a time-lag consideration that is at play. Construction of meaning comes from the ability of the different parts of the system to be aware of each other and the enactive processes coming out of dependent relationships between the different parts. This is done through a processual approach rather as the elements have been de-ontoligized (Luhmann, 1995). The bridging between the different parts of the system (be these within an organisation or as part of a sector) to create ongoing working relationships creating a complementarity of expectations based on shared norms (Parsons, Bales, & Shils, 1953). There is a double contingency in place where one's actions and the other's reaction to what is done shape awareness and participation (Parsons, 1981/1951). From this emanate strong anticipations that influence intentions and, subsequently, meaning behind acts (Leydesdorff, 2008). Steering to ensure intentions is inherent to this process and based on whose position prevails and drives the defining elements of quality. Steering in this sense is an attempt to reduce the difference between different intentions and perceptions; however, it can also be a form of government shoring itself up through corporate techniques (King & Thornhill, 2003; Luhmann, 1997).

What Is Quality in Professional Education?

As with any educational purpose, there is a personal and social component that *en toto* make up a view of quality in professional education. There are different views of quality because of the individual and collective aspects to educating professionals. Receivers of the educational preparation process wants utilitarian benefits that lead to personal advancement in self-worth and professional terms. Communities and employers want to see utilitarian benefits from the perspective of adding capacity to the workforce and contributing to the community's social fabric. Education in the broadest sense thus is both a personal benefit and a public good. At present, the emphasis is on personal benefit in terms of who pays; conversely, the focus in defining the quality of programs is on employability and the *homo economicus* (Padró & Green, in press), possibly at the expense of personal development and growth. Most of the quality attributes point towards the logic behind this external perspective. Autopoiesis does exist within the profession as it evolves in its practice and underlying theories of practice; yet, as educational institutions and programs are parts of a wider system, autopoiesis is bounded and guided by the larger normative expectations of society. Quality is an autopoietic mechanism indicating appropriateness, processual and applications focused and usually predicated on positivistic elements. The quality mechanism also serves as timekeeper in that processes are designed to continuously evaluate appropriateness in terms of fitness 'for purpose' more than 'of purpose'. The argument can be made that the 'for purpose' aspect prevails over 'of purpose' because the immanent and temporal aspects foci are outcome specific, linked to current performance based on recent performance. Fitness 'of purpose' is a more complex aspect of quality when it comes to professional education because of the reciprocal, double contingent nature of the profession and stakeholders. The professions, usually through professional associations or equivalents, determine the accepted standards of practice and define professionalism (Press, 2018). The workforce applies these while also influencing the professional association 'of purpose' element from its experience lens. Both then influence university programs and government agencies who oversee the professions. Fitness 'of purpose' therefore becomes a mediated steering proposition.

Developing a professional identity is essential to the success of a practitioner within a profession (Hershey, 2007). Although not always fully articulated as a learning outcome, it is an overarching concern in professional education programs. As curriculum moves from just a face-to-face to blended or fully online delivery modes, one issue that comes forth is how to ensure professional identity is embedded as part of the curriculum. A definition of quality does consider this in its monitoring and throughput processing that exists within the curriculum. The more recent developments regarding the importance of dispositions and ethical practice reflects this interest in professional identity.

Transformation is the developmental outcome in professional education. As such, quality from a preparation perspective should entail inclusion and monitoring of the 'frontier effects' (Hall, 1996) of meaning formation and the contextualization of information and knowledge into a personal theory of action that characterizes individual practice in a work environment setting. Such an approach is in keeping with the modern view of curriculum linking organized content or subject matter with the experiences of the learner (Lunenburg, 2011). Graduate quality often relates to concerns surrounding preparation and acquired work-ready skill-sets and providing competing ideas on how to succeed. As Press

(2018) indicated, "[in] the area of professional education curricula, the literature poses questions on the quality of educational outcomes and influencing factors (e.g., limitations of existing curricular and pedagogical practices, the impact of prescriptions, standardisation, professionalism, learning and teaching transactions, etc.)" (p. 5). Professionals are considered to be the most highly educated group in a society (Freidson, 2001). Their preparation should embody and educationally right practice, which is per force the definition of quality within an educational program.

Online learning is a frontier that is disrupting the notion of quality within programs. The yardstick is that online learning should have the same effect as face-to-face learning experiences. The challenge rests in that in-between, third space where professional identity is conceptualised. Interactions are paramount in accordance to the literature in online learning (Abrami, Bernard, Bures, Borokhovski, & Tamim, 2012). The in-between spaces where leaners and learners, teachers and learners, and learners and content interact shed light to how the ambiguities between pre-course experience beliefs and new learning and values translates the uncertainty difficulties to a utility-focused rather than merely pragmatic oriented characterised personal epistemology (Moore, 1989; Savin-Baden, 2008).

All told, professional education in its quest for quality from a curricular perspective should focus on:

1. The establishment, shaping and maintenance of intersubjectivity to establish intentionally, among other things, intention and relevance.
2. Relating events, utterances and acts relating to the instrumentality and organisation of action.
3. Creating a normative context relating to 'requiredness' (constraints) limiting the previous two modes due to identified obligations, general standards, acceptable behaviours and exceptions.
4. Making of propositions based on recognising formal necessities imposed by rules of the symbolic, syntactic and conceptual systems used by individuals to achieve decontextualised meaning.
5. Becoming critical of one's own and other's tacit assumptions and expectations, and assessing their relevance for making an interpretation of what is being learned (Bruner, 1996; Mezirow 2000).

Together, these provide professional education programs with points of reference that, in applied form, can then shape the identity and notions of quality of a good program held by the broader community, government and workforce stakeholders interested in their graduates.

This introductory chapter to the second volume of Ensuring Quality in Professional Education has delved into the notions of quality and how these are perceived influence praxis and programming. Quality is primarily an outside-in look at organisational performance because, as Deming (1994) said, an organisation cannot know itself. Quality is also a systems-based perspective and therefore provides an internal-external approach toward performance. The second chapter then continues with discussion of the use of surveys and other tools to make improvements in quality in teaching, learning, student experience and employability. Student experience surveys have long been used by lecturers to provide feedback for continuous improvement of courses, but results are now also being regularly used by management of higher education institutions and reports scrutinised across the sector by governments internationally to evaluate institutions. There are significant pressures on lecturers, senior managers and leaders to raise the quality of student experience given that results of satisfaction and employability surveys are published in the public domain in many countries, and this chapter discusses pragmatic and responsible use of such survey data. Chapter 3 looks more broadly at international quality assurance indicators and accreditation and their impact in a competitive global higher education market. The requirement to demonstrate quality is influenced by performance measures designed to demonstrate value for money in an era of austerity that creates a challenge for universities, and Irish universities are the focus in this chapter.

Theoretical aspects of professional learning are contextualised through frameworks and visualised through concept mapping in Chap. 4. The knowledge structures discussed have implications for curriculum design in professional education and also for evaluation of teaching. Contextualised education and the ethics of professional education and practice are particularly important in the development of quality education for professional practice in developing countries where significant emphasis has been placed on 'knowledge transfer' from highly developed nations but also concern over international comparability of standards.

Chapter 5 offers a perspective on the challenges of providing quality professional education in countries like Papua New Guinea (PNG) where not all higher education is undertaken in universities and where there is a potentially weak professional ethos. The challenge of offering a quality learning experience to a wider and growing population is one that can be supported with new technology and methods of learning.

The following chapters in this volume look to the Enterprise/Production field of engineering and begins with a dual site case study of the provision of extension learning for engineers by two universities in Australia and Venezuela. Extension learning refers to continuing professional development in agriculture, engineering and science, whereby practitioners engage in further, formalised training. The discussion highlights the contextualised and increasingly politicised character of the provision of extension learning, but also provides evidence of the ongoing effectiveness of that provision for generating quality practice in this professional field. Chapter 7 reviews a postgraduate engineering management course. Historically engineering degrees have had a significant emphasis on knowledge content and have aimed to expose a student to a multitude of engineering knowledge based problems relevant to a particular discipline of engineering. This newly developed course which aims to play a leading role in the development of the project management knowledge, skills and application of professional engineers is evaluated against project success criteria, professional engineering requirements, the Australian Qualifications Framework requirements for postgraduate courses, and learner feedback. Close liaison and consultation with industry and relevant professional organisations are considered essential to assure alignment with respect to the project management skills and knowledge of professional engineers required for successful delivery on complex projects in the field. Chapter 8 argues that engineering education needs to refocus towards a more rounded approach with more emphasis on application skills, personal and professional skills and real world engineering problem solving. They describe a scaffolded approach that incorporates both discipline knowledge and applications, and professional competencies required by industry such as teamwork. This is achieved via participation in authentic projects, the implementation of ePortfolios, and development of capacity for self-assessment, reflective practice and critical thinking. The final engineering chapter provides a discussion of an evolving area of engineering curriculum focus. Sustainable engineering has emerged as an important and complex area that takes account of social, political and economic contexts. This chapter highlights the need for increased uniformity of delivery of the broader sustainability concepts alongside the requirement for stimulation of challenge and debate in this conceptually challenging field.

The final Chap. 10 considers returns to notions of quality in professional education, focusing on the conceptual complexities of quality assurance in higher education for the professions in relation to the multiple outcomes of employability, institutional and other requisite standards. This chapter links back to the transformational aspects of curriculum change, pedagogy and educational quality explored in the previous case study chapters for achieving quality graduate outcomes for the professions through higher education.

References

Abrami, P. C., Bernard, R. M., Bures, E. M., Borokhovski, E., & Tamim, R. M. (2012). Interaction in distance education and online learning: Using evidence and theory to improve practice. In L. Moller & J. B. Huett (Eds.), *The next generation of distance education: Unconstrained learning* (pp. 49–69). New York: Springer.

Alba, J. W., & Hutchinson, J. W. (1987). Dimensions of consumer expertise. *The Journal of Consumer Research, 13*(4), 411–454.

Askenazy, P., & Galbis, E. M. (2007). The impact of technological and organizational changes on labor flows. Evidence on French establishments. *Labour, 21*(2), 265–301.

Audi, R. (1988). *Epistemology: A contemporary introduction to the theory of knowledge*. New York: Routledge.

Banks, S. (2010). Integrity in professional life: Issues of conduct, commitment and capacity. *British Journal of Social Work, 40*, 2168–2184.

Bekkers, V., & Edwards, A. (2007). Legitimacy and democracy: A conceptual framework for assessing governance practices. In V. Bekkers, G. Dijkstra, A. Edwards, & M. Fenger (Eds.), *Governance and the democratic deficit: Assessing the democratic legitimacy of governance practices* (pp. 35–60). Aldershot, Hampshire: Ashgate.

Biggs, J., & Tang, C. (2007). *Teaching for quality at university: What the student does* (3rd ed.). Berkshire, UK: Open University Press, McGraw-Hill Education.

Billett, S. (2010). Emerging perspectives of work: Implications for university learning and teaching. In J. Higgs, I. Goulter, S. Loftus, J. Reid, & F. Trede (Eds.), *Education for future practice* (pp. 97–112). Rotterdam, Netherlands: Sense Publishers.

Bird, B. (1988). Implementing entrepreneurial ideas: The case for intention. *The Academy of Management Review, 13*(3), 442–453.

Bråten, I., & Strømsø, H. I. (2008). Job values in professional education: The role of achievement goals. *Scandinavian Journal of Educational Research, 52*(3), 259–277.

Bronfenbrenner, U., & Morris, P. A. (2006). The bioecological model of human development. In W. Damon & R. M. Lerner (Eds.), *Handbook of child psychology* (6th ed., pp. 793–828). Hoboken, NJ: Wiley.

Brown, S. L., & Eisenhardt, K. M. (1997). The art of continuous change: Linking complexity theory and time-paced evolution in relentlessly shifting organizations. *Administrative Science Quarterly, 42*(1), 1–34.

Bruner, J. (1996). Frames for thinking: Ways of making meaning. In D. R. Olson & N. Torrance (Eds.), *Modes of thought: Explorations in culture and cognition* (pp. 93–105). Cambridge, UK: Cambridge University Press.

Büthe, T. (2002). Taking temporality seriously: Modeling history and the use of narratives as evidence. *The American Political Science Review, 96*(3), 481–493.

Cameron, J., Banko, K. M., & Pierce, W. D. (2001). Pervasive negative effects of rewards on intrinsic motivation: The myth continues. *The Behavior Analyst, 24*, 1–44.

Chaudhuri, D., Mukhopadhyay, A. R., & Ghosn, S. K. (2011). Assessment of engineering colleges through application of the six sigma metrics in a state of India. *International Journal of Quality & Reliability Management, 28*(9), 969–1001.

Cheng, M. (2016). *Quality in education: Developing a virtue of professional practice*. Rotterdam, Netherlands: Sense Publishers.

Crowe, J. (2007). Dworkin on the value of integrity. *Deakin Law Review, 12*(1), 167–180.

Dahl, R. A. (1957). The concept of power. *Behavioral Science, 2*(3), 201–215.

Dall'Alba, G. (2009). Learning professional ways of being: Ambiguities of becoming. *Educational Philosophy and Theory, 41*(1), 34–45.

Deleuse, G., & Guattari, F. (1987). *A thousand plateaus: Capitalism and schizophrenia* (B. Massumi, Trans.). Minneapolis, MN: University of Minnesota Press.

Deming, W. E. (1994). *The new economics for industry, government, education* (2nd ed.). Cambridge, MA: MIT Press.

Dewey, J. (1887). *Psychology*. New York: Harper & Brothers.

Dworkin, R. (1986). *Law's empire*. Cambridge, MA: Belknap Press.

Edgar, A., & Pattison, S. (2011). Integrity and the moral complexity of professional practice. *Nursing Philosophy, 12*, 94–106.

Elassy, N. (2015). The concepts of quality, quality assurance and quality enhancement. *Quality Assurance in Education, 23*(3), 250–261.

Emerson, R. M. (1962). Power-dependence relations. *American Sociological Review, 27*(1), 31–41.

Ericsson, K. A. (2008). Deliberate practice and acquisition of expert performance: A general overview. *Academy Emergency Medicine, 15*, 988–994.

Eriksen, A. (2015). What is professional integrity? *Nordic Journal of Applied Ethics, 9*(2), 3–17.

Feigenbaum, A. V. (1983). *Total quality control* (3rd ed.). New York: McGraw-Hill.

Freeman, R. E., Harrison, J. S., Wicks, A. C., Parmar, B., & de Colle, S. (2010). *Stakeholder theory: The state of the art*. Cambridge, UK: Cambridge University Press.

Freidson, E. (2001). *Professionalism: The third logic—On the practice of knowledge*. Chicago: University of Chicago Press.

French, J. R. P., Jr., & Raven, B. (1959). The bases of social power. In D. Cartwright (Ed.), *Studies in social power* (pp. 150–167). Ann Arbor, MI: Institute of Social Research, University of Michigan.

Friedman, L. (1995). C.S. Peirce's transcendental and immanent realism. *Transactions of The Charles S. Peirce Society, 31*(2), 374–392.

Giddens, A. (1968). 'Power' in the recent writings of Talcott Parsons. *Sociology, 2*(3), 257–272.

Gobet, F., Lane, P. C. R., Croker, S., Cheng, P. C.-H., Jones, G., Oliver, I., & Pine, J. M. (2001). Chunking mechanisms in human learning. *Cognitive Sciences, 5*(6), 236–243.

Hagström, L., & Scheja, M. (2014). Using meta-reflection to improve learning and throughput: Redesigning assessment procedures in a political science course on power. *Assessment & Evaluation in Higher Education, 39*(2), 242–252.

Hall, S. (1996). Who needs identity. In S. Hall & P. du Gay (Eds.), *Questions of cultural identity* (pp. 1–17). London: SAGE.
Harvey, L., & Green, D. (1993). Defining quality. *Assessment & Evaluation in Higher Education, 18*(1), 9–34.
Heidegger, M. (2008/1927). Being and time (J. Macquarrie & E. Robinson, Trans.). New York: HarperPerennial.
Hershey, J.L. (2007). *The lived experience of becoming a professional nurse for associate degree nursing graduates: A phenomenological study*. Doctoral dissertation, The Pennsylvania State University.
Higgs, J., & Titchen, A. (2001). Rethinking the practice-knowledge interface in an uncertain world: A model for practice development. *British Journal of Occupational Therapy, 64*(11), 526–533.
Hindle, K., Klyver, K., & Jennings, D. F. (2009). An 'informed' intent model: Incorporating human capital, social capital, and gender variables into the theoretical model of entrepreneurial intentions. In A. L. Carsrud & M. Brännback (Eds.), *Understanding the entrepreneurial mind: Opening the black box* (pp. 35–50). Dordrecht, Netherlands: Springer Science + Business Media.
Hollander, E. P., & Willis, R. H. (1967). Some current issues in the psychology of conformity and nonconformity. *Psychological Bulletin, 68*(1), 62–76.
Howard, S. A. (2015). Metaemotional intentionality. *Pacific Philosophical Quarterly, 98*, 406–428.
Husserl, E. (1931). *Ideas: General introduction to pure phenomenology* (W. R. B. Gibson, Trans.). London: George Allen & Unwind LTD.
James, W. (1890). *The principles of psychology. Volume I*. New York: Henry Holt and Company.
Jarvis, P. (1999). *The practitioner-researcher: Developing theory from practice*. San Francisco: Jossey-Bass.
Juran, J. M., & Godfrey, A. B. (1999). The quality control process. In J. M. Juran, A. B. Godfrey, R. E. Hoogstoel, & E. G. Schilling (Eds.), *Juran's quality handbook* (5th ed., pp. 4.1–4.29). New York: McGraw-Hill.
Juran, J. M., & Gryna, F. M., Jr. (1970). *Quality planning and analysis: From product development through usage*. New York: McGraw-Hill.
Kahneman, D., & Tversky, A. (1979). Prospect theory: An analysis of decisions under risk. *Econometrica, 47*(2), 263–291.
Karapanos, E., Zimmerman, J., Forlizzi, J., & Martens, J.-B. (2009). User experience over time: An initial framework. In *Proceedings of the 27th International*

Conference on Human Factors in Computing Systems, CHI 2009 (pp. 729–738). Boston, MA, 4–9 April 2009.

Katz, D., & Kahn, R. L. (1978). *The social psychology of organizations* (2nd ed.). New York: Wiley.

Kemmis, S. (2005). Knowing practice: Searching for salience. *Pedagogy, Culture and Society, 13*(3), 391–426.

King, M., & Thornhill, C. (2003). *Niklas Luhmann's theory of politics and law*. Hampshire, UK: Palgrave Macmillan.

Larkin, J. H., & Simon, H. A. (1987). Why a diagram is (sometimes) worth ten thousand words. *Cognitive Science, 11*, 65–99.

Lee, D. H., & Olshavsky, R. W. (1994). Toward a predictive model of the consumer inference process: The role of expertise. *Psychology & Marketing, 11*(2), 109–127.

Leydesdorff, L. (2008). The communication of meaning in anticipatory systems: A simulation study of the dynamics of intentionality in social interactions. In D. M. Dubois (Ed.), *Proceedings of the 8th International Conference on Computing Anticipatory Systems CASYS'07, Liège, Belgium, 6–11 August 2007* (Vol. 1051, pp. 33–49). Melville, NY: American Institute of Physics Conference Proceedings.

Lieberherr, E. (2013). *The role of throughput in the input-output legitimacy debate: Insights from public and private governance modes in the Swiss and English water sectors*. Paper presented at ICPP 2013, Panel 39: The New Policies of Privatization, June 26–28, Grenoble, France. Retrieved from http://archives.ippapublicpolicy.org/IMG/pdf/panel_39_s2_lieberherr.pdf

Lindberg, M. (2014). Implications of the Bologna process for throughput in the higher education sector: An empirical illustration based on a Finnish-British comparison. *European Journal of Education, 49*(2), 259–271.

Locke, J. (1689/1952). *An enquiry concerning human understanding*. Chicago: Encyclopedia Britannica.

Lomas, L. (2004). Embedding quality: The challenges for higher education. *Quality Assurance in Education, 12*(4), 157–165.

Luhmann, N. (1995). *Social systems* (J. Bednarz & D. Baecker, Trans.). Stanford, CA: Stanford University Press.

Luhmann, N. (1997). The limits of steering. *Theory, Culture and Society, 14*(1), 41–57.

Lunenburg, F. C. (2011). Theorizing about curriculum: Conceptions and definitions. *International Journal of Scholarly Intellectual Diversity, 13*(1), 1–6.

Maturana, H., & Varela, F. J. (1980). *Autopoiesis and cognition: The realization of the living*. Dordrecht, Netherlands: D. Reidel Publishing Company.

Mezirow, J. (1997). Transformative learning: Theory to practice. In P. Cranton (Ed.), *Transformative learning in action: Insights from practice—New directions for adult and continuing education, no. 74* (pp. 5–12). San Francisco: Jossey-Bass.

Mezirow, J. (2000). Learning to think like an adult: Core concepts of transformation theory. In J. Mezirow (Ed.), *Learning as transformation: Critical perspectives on a theory in Progress* (pp. 3–34). San Francisco: Jossey-Bass.

Miles, R. E., & Snow, C. C. (1978). *Organizational strategy, structure, and process*. New York: McGraw-Hill.

Miller, G. A. (1956). The magical number seven, plus or minus two: Some limits on our capacity for processing information. *Psychological Review, 101*(2), 343–352.

Mitchell, R. K., Agle, B. R., & Wood, D. J. (1997). Toward a theory of stakeholder identification and salience: Defining the principle of who and what really counts. *Academy of Management Review, 22*(4), 853–886.

Mockler, N. (2018). *Teaching quality is not teacher quality. How we talk about 'quality' matters, here's why*. EduResearch Matters (blog). Retrieved from Australian Education Research Association website: http://www.aare.edu.au/blog/?p=2845&utm_campaign=website

Moore, M. G. (1989). Editorial: Three types of interaction. *The American Journal of Distance Education, 3*(2), 1–7.

Noordegraaf, M. (2011). Remaking professionals? How associations and professional education connect professionalism and organizations. *Current Sociology, 59*(4), 465–488.

Padró, F. F. (1988). *Quality circles and their existence in present-day school administration*. Doctoral dissertation, The University of Arizona.

Padró, F. F., & Green, J. H. (in press). Education administrators in wonderland: Figuring out how policy-making and regulatory compliance when making decisions. In K. Trimmer, R. Dixon, & Y. Findlay (Eds.), *Education and the law: Considering the legal context of schools*. Dordrecht, Netherlands: Springer International Publishing AG.

Padró, F. F., & Hawke, M. F. (2003). A perceptual model of organization behavior. *National Social Sciences Journal, 19*(2), 102–112.

Padró, F. F., Hawke, M. F., & Hawke, L. M. (2016). Assessment and quality: Policy-steering and the making of a *deus ex machina*. In J. Bower & P. L. Thomas (Eds.), *De-testing and de-grading schools: Authentic alternatives to accountability and standardization* (Revised ed., pp. 33–50). New York: Peter Lang.

Parsons, T. (1963). On the concepts of political power. *Proceedings of the American Philosophical Society, 107*(3), 232–262.

Parsons, T. (1981/1951). *The social system*. London: Routledge.

Parsons, T., Bales, R. F., & Shils, E. A. (1953). *Working papers in the theory of action*. New York: Free Press.

Pascale, R. T. (1999). Surfing at the edge of chaos. *Sloan Management Review, 40*(3), 83–94.

Peirce, C. S. (1958). *Values on a universe of chance: Charles S. Peirce: Selected writings* (P. P. Wiener, Ed.). New York: Dover Publications.

Peirce, C. S. (1994). *The collected papers of Charles Sanders Peirce: Electronic edition* (C. Hartshorne & P. Wiess, Eds., vols. 1–6, 1935; A. W. Burk, Ed., vols. 7–8, 1958). Retrieved from https://colorysemiotica.files.wordpress.com/2014/08/peirce-collectedpapers.pdf

Pitsoe, V. J., & Letseka, M. (2018). Heidegger and Althusser on quality management systems in open and distance learning. In L. Kounis (Ed.), *Quality management systems: A selective presentation of case-studies showcasing its evolution* (pp. 47–60). London: IntechOpen.

Press, N. I. (2018). *Educating for a profession: A phenomenological case study of professional practice preparation for the Nursing discipline from a sociocultural perspective*. Doctoral dissertation, University of Southern Queensland.

Press, N., & Padró, F. F. (2017). Educating for a profession: Curriculum as transformation and curriculum transformation. In R. G. Walker & S. B. Bedford (Eds.), *Research and development in higher education: Curriculum transformation, 40* (pp. 313–322). Sydney, Australia, 27–30 June 2017.

Reeves, C. A., & Bednar, D. A. (1994). Defining quality: Alternatives and implications. *The Academy of Management Review*, Special Issue: "Total Quality", *19*(3), 419–445.

Robinson, A. (2010). *Trinity, evolution, and the metaphysical semiotics of C.S. Peirce*. Leiden, Netherlands: Brill.

Roest, H., & Rindfleisch, A. (2010). The influence of quality cues and typicality cues on restaurant purchase intention. *Journal of Retailing and Consumer Services, 17*, 10–18.

Rogers, A. (2014). *The base of the iceberg: Informal learning and its impact on formal and non-formal learning*. Opladen, Germany: Budrich.

Sahi, G., Gupta, M. C., & Patel, P. C. (2017). A measure of throughput orientation: Scale development and nomological validation. *Decision Sciences, 48*(3), 420–453.

Savin-Baden, M. (2008). *Learning spaces: Creating opportunities for knowledge creation in academic life*. Maidenhead, UK: Open University Press.
Schumpeter, J. A. (2003). *Capitalism, socialism and democracy*. London: Routledge.
Seidl, D. (2004). *Luhmann's theory of autopoietic social systems*. Munich Business Research Paper 2004-2. Munich, Germany: Ludwig-Maximilians-Universität München.
Sheehan, T., & Palmer, R.E. (Eds.). (1997). *Edmund Husserl, Psychological and transcendental phenomenology and the confrontation with Heidegger (1927–1931): The Encyclopedia Britannica Article, the Amsterdam Lectures, 'Phenomenology and Anthropology', and Husserl's Marginal Notes in Being and Time and Kant and the Problem of Metaphysics. Collected Works, Volume 6*. Dordrecht, Netherlands: Kluwer Academic Publishers.
Steinbock, A. J. (2001). (Transl.). *Edmund Husserl: Analyses concerning passive and active synthesis: Lectures on transcendental logic*. Dordrecht, Netherlands: Kluwer Academic Publishers.
Swan, D. (1998). The changing university: Fitness of purpose. *Irish Educational Studies, 17*(1), 272–283.
Taylor, E. W. (2009). Fostering transformative learning. In J. Mezirow, E. W. Taylor, & Associates (Eds.), *Transformative learning in practice: Insights from community, workplace, and higher education* (pp. 3–17). San Francisco: Jossey-Bass.
Tversky, A., & Kahneman, D. (1992). Advances in prospect theory: Cumulative representation of uncertainty. *Journal of Risk and Uncertainty, 5*(4), 297–323.
Van Meerkerk, I., Edelenbos, J., & Klijn, E.-H. (2015). Connective management and governance network performance: The mediating role of throughput legitimacy. Findings from survey research on complex water projects in the Netherlands. *Environment and Planning C: Government and Space, 33*(4), 746–764.
Vanderstraeten, R. (2002). Parsons, Luhmann and the theorem of double contingency. *Journal of Classical Sociology, 2*(1), 77–92.
Weick, K. E. (1979). *The social psychology of organizing* (2nd ed.). Reading, MA: Addison-Wesley.
Westbroek, H. B., Klaassen, K., Bulte, A., & Pilot, A. (2010). Providing students with a sense of purpose by adapting a professional practice. *International Journal of Science Education, 32*(5), 603–627.
Wong, Q. Y.-Y. (2012). An alternative view of quality assurance and enhancement. *Management in Education, 26*(1), 38–42.

Wittgenstein, L. (1986). *Philosophical investigations* (G. E. M. Anscombe, Trans.). Oxford, UK: Basil Blackwell.

Yielder, J. (2004). An integrated model of professional expertise and its implications for higher education. *International Journal of Lifelong Education, 23*(1), 60–80.

2

Evaluating the Student Experience: A Critical Review of the Use of Surveys to Enhance the Student Experience

Rhona Sharpe

Introduction

Universities and colleges now use a range of surveys to collect feedback from students at all stages of their journey from open days to graduation (Kember & Ginns, 2012). Surveys are also important sources of data in government approved datasets and newspaper league tables. This widespread use of surveys has resulted in a large international research literature examining their validity and reliability. However, this research often shows biases such as in responses to the UK's National Student Survey (HEFCE, 2014) and North American student evaluations of teaching (Onweugbuzie et al., 2007). Despite these recognised biases, the use of these surveys as key institutional measures of quality has been accepted and adopted widely. The introduction of the UK Teaching Excellence Framework (BIS, 2016), which uses responses to questions from the National Student Survey and Destination of Leavers from Higher Education as key metrics, provides a timely prompt to review the validity

R. Sharpe (✉)
University of Surrey, Guildford, UK
e-mail: r.sharpe@surrey.ac.uk

and value of these measures used to monitor the student experience of professional education and to suggest tools and practices to complement the use of surveys.

The National Context

Surveying students about their experiences has long been a tool used by lecturers to collect feedback on their teaching (Angelo & Cross, 1993). However, as the student experience has become a strategic priority for higher education institutions, surveys have come to be the dominant tool for academic managers to measure and monitor the quality of teaching. These days, any discussion of surveys needs to take account of the consumer-orientated context in which students are learning; the result of the marketization of higher education (Bunce, Baird, & Jones, 2016). In the UK, successive governments have intervened to create, and then increase tuition fees, remove controls on the number of students who can enter higher education and lower the barriers to entry for new providers. Combined with a demographic fall in the number of 18-year olds that will last until 2024 (UCAS, 2016), this has increased competition between universities to recruit and retain students.

University leaders' obsession with survey results is partly a desire for improvement in difficult market conditions. It has also been driven by the use of survey data by governments. Internationally, government agencies have promoted surveys as an easily accessible tool to produce data which can be used to manage the reputation of their country's higher education system in order to aid international recruitment, and to identify institutions that may require intervention. In the UK a single measure has dominated the discourse. The National Student Survey (NSS) has become the de facto key performance indicator for the increasing number of senior managers with 'student experience' in their job title. Alongside the Destination of Leavers in Higher Education (DLHE), the results for from the NSS are made publicly available on the *UniStats* website and are widely reported in the media (e.g. Merrifield, 2016). Australia operates a similar system where a government co-ordinated survey is distributed to recent graduates twice a year and includes the Course

Experience Questionnaire (CEQ) and the Graduate Destination Survey. Results are used widely by institutions and reported on the *Good Universities* website and are used to rank universities on a 1–5 starred rating scale. Although the USA does not have a nationally required survey, student evaluations of teaching are common, and in 2017, 720 colleges also participated in the National Survey of Student Engagement (NSSE). This was a considerable increase from 557 participating colleges the year before, showing how these surveys are continuing to gain popularity even without government intervention (http://nsse.indiana.edu/html/announcements.cfm).

Much has been hypothesized about the impact of marketization on student attitudes towards higher education and how they respond to feedback surveys. Bunce et al. (2016) found relationships between consumer attitudes, learner identity and attainment which suggest that students who view themselves as consumers are less likely to be engaged in intellectual pursuit of knowledge and have lower grades. They also found more consumerist attitudes in students studying STEM subjects. Perhaps students' attitudes are also driving the uptake of surveys. Consumers expect to be asked about their experience and that their feedback will be acted upon. Certainly, there is a noticeable willingness of students and their parents to share their experiences on consumer focussed web sites such as The Student Room (http://www.thestudentroom.co.uk) and MumsNet (http://www.mumsnet.com). In the professions, where students have chosen degrees with clear routes to employment, and an expectation of higher than average graduate salaries, it is important to understand how students rate their lecturers and their courses and the impact of the wider context of higher education on their expectations.

The Institutional Context

In such a climate, being able to show the quality of the higher education experience for potential students is of great value to an institution, as is the ability to examine the strengths of their services and to identify any areas that require additional attention and investment. Data from student feedback surveys are now regularly combined, summarised, compared and shared across an institution and used in decision making (Bedggood & Donovan, 2012). The pressure to monitor the student experience extends beyond the academic programme. Although students are legally adults, for many students coming to university is the first time they have lived away from home and studied independently. Universities therefore offer a range of support services which influence the overall experience of being at university. However, the act of asking questions about an area sets expectations that it is under the university's control. Student experience surveys should only encompass those aspects of the learners' journey that are within the university's remit to influence. These can be grouped as hygiene factors, transactional experiences, transformational experiences and graduate outcomes (Fig. 2.1).

Aspects of the student experience	Examples of what is experienced	Indicators of the student experience
Graduate outcomes	e.g. employability, graduate attributes, alumni benefits.	Destination of Leavers Higher Education
Transformational experiences Teaching and learning, community	e.g. courses, assessment, wellbeing services, student societies.	National Student Survey UK Engagement Survey Course Representatives
Transactional Interactions with university services	e.g. online enrolment, assignment submissions, office hours, appointments	National Student Survey Usage statistics IT Service Desk logs Library survey Graduation survey Barometer Survey
Hygiene factors Shelter, safety	e.g. built environment, learning spaces, learning resources, transport, catering, accommodation.	Estates Service Desk logs Complaints and appeals Open day survey Decliners survey

Fig. 2.1 Aspects of the undergraduate student experience and typical UK indicators

Table 2.1 Oxford Brookes University undergraduate student surveys 2015/16

Survey	Distributed to	When
Open day surveys	Potential students	October or June
Applicant day evaluation	Applicants	March
Decliners survey	Decliners	July
Induction evaluation survey	First years	September
New student survey	All	September
Clearing and adjustment survey	First years admitted through clearing	September
Module evaluation survey	All	End of each semester
National Student Survey	Final years	February
Engagement Survey	Non final years	April alternate years with Barometer
Student Barometer	Non final years	April alternate years with Engagement Survey
Graduation ceremony evaluation	Graduates	June or September
Destination of leavers from higher education institutions	Graduates	January after graduation

Table 2.1 shows the student surveys currently distributed to potential, current and alumni undergraduates in the author's own university. This list includes two surveys required in the UK (NSS and DLHE) and 10 others that the university has elected to use. In addition, students may be approached to respond to national consumer surveys e.g. Student Academic Experience Survey co-ordinated by HEPI and the Higher Education Academy (https://www.heacademy.ac.uk/institutions/surveys/student-academic-experience-survey), The Which? University Student Survey (http://university.which.co.uk/advice/which-university-student-survey) and the Times Higher Education Student Survey (https://www.timeshighereducation.com/student/news/student-experience-survey-2017-results).

Although this initially looks like a long list of surveys, Table 2.1 shows that most are distributed to different groups of students at different stages in their journey. The exception is the module evaluation survey which all students are asked to complete at the end of each semester for every module. In response to criticisms of survey fatigue other universities take a different approach. The University of Sydney adopts stratified sampling methods where only selected students are sent surveys (reported in Kember & Ginns, 2012). Such carefully constructed sampling provides just as trustworthy results as researching an entire population. However, it may not be what the student-as-consumer expects. This leads to pressure to continue to survey all students, despite poor response rates.

The Academic Programme Context

In professional education, as elsewhere in higher education, the visibility of data arising from surveys to academic managers is putting pressure on programme teams to raise the quality of the student experience and improve student satisfaction. A key debate since the introduction of the NSS in the UK 2005 has been about what it purports to measure. These criticisms highlight a tension between obtaining high approval ratings and providing a high quality learning experience, as expressed by Rienties (2014) in an evaluation of a university wide adoption of an online module evaluation survey:

> *Indeed, several academics felt that getting a high score on student evaluations was more important than concentrating on providing a valuable learning experience for students in the long run.* (Rienties, 2014, p. 998)

Originally derived from the Course Experience Questionnaire (CEQ), which asked Australian graduates to rate aspects of their course (Ramsden, 1991), the UK NSS is distributed to students in their final semester. Results for each academic programme are reported as part of the Key Information Set on the *UniStats* website. The CEQ was based on student learning theory which seeks to understand how students approach their learning in response to the perceived demands of the learning environment (e.g. Biggs, Kember, & Leung, 2001; Entwistle & Ramsden, 1983). The essence of this argument has been that despite its roots in student learning theory, the NSS is not a valid proxy for educational quality (Gibbs, 2010). That is, we should not expect students who are learning to be satisfied, as expressed by one lecturer in the Guardian newspaper "If university does not leave students at least a little dissatisfied, it means they haven't been sufficiently challenged or pushed outside of their intellectual comfort zone—and they should ask for their money back." (Williams, 2015). Evidence from a large-scale analysis of course evaluation ratings collected from Open University students supports this claim. Rienties and Toetnel (2016) report that satisfaction was not related to academic progression, and that student-centred learning activities were associated with decreased satisfaction even where the association with academic progress was positive. This is the first large scale study which seems to support the claim often made by teachers that learning is not always pleasant. Indeed, the authors conclude that

> *If our findings are replicated in other contexts, a crucial debate with academics, students and managers needs to develop whether universities should focus on happy students or customers, or whether universities should design learning activities that stretch learners to their maximum abilities and ensuring that they eventually pass the module.* (p. 340)

The issue of subject difficulty often arises in professional education and there are concerns about this might affect ratings. At the University of Nottingham's Malaysia Campus, the Faculty of Engineering developed a new tool for students to evaluate their modules. The new survey identifies 'difficult' modules, why they are perceived as difficult and how students are overcoming this (Lim, Gan & Ng, 2010). As might be expected, those modules identified by students as difficult were those that required the application of concepts through mathematical manipulations. However, the focus on the learning rather than satisfaction encouraged constructive conversations about the teaching of these modules.

Australian researchers have also tried to distinguish between student learning and student satisfaction. Bedggood and Donovan (2012) reported on an earlier study where they examined the content of 30 teacher evaluation surveys from eight Australian universities and found that most are measures of satisfaction rather than teaching quality, concluding that 'As it stands, the use of student satisfaction to evaluate teaching quality is unjustifiable, yet this is common practice' (p. 826). They developed two distinct measures for these separate constructs, arguing that as university managers were going to go on using surveys regardless, they should know what they are measuring.

An alternative survey which does claim links between its scores and academic performance is the National Survey of Student Engagement (NSSE) developed by George Kuh and colleagues at Indiana University to measure the 'quality of effort students themselves devote to educationally purposeful activities that contribute directly to desired outcomes' (Hu & Kuh, 2002, p. 555). Kuh et al. (2005) define two key aspects measured by the NSSE: the extent to which students engage in the activities that are offered to them (in terms of time and effort) and the extent to which the institution allocates resources and design courses in ways which encourage students to engage in educational purposeful activities. The NSSE was first distributed in North America in 2000 and variants are available in the UK, Ireland, Australasia, China and South Africa (Coates & McCormick, 2014).

Table 2.2 illustrates the difference between satisfaction and engagement style questions. The NSS questions set student expectations for what services they can expect their university to *provide*. In contrast, the UK Engagement Survey (UKES) sets expectations for what learners need to *do* in order to gain from their education. It is the latter which is related to educational outcome.

Table 2.2 Comparison of satisfaction and engagement style questions

Area of questions	National Student Survey (NSS)	UK Engagement Survey (UKES)
Staff	Staff are good at explaining things Staff have made the subject interesting	About how often have you discussed ideas from your course with teaching staff outside taught sessions, including by email/online?
Assessment and feedback	I have received detailed comments on my work	About how often have you made significant changes to your work based on feedback?
Course challenge	The course is intellectually stimulating	During the current academic year, how much has your course challenged you to do your best work?
Academic support	I have received sufficient advice and support with my studies	How often have you discussed your academic performance and/or feedback with teaching staff?

The UK Higher Education Academy sponsored a trial of a version of the NSSE adapted for the UK context and a number of universities have continued to use this alongside the NSS (Buckley, 2013, 2014). One of the most interesting recent developments has been the way in which UK universities have extended the engagement survey, using the principles of educationally purposeful activities and applying them to institution specific activities. For example, Oxford Brookes University has developed and added scales on the extent to which students engage in activities designed to develop each of the five institutional graduate attributes (Sharpe, O'Donovan, & Pavlakou, 2014).

Surveys to monitor graduate outcomes suffer from similar problems of uncertainty about what is being measured. In the UK two questions asked of graduates in the DLHE six months after graduation (whether you are in employment and the type of employment you are in), now form part of the required metrics for the Teaching Excellence Framework which rated institutions as gold, silver or bronze. A sector wide consultation in 2016 (HESA, 2016) about what should replace the DLHE overwhelming found that a survey was needed but there was no consensus on the alternative measures of graduate outcomes to replace or complement the much-criticised questions about Standard Occupational Classification of jobs and salary as 'common determinants of success'. Even a question as seemingly simple as whether or not you are working in a minefield, when incorporated into a survey.

The Lecturer's Context

For the individual lecturer, the primary concern is how survey data will be used. Rienties (2014) highlighted faculty concerns with the use of student evaluations in tenure and promotion decisions. It appears such concerns are well founded. In a comprehensive literature review examining the validity and reliability of North American student evaluations of teaching, Onweugbuzie et al. (2007) show that certain groups of staff consistently receive lower ratings: women, non-native English speakers and staff from black and minority ethic (BME) backgrounds and it appears these biases extend to online professional education settings (Doubleday & Lee, 2016)

Certain types of courses typically also receive lower ratings: large classes, introductory courses and subjects students find difficult. In professional education it may also be that the questions asked in standard surveys are just not suitable to evaluate the lecturer within their specific mode of teaching. Arah, Hoekstra, Bos, and Lombarts (2011) developed a survey tool for providing feedback to medical faculty suitable which is suitable for use in residency settings. It has scales for learning climate, professional attitude and behaviour, communication of goals, evaluation of residents and feedback. Other than feedback which does appear in the NSS, these are qualities of teaching which are highly contextualised to medical education.

At the same time as lecturers are being encouraged to develop creative, innovative responses to the challenges of teaching in an expanding, globalised, digital age, student evaluations of teaching reward a transmission model of teaching (Titus, 2008). Lecturers who try more innovative or critical pedagogies are at risk of receiving lower than average student ratings. Lecturers engaged in the scholarship of teaching, who wish to evaluate their experimentation with different pedagogies, find the institutionally valued surveys to be too general to be of use to them. Kember and Ginns (2012) in their evaluation handbook cite some of their own research in which they reviewed 90 action research projects and found 'virtually none' had found any value in such survey data (Kember, 2000). They consider that these tools are not sufficiently tailored to the expected outcomes of the innovation and argue instead that teachers should be supported in developing skills in evaluation design and analysis, so that they can construct their own evaluations.

Interpreting and Using Survey Data

Surveys appear to be so well ingrained into the management of teaching and learning that it is unlikely they will be removed. Perhaps a more pragmatic approach is to share more widely what is known about the resulting data, so that survey findings can be interpreted more responsibly. While the findings of biases in student evaluations of teaching that individual lecturers are subjected to are striking, similar cautions can be offered at the examination of data at the institutional level. Researchers have warned that neither the Australian CEQ nor the UK's NSS should be used for institutional benchmarking because differences between universities explain so little of the variance in the data (Marsh, Ginns, Morin, Nagengast, & Martin, 2011; Marsh & Cheng, 2008, cited in Kember and Ginns). The largest variation in NSS ratings is between subjects of study, with a range of over 15 percentage points (HEFCE, 2014). This means that an institution that has more programmes from the humanities is likely to have a higher overall satisfaction rating than an institution that offers mostly science and/or law courses, purely on the basis of what courses it provides. Such differences in ratings may be due to genuine differences in satisfaction or to variations in how students interpret the questions. During cognitive testing to create a UK version of the NSSE, Kandiko Howson and Matos (2014) found differences in students' understanding of questions by subject studied and whether students were studying at a teaching intensive or research intensive university.

Interpretation of data must also be based on an understanding of the sample who completed it. In an analysis of nine years of NSS data (2003–2015) the overall satisfaction of Black Caribbean students was found to be lower compared to White students or that the proportion of Black African students who agree with the overall satisfaction question is higher compared with White students. Those declaring a disability are consistently less satisfied that those without a disability (HEFCE, 2014). Survey data has the potential to help us to manage the student experience in a more differentiated way by examining the experiences of different groups of students.

Our interpretation and reporting of data must be based on an understanding of how students' complete surveys. Titus (2008), having conducted 75 in depth interviews with American faculty and students found a halo effect where students rate the course as a whole as a good experience:

> *Many students report that rather than reading the actual rating items, they locate a column on the form to reflect their general level of enjoyment in the course and then mark all of the rating items in that same column at that same value.* (Titus, 2008, p. 403)

Similarly, in analysing NSS data from nine years, HEFCE (2014) found an increase in yea-sayers (who give the same answer to every question) from 1% in 2005 to 5.4% in 2013, highlighting the scale of this issue with the statistic that over 1 in 20 respondents chose the same answer to each of the 22 questions in the survey. This suggests the detailed scrutiny of percentages of students responding to individual survey items may be less useful than talking to students about what influences their general level of enjoyment with a course.

Individual lecturers and programme teams should be supported to interpret survey data. For teachers, we know that survey data on its own does not change practice. Marsh and Roche (1993) found that student ratings only improve if teachers are supported to engage with the student feedback through effective counselling e.g. from academic developers. This is a step that is sorely missing in most institutional adoptions of student feedback surveys.

Complementary Methods to Monitor the Student Experience

Although we know student evaluations of teaching are imperfect measures of teaching quality, the real problem with these surveys is that they are being used as the sole method for monitoring and measuring teaching quality (Titus, 2008; Kember & Ginns, 2012). The value of the data they provide is dependent on how academic lecturers and managers use, and encourage the use of, data as part of improvement processes (Buckley, 2012; Pymount, 2016). This final section makes some recommendations for managers of professional education.

Alongside completing a plethora of surveys during their journey, students are asked to engage actively in quality assurance and enhancement activities. In the UK the traditional 'course reps' system has been subject to scrutiny with concerns raised about how the system works for all groups of students (van der Velden, Pool, Lowe, Naidoo, & Pimentel Botas, 2013) and how student representatives are prepared for their roles (Pymount, 2016). The expectation from the Quality Assurance Agency's quality code is that 'Higher education providers take deliberate steps to engage *all* students, individually and collectively, as partners in the assurance and enhancement of their educational experience' (my emphasis, QAA, 2012, p.6). The code makes it clear that relying on a single formal student representation system is not sufficient and that higher education institutions should be proactively initiating frequent conversations with students e.g. student involvement in new projects, or student dialogue with decision makers. Such activities should be a valuable complement to survey-based activity.

Participative research methods are increasing in popularity as a way of both collecting rigorous research data and initiating conversations with students about their experiences (Seale, 2010). For example, libraries have embraced ethnography as an approach to study the ways in which students use libraries (Fried Foster, 2013; Gibbons, 2013). In an environment where most data is collected in order to review hygiene and transactional elements of the student experience (see Fig. 2.1), participative evaluations are useful in being student rather than service orientated. Institutional research is frequently service orientated, evaluating e.g. library resources, the upgrade of a virtual learning environment/learning management system or the student experience of academic advice. A notable exception is an examination of the experience of BME students in a predominantly white university, which uses BME student interviewers and presents the findings as student vignettes (Currant, 2015). Such methodologies are valuable for evaluating the transformational experiences of learning and should serve as models for future institutional research particularly where they are embedded as regular review points rather than one off projects.

Whichever combination of methods is chosen to collect student feedback, both staff and students need to understand and trust the measures in use and be encouraged to engage with them. Rienties (2014) followed up a university wide implementation of a module evaluation survey with an investigation of staff perceptions, finding that some academic staff remained concerned about the suitability of the survey for their discipline, how response rates influenced validity and how managers were going to use the results. Similarly, Pymount's (2016) recommendations having interviewed a range of staff and students focus on how university managers communicate with staff and students to ensure they are aware of the surveys in use and how their findings are interpreted and acted upon. Closing the feedback loop is particularly important. It demonstrates that traditional practices can be changed and encourages sharing of good practices around the institution

Conclusions

Over the last 20 years, the higher education sector has invested heavily in tools and systems to monitor student experiences and engage students in discussions and decision-making about issues which relate to their experiences. Over this time, student satisfaction with university has risen steadily (HEFCE, 2014). However, we must not be complacent. Expertise is developing, informed by research, in how to collect, analyse and interpret student experience data, and this knowledge must be shared more widely. Teachers should be trained in conducting their own evaluations which suit their local circumstances and supported to interpret the findings. Institutional researchers should explore participative research methods to complement the use of surveys. Academic managers should engage staff and students in dialogue about which tools are used, how the data informs decision making and what improvements have been made. Researchers could further explore the effects of student-as-consumer attitudes on responses. Overall, this review has shown a need to adopt a more student-orientated approach to the design and analysis of student experience measures to include transformational learning and impact on gradate outcomes.

References

Angelo, T. A., & Cross, K. P. (1993). *Classroom assessment techniques: A handbook for college teachers* (2nd ed.). Jossey-Bass.

Arah, O., Hoekstra, J., Bos, A., & Lombarts, K. (2011). New tools for systematic evaluation of teaching qualities of medical faculty: Results of an ongoing multi-center survey. *PLoS ONE, 6*(10). https://doi.org/10.1371/journal.pone.0025983

Bedggood, R. E., & Donovan, J. D. (2012). University performance evaluations: What are we really measuring? *Studies in Higher Education, 37*(7), 825–842.

Biggs, J. B., Kember, D., & Leung, D. Y. P. (2001). The revised two factor study process questionnaire: R-SPQ2F. *British Journal of Educational Psychology, 71*, 133–149.

BIS. (2016, September). Teaching Excellence Framework: Year 2 specification. Department for Business Innovation and Skills. Retrieved from https://www.gov.uk/government/publications/teaching-excellence-framework-year-2-specification

Buckley, A. (2012). *"Making it count": Reflecting on the National Student Survey (NSS) in the process of enhancement.* York: Higher Education Academy Retrieved from https://www.heacademy.ac.uk/making-it-count-reflections-national-student-survey-nss-process-enhancement

Buckley, A. (2013). *Engagement for enhancement: Report of a UK survey pilot.* York: Higher Education Academy.

Buckley, A. (2014). *The UK Engagement Survey 2014: The second pilot year.* York: Higher Education Academy.

Bunce, L., Baird, A., & Jones, S. E. (2016). The student-as-consumer approach in higher education and its effects on academic performance. *Studies in Higher Education.* https://doi.org/10.1080/03075079.2015.1127908

Coates, H., & McCormick, A. (Eds.). (2014). *Engaging university students: International insights from system-wide studies.* London: Springer.

Currant, N. (2015) Strategies of belonging: Counterstories of Black students at a predominately white university. *Brookes eJournal of Learning and Teaching, 7* (2). Retrieved from bejlt.brookes.ac.uk

Doubleday, A., & Lee, L. (2016). Dissecting the voice: Health professions students' perceptions of instructor age and gender in an online environment and the impact on evaluations for faculty. *Anatomical Sciences Education, 9*(6), 537–544.

Entwistle, N., & Ramsden, P. (1983). *Understanding student learning.* London: Croom Helm.

Fried Foster, N. (Ed.). (2013). *Studying students: A second look.* Chicago: Association of College and Research Libraries.

Gibbons, S. (2013). Techniques to understand the changing needs of library users. *IFLA Journal, 39*(2), 162–167.

Gibbs, G. (2010). *Dimensions of quality*. York: Higher Education Academy.
HEFCE. (2014). *UK review of the provision of information about higher education*. National Student Survey results and trends analysis 2005–2013. Retrieved from http://www.hefce.ac.uk/pubs/year/2014/201413/
HESA. (2016, October). *Synthesis of consultation responses in support of HESA's fundamental review of destinations and outcomes data for graduates from higher education*. Higher Education Statistics Agency.
Hu, S., & Kuh, G. (2002). Being (dis)engaged in educationally purposeful activities: The influences of student and institutional characteristics. *Research in Higher Education, 43*(5), 555–575.
Kandiko Howson, C., & Matos, F. (2014). *UK Engagement Survey 2014: Full report of cognitive testing*. York: Higher Education Academy. Retrieved from https://www.heacademy.ac.uk/system/files/resources/ukes_2014_cognitive_testing_report.pdf
Kember, D. (2000). *Action learning and action research: Improving the quality of teaching and learning*. London: Kogan Page.
Kember, D., & Ginns, P. (2012). *Evaluating teaching and learning*. New York: Routledge.
Kuh, G. D., Kinzie, J., Shuh, J. H., Whitt, E. J., & Associates (Eds.). (2005). *Student success in college: Creating conditions that matter*. San Francisco: Jossey-Bass.
Lim, P. H., Gan, S., & Ng, H. K. (2010). Student evaluation of engineering modules for improved teaching-learning effectiveness. *Engineering Education, 5*, 52–63.
Marsh, H. W., & Cheng, J. H. S. (2008). Dimensionality, multi-level structure and differentiation at the level of the university and discipline: Preliminary results. Retrieved from https://www.heacademy.ac.uk/resource/national-student-survey-teaching-uk-universities-dimensionality-multilevel-structure-and
Marsh, H. W., Ginns, P., Morin, A. J. S., Nagengast, B., & Martin, A. J. (2011). Use of student ratings to benchmark universities: Multilevel modelling of responses to the Australian Course Experience Questionnaire (CEQ). *Journal of Educational Psychology, 103*, 733–748.
Marsh, H. W., & Roche, L. (1993). The use of students' evaluations and an individually structured intervention to enhance university teaching effectiveness. *American Education Research Journal, 30*, 217–251.
Merrifield, N. (2016, August 31). Best and worst UK universities for nursing, as rated by students. *Nursing Times*.

Onweugbuzie, A., Witcher, A., Collins, K., Filer, J., Wiedmaier, C., & Moore, C. (2007). Students' perceptions of characteristics of effective college teachers: A validity study of a teaching evaluation form using a mixed-method analysis. *American Educational Research Journal, 44*(1), 113–160.

Pymount, S. (2016, January) *The effectiveness of the National Student Survey and local institutional surveys as a management tool for setting effective strategies in higher education.* Thesis submitted for Doctor of Business Administration, Nottingham Business School.

Quality Assurance Agency. (2012). *Chapter B5: Student engagement.* UK Quality Code for Higher Education.

Ramsden, P. (1991). A performance indicator of teaching quality in higher education: The Course Experience Questionnaire. *Studies in Higher Education, 16*(2), 129–150.

Rienties, B. (2014). Understanding academic resistance towards (online) student evaluation. *Assessment and Evaluation in Higher Education, 39*(8), 987–1001.

Rienties, B., & Toetnel, L. (2016). The impact of learning design on student behaviour, satisfaction and performance: A cross-institutional comparison across 151 modules. *Computers in Human Behaviour, 60,* 333–341.

Seale, J. (2010). Doing student voice work in higher education: An exploration of the value of participatory methods. *British Educational Research Journal, 36*(6), 995–1015.

Sharpe, R., O'Donovan, B., & Pavlakou, M. (2014). Using the framework of engagement surveys to evaluate institutional student enhancement initiatives. In *Surveys for Enhancement Conference,* Birmingham, 4 June 2014.

Titus, J. J. (2008). Student ratings in a consumerist academy: Leveraging pedagogical control and authority. *Sociological Perspectives, 51*(2), 397–342.

UCAS. (2016). *UK application rates by the January deadline: 2016 cycle.* UCAS Analysis and Research, 4 February. Retrieved from https://www.ucas.com/sites/default/files/jan-16-deadline-application-rates-report.pdf

Van der Velden, G., Pool, A. D., Lowe, J. A., Naidoo, R., & Pimentel Botas, P. C. (2013). *Student engagement in learning and teaching quality management: A good practice guide for higher education providers and students' unions.* QAA and University of Bath.

Williams, J. (2015, August 13). The National Student Survey should be abolished before it does any more harm. *The Guardian.*

3

'Quality' in an Era of Austerity: Challenges for Irish Universities

Marie Clarke

Introduction

The increasing demand for higher education has been accompanied by a decrease in resources to the higher education sector (Martin & Stella, 2007). Policy-makers in the USA and Europe since the 1980s have focussed on academic quality new policy instruments to assure and improve the quality of teaching and student learning in the tertiary sector (Liu, 2016). Governments now expect universities to be accountable for the quality of services and resources invested. The global demand for skilled human capital has resulted in changes in the degree frameworks of many countries as policymakers seek international recognition of the credentials granted by their country's higher education institutions (Dill, 2007).

The onset of austerity since 2008, has promoted policies in higher education that has placed the system in a constantly shifting political context where its value is under constant review (Davies & O'Callaghan,

M. Clarke (✉)
University College Dublin, Dublin, Ireland
e-mail: marie.clarke@ucd.ie

2014). For some countries, the consequences of the financial crisis have resulted in a reframing of the discourse around graduate employability as large numbers of graduates have found themselves unemployed or underemployed (Cerdeira et al., 2016). Within this narrative, universities have been assigned both some share of the blame for the 'Great Recession' in not producing the right skills, and some responsibility for driving skills and innovation to bring the economy out of recession (Arora, 2015).

This chapter explores the Irish context and the impact of austerity on policy instruments and the impact of these approaches on quality assurance. The period of austerity in Ireland witnessed an increase in regulatory and oversight approaches within the higher education sector and greater emphasis on linking universities to an employability and skills agenda. Within this context the complexities and challenges surrounding quality assurance and professional accreditation become very clear.

Quality Assurance and Government Regulation

Lowi (1972) suggests that any analysis of public policy should focus on the choices made in relation to the way state power is applied and not on the goals of those policies. His policy typology included four policy types: distributive, regulatory, redistributive, and constituent. Distributive policies are government policies that impact on spending in relation to public services where benefits and costs are shared. Regulatory policies limit the power of individuals and agencies and compel certain types of behaviours. Constituent policies create executive power entities and deal with laws. Redistributive powers are dynamic and occur as a result of implementation sometimes with unforeseen consequences. Policy choices in Lowi's (1972) view are an independent variable in the political process. Policy analysis is not about issues but about the ways in which the power of the state is made manifest (Nicholson, 2002).

Contemporary governments use a variety of approaches to regulate state supported activities. Hood (2004) contends that these approaches contain three main elements: information based, authority based, and organization based. Information-based policy instruments are used by governments to address citizens directly providing information about new policies or as a way of influencing public opinion (Hassel, 2015). Authority-based policy instruments are regulatory government tools that cover most policy fields. The regulations include rules, standards, directives and legislation (Hassel, 2015). Self-regulation or delegated self-regulation is when actors who are the recipients of regulation can influence and participate in the setting of the regulation. Organisation-based instruments are used by governments to regulate either directly or through agencies under governmental control. Very often governments employ a mixture of all instruments in order to implement public policies (Hassel, 2015). Many policy instruments are hybrids in nature (Hood, 2004) and employ different control mechanisms.

Government Regulation and Universities

Government direct regulation in higher education can take many forms. A state may choose to define academic standards, to evaluate and enforce standards or employ legal, financial, and monitoring instruments (Dill, 2007). The state can control academic quality by steering professional self-regulation and market regulation. In the university context, direct regulation assumes the sovereignty of the state in defining and enforcing academic standards and can include the definition of academic degree frameworks, state conducted accreditation of programs and/or institutions, performance funding and contracts, and regulations influencing the public provision of academic information such as state-mandated exams or surveys. These methods have frequently been used as an important external quality assurance practice in many countries (Cave, Hanney, Henkel, & Kogan, 1997).

The use of performance indicators as policy tools in higher education has increased worldwide, principally as a result of growing pressure for public accountability (Ewell, 1999). In response to the changing environment of higher education a number of countries have adopted new national qualifications frameworks (Young, 2003). The initial rationale for these frameworks was to provide international recognition to attract foreign students as well placing graduates in the global market. By providing broad descriptors of learning outcomes specific to each level of academic degrees, academic qualification frameworks also provide some potential reference points for external quality assurance practices (McInnis, 2005).

Dill and Beerkens (2013) argue that in many countries, the design of academic quality assurance policies is contested between the state and universities. Governments are interested both in accountability and improvement. Universities tend to focus on quality improvement and are concerned with the provision of high quality education within the conditions set by the government (Kis, 2005). Almost all European countries have an agency co-coordinating quality assurance. They are generally established either by the national or regional government or by universities themselves, often at the request of government (ENQA, 2003). While these agencies are viewed as being independent, however both government and institutions may be represented on the board of the quality assurance agency or contribute to the funding of the agency or evaluations. In Europe, the main source of funding of quality assurance in higher education is the government, but higher education institutions may also provide funding in certain countries (ENQA, 2003).

Market mechanisms also impact on universities and include commercially produced rankings (Dill, 2007). Rankings are different to quality assurance processes. The stated purpose of most rankings is to identify 'excellence', in terms of the best higher education institutions. Rankings by commercial publications often rely upon information gleaned from reputational surveys, input measures such as student test scores or financial resources, and indicators of research quality (Dill & Soo, 2005). These rankings have become highly influential on academic behaviour, often encouraging institutions and programs to invest time, resources, and effort in improving their rated reputations. The most undesirable impact of rankings include 'data massage' to improve the ranking position, homogenisation of higher education provisions, and academic drift (Wächter et al., 2015). Accreditation is also a widely used method in quality assurance (Kis, 2005).

Professional accreditation has become more important as qualifications are effectively becoming gateways for higher professional positions

(Coles, 2015). Accreditation is an evaluation of whether an institution or programme meets a threshold standard and qualifies for a certain status. Professional accreditation can be either regulated or non-regulated. Governments regulate some professions where they wish to assure public safety (El-Khawas, 2000). In unregulated professions, professional associations may establish an accreditation function as part of their wider professional services and operations. In universities, the programmes that are subject to professional review are those generally tied to health care, teacher education and other professions such as architecture, engineering and law (El-Khawas, 2000). Regulatory bodies are focused on public protection. They are concerned that students are well prepared for placements and that they will be adequately supported once in role. Professional associations tend to focus on professional competence ensuring that skills and core competencies are achieved (Friedman, Hogg, Nadarajah, & Pitts, 2017). Accreditation according to Eaton (2012), is becoming increasingly government-controlled, serving more and more as an instrument of government policy to ensure that institutions comply with government law and regulation. Obtaining accreditation may have implications for the university itself such as permission to operate a programme. Accrediting organisations publish their reports and provide detailed descriptions of how standards are met or not met. If accreditation is denied the press in its coverage also contributes to the quality debate (Eaton, 2012).

The extent to which indicators of quality have shaped both the politics of higher education and institutional priorities is not a new phenomenon (Patrick & Stanley, 1998). Universities are influenced by government policies, external quality accreditation bodies, changes in the labour market and diverse societal expectations of the higher education sector (Mizikaci, 2006). The demands emerging from government interest and oversight, can influence and steer the direction and scope of program design, skill sets found within programs and courses, and student experiences mandated to students within the curriculum and the co-curriculum. A key government policy in all countries is the issue of employment and this has become an important indicator of quality in higher education (Kis, 2005).

Graduate Employability and Quality Assurance

Employability can be viewed through a range of different lenses related to the needs of different stakeholders: government, employers, students and universities (Artess, Hooley, & Mellors-Bourne, 2016). Some countries have integrated the employability agenda into their higher education systems (Bridgstock & Cunningham, 2016). The development of less predictable careers, now extends to all segments of the labour market, including to occupations for which a degree is usually necessary (Heery & Salmon, 2000). Within EU policy, there is a renewed focus on higher education to promote excellence in skills development, to promote inclusive and connected systems and promote innovation (Lynch, 2017). A number of European policy instruments and mobility tools have been developed to support the employability agenda. These include reforms in national qualifications systems including the European Qualifications Framework (EQF) for Lifelong Learning, the European Credit and Transfer System (ECTS) for higher education, the European Credit System for Vocational Education and Training (ECVET) and EUROPASS.

Various barriers sit between higher education and the labour market. Rich (2015) argues that the employment of graduates on completion of their studies is one kind of policy goal, ensuring that their skills are effectively used is a different policy goal and contends that universities should take a longer-term perspective and support graduates to establish a career. The quality of universities is often measured using employability metrics. In response to government and employer expectations many universities actively create strategies, frameworks and other kinds of institutional narratives to address employability. These include: changing structures to make the institution more effective in delivering employability. Such structural change often impacts on faculty recruitment, allocation of resources, reorientation of curricula and the development of new qualifications (Artess et al., 2016). Programme development usually includes an increase in employer involvement; the introduction of employability modules or employability elements to support graduate employability; and the provision of career and employability services (Artess et al., 2016).

The skills agenda has been criticised as reflecting a narrow view of educational aims and a threat to academic freedom (Morley, 2001). According to Cranmer (2006) there are difficulties inherent in the employability agenda, from definition to measurement and development. Employment data is also difficult to interpret. Harvey, Locke, and Morey (2002), criticises current methods for measuring employability outcomes based on the proportion of graduates who achieve a full-time job within the first six months after graduation. They contend that this approach measures graduate success only in the short term, and, assesses employability as an institutional achievement rather than that of the individual graduate. Morley (2001) argues that employability has become a performance indicator within higher education, which overlooks how other social factors interact with labour market opportunities. Smith, McKnight, and Naylor (2000) argue that employability is affected by region and locality in terms of employment opportunities; employment patterns change over time and responses by universities can be different in terms of providing for those changes and can be affected by social mix of students and the range of subjects provided by institutions. Employers tend to demand immediate expertise, whereas universities emphasise adaptable expertise that enables graduates to operate in unpredictable new situations (Schwarz & Westerheijden, 2004) which requires different approaches to the educative process (Gibbs, 2010). This is especially the case in professional education delivered in university contexts.

Professional education has always been central to the university (Levi, 1972). Universities have a public mission which includes providing an education that prepares students for the public service professions; informing debate in the public sphere; preparing citizens to participate in society; producing new technologies and advancing social mobility (Calhoun, 2006). In professional education an emphasis on the dominance of utilitarian and technocratic approaches has been criticised (Jarvis & Gouthro, 2013). The intellectual discipline provides opportunities for reflection (Eraut, 1994) and learning and insight (Levi, 1972). The university must also produce skilled professionals with a commitment to professional standards and codes of conduct (East, Stokes, & Walker, 2014).

Howieson et al. (2014) argues that while university education is important to future practitioners, there are limits imposed by scarce resources, the generalised context within which university learning occurs, and the varied nature of expertise. Many of these challenges were exacerbated in the Irish higher education system during the period of austerity.

The Irish Higher Education System

The Irish public higher education system consists of seven universities and Dublin Institute of Technology (which have self-awarding powers) and 13 other Institutes of Technology (which have delegated authority to make their own awards from QQI) and which offer Bachelor and Master programmes in a growing range of subject areas. There are other public and private higher education institutions in specialised areas. In 2015/16, there were 222,618 student enrolments in public higher education institutions in Ireland of which 119, 798 are enrolled in the university sector. In 2014/15, over 15,000 whole-time equivalent, full-time students in Irish higher education were international: that is, approximately 9% of full-time numbers, an increase from 7% in 2012/13. It is expected that entrants to third level education will increase by 124% in the period 2013–2028 (HEA, 2017). The development of Technological Universities is currently being legislated for as a result of mergers between Institutes of Technology. It is envisaged that the creation of these universities will allow funding to be channelled towards addressing regional skills needs. The post-Brexit environment will present a range of challenges and opportunities for the Irish higher education sector in relation to student mobility, international educational programmes and funding (HEA, 2017). In 2015, there were 17,699 core faculty and non-faculty staff in Irish public higher education institutions. This was supplemented by temporary research and specialist staff of 4882, bringing overall staffing levels in the sector to 23,544. The faculty/non-faculty split in universities is, 47% of core staff in universities are faculty members and 53% are non-faculty (HEA, 2017).

Quality Assurance and Professional Accreditation in Irish Higher Education

The Higher Education Authority (hereafter HEA) has a statutory responsibility, at central government level, for the effective governance and regulation of higher education institutions and the higher education system (HEA, 2017). A more regulatory approach to higher education in Ireland has been in evidence since 2009 when Ireland became one of the first countries to reference its National Framework Qualification levels to the European Qualifications Framework. Ireland is part of the European wide Bologna Process. In 2012, the Qualifications and Quality Assurance (Education and Training) Act was introduced which amalgamated four existing bodies who were tasked with quality assurance in the higher and further education sectors. Quality and Qualifications Ireland was established under the Act and is the primary oversight body for quality in the university sector which conducts five-yearly external institutional review process. QQI is the guardian of the National Framework of Qualifications (NFQ) and is also responsible for the recognition of professional and other awarding bodies. It has national responsibility for overseeing a number of European mobility tools, which enhances the employability of Irish graduates going abroad and assists holders of foreign qualifications who come to Ireland to learn or to work. The Irish Survey of Student Engagement Survey (hereafter ISSE), was introduced in 2013. This survey in keeping with similar international surveys captures data on a range of indicators of the student experience and overall student satisfaction levels.

The accreditation landscape in Ireland is both varied and complex and reflects the structure, representation and regulation of the professions whose associations operate independently of each other (Friedman et al., 2017). There are professional associations that represent a profession; regulatory bodies that regulate a profession; other institutions that have a remit for regulating professional and other accrediting agencies (non-professional bodies). Some professional associations are defined by statute and membership is compulsory in order to practice. There are also some organisations which are specialist accrediting bodies who do not have professional members (Friedman et al., 2017).

In many professions, a quota system exists in terms of entry to programmes in universities. In medicine and nursing, there is a quota on the number of Irish and EU students that universities can accept on undergraduate medical degree programmes. The intake of students to publicly-funded initial teacher education (ITE) programmes for primary teachers in regulated by the Department of Education and Skills (Teaching Council, 2017). The intake to post primary consecutive programmes, provided by universities, is not regulated, except for a relatively short period between 1994 and the early 2000s, when with the agreement of the universities involved, the number of students entering consecutive higher diploma programmes was limited (Teaching Council, 2017). There is no quota system in engineering or law.

Austerity and Quality Assurance in the Irish Higher Education Sector

The resourcing of the Irish higher education sector is predominantly through public funding administered by the Higher Education Authority (hereafter, HEA). It has three major components: institutional funding, capital funding, and research funding. Institutional funding, is informed by a formula based unit cost calculation (termed RGAM) and a grant is made in lieu of undergraduate tuition fees. The funding approach is similar to nearly all international higher education systems: a block grant which allocates public funding on the basis of broad performance, subject to meeting accountability and transparency standards, while also allowing institutional autonomy on how this is spent (HEA, 2017).

The pace of economic and social change in Ireland was extremely rapid between 1995 and 2008 and the higher education sector was viewed as central to developing a knowledge economy. At the start of the 2000s, Ireland did not escape the general economic downturn following 11 September 2001. One result of this was a delayed cut of effectively 10% in the universities' operating budgets in 2003/04. While the national economic climate improved again during 2004, the OECD found that more investment in higher education was needed if Ireland's national goals were to be realized, and that system-wide structural and other issues need to be addressed for such investment to be effective (OECD, 2004). Ireland's investment in its education system in 2004 was lower than the OECD average (OECD, 2004).

The global recession in 2008 had a significant impact on the Republic of Ireland, which is a small open economy. The impact of the Irish sovereign debt and the consequent economic reforms mandated under the National Recovery Plan 2011–2014, as well as the Programme of Financial Support for Ireland, which the EU and the International Monitory Fund (IMF) provided for Ireland resulted in almost ten years of austerity measures. The state's public-sector Employment Control Framework (hereafter ECF, in place since 2009) imposed a recruitment embargo and coupled with early retirement incentivised schemes many professions experienced severe cuts. In the professional areas, a number of trends emerged during the recessionary period. Between 2008 and 2012 the staff numbers engaged in the legal sector fell by 16% (Law Society of Ireland, 2014). In the period 2007–2010 the number of people employed by accountancy practices decreased by seven per cent (Hays, 2010). The number of nurses registered on the active register decreased by 6% between 2008 and 2014 (Humphries, McAleese, Matthews, & Brugha, 2015). In order to address the supply issues a graduate nurse employment scheme was launched in 2013 which offered 1000 new nursing positions at reduced salary rates. This proved to be controversial and was the focus of a boycott by the Irish Nursing and Midwifery Organisation (INMO). The cuts implemented during the financial crisis reduced the number of doctors in general practice and there is an expected shortage of over 2000 doctors by 2025 as many current GPs are scheduled to retire in the coming years. There are 1600 fewer consultants working in the Public Health Services now than should be the case under the most recent targets set (IMO, 2017). Teachers recruited since January 2011 were placed on significantly lower pay-scales than their colleagues due to austerity-era cuts. This proved controversial with teacher unions. Engineering graduates were particularly affected by the recession. In 2012, the highest emigration rate was among engineering Level 8 graduates at 17%.

The austerity period had a major impact on the higher education sector. Over the period 2007/08 to 2014/15 there was a fall in state grants for higher education of 38% (Clarke, Drennan, Harmon, Hyde, & Politis, 2015). Overall funding for the higher education sector fell by at least 13.5% while the overall number of full-time students has increased by 25%. This resulted in an overall decrease in the total funding per student of 22% (Clarke et al., 2015). At the same time the numbers employed in higher education institutions fell by 13% a real term reduction of 4000 staff (Boland, 2015). In the university sector, the most recent audited accounts (2016) highlighted an overall aggregate deficit. Given the OECD recommendation of a 3% annual surplus to maintain institutional sustainability, the deficit position across higher education is a major concern (HEA, 2017).

These austerity measures were accompanied by a series of policy initiatives designed to make universities more responsive to government policy and demanded more accountability. In 2011, the *National Strategy for Higher Education to 2030* was published which set out a long-term vision of higher education as a central driver of innovation, competitive enterprise and academic excellence. A major restructuring of the higher education sector was proposed in terms of reducing the number of HEIs and providing for the introduction of a new type of institution, a technological university. The need for a sustainable and equitable funding model was also signalled where universities were required to agree compact agreements with the HEA to deliver key outcomes (HEA, 2016). This developed into a formal process of strategic dialogue and institutional compacts, where three-year plans for delivering on policy objectives were agreed with individual HEIs and monitored via an annual process with the HEA. Embedded within this was the provision to withhold up to 10% of HEI funding if performance was considered unsatisfactory. This was a clear accountability measure to assess performance against specific objectives. No reward based mechanism was built into the performance funding approach for institutions that exceeded targets.

The role of universities to deliver on national objectives was linked to other government initiatives such as the *Action Plan for Education 2017; National Plan for Equity of Access to Higher Education 2015–2019*; the

National Skills Strategy 2025; *Innovation 2020*; *Irish Educated, Globally Connected* and the *National Review of Gender Equality in Irish Higher Education Institutions*. It is evident that universities are expected to respond to a diverse set of priorities and responsibilities, as set out in government policy. The future funding of Irish higher education is currently under review.

The funding challenge is widely recognised in the Irish higher education system. In 2016, a report entitled *Investing in National Ambition: a Strategy for Funding Higher Education* was published. It acknowledged that there was little scope to secure further efficiencies and maintain quality without increased investment. It recommended additional annual funding of €600 million to be provided by 2021 and €1 billion by 2030 to deliver higher quality outcomes and provide for increased demand. A necessary condition of additional funding is an acceptance that the higher education system delivers efficiently, effectively and demonstrably against public and governmental expectations. The report placed a significant focus on the value of higher education and its role in the creation of jobs, the restoration of living standards and the enhancement of social services. The Department of Education and Skills has indicated that the funding approach will be underpinned by a series of core principles, including the need for it to be metric and outcome based and reflective of national policy. A key consideration will be the development of a funding model to ensure that institutions are agile and responsive in meeting evolving skills needs (DES, 2017). As part of the funding options for higher education the government has proposed that employers increase their contributions to the National Training Fund (DES, 2017) and in the 2018 budget, employers through the National Training Fund (NTF) were requested to contribute €200 million to higher education over a three-year period. The government will monitor how these funds are channelled into skills development areas. The development of apprenticeships is promoted by government as a significant opportunity for Irish higher education institutions to secure additional funding. Institutions are invited to apply for additional resources towards the development of courses in identified areas there are skills gaps.

The Impact of Austerity on Quality Assurance Processes in Irish Universities

The QQI quality review reports for the period 2008–2015 from the university sector reflected the recurring theme of austerity and resource cuts. The reduction in the state capital grants together with the less flexible approach available to the annual core operating budgets to offset acute shortfalls; has resulted in well publicised gaps in funding for capital maintenance, upgrades and developments in Irish universities (QQI, 2016). Engineers Ireland (2017) noted from its accreditation process the lack of investment in laboratory facilities in universities. There was a constant perceived tension between a continual drive to contain or reduce costs and an enhanced focus on income generation from new sources of revenue (QQI, 2016). The main challenge identified was the delivery of current programmes within a reduced resource environment. Issues such as reduced staffing levels the increase in student numbers, increased workload, reduced promotion opportunities; reduced staff development opportunities and increased tensions between time spent on teaching and time spent on research were mentioned frequently in institutional reports (QQI, 2016). It also emerged that faculty felt under increased strain and were reluctant to take on additional duties in the context of pay cuts.

The reduction in available staff due to the conditions imposed by the ECF resulted in an increased staff-student ratio currently at 1:19 which is well above the OECD average of 1:15.6 (QQI, 2016). The perceived impact of austerity on the quality of the student learning experience focussed on the learning and teaching environment particularly the continued maintenance of facilities and equipment, the need to update IT infrastructure and the lack of library resources. Students were unhappy with the facilities available to them, and while institutions and individual departments were aware of the short-comings indicated that there were no immediate solutions available to address these concerns (QQI, 2016). Reports noted that despite faculty and staff efforts to contain these issues to 'protect' students that over time these were now coming to the fore and some reports took the opportunity to 'warn' about quality of the Student Learning Experience (SLE). Other reports noted that impacts were apparent in the reduced provision of tutorials, academic student support, services available to students and assessment feedback provided to students. The cuts to resources impacted negatively on the capacity of institutions to attract international students, who were viewed as a source of important additional income. Similar themes emerged from recent ISSE surveys. A recurrent and emerging theme across the ISSE surveys was the low interaction between undergraduates and faculty (ISSE, 2016). The results from the ISSE survey reflect the concerns expressed by faculty in the institutional quality review reports.

QQI is focussed on optimising resources, following the period of austerity (Friedman et al., 2017). A study entitled *Professional Body Accreditation in Higher Education Institutions in Ireland* was commissioned by QQI to examine the ways in which professional body activity impacted upon the higher education institution quality assurance contexts (Friedman et al., 2017). Professional body accreditation has had a major impact on university resources (Friedman et al., 2017). Over a three-year period, many universities had to increase resources for accreditation for a variety of reasons including: the accreditation of more programmes, increased fees, increased student numbers, investment in online resources, and changes in accrediting body requirements (Friedman et al., 2017). It also emerged from the study that professional body accreditation requirements changed regularly which also increased the level of resources required. Single programmes can require accreditation from more than one professional body and approaches sometimes clash thus causing added complexities. Many faculty were not motivated to engage and were of the view that professional accreditation led to an ever-narrowing academic standardisation at the expense of innovation (Friedman et al., 2017). However, it was generally recognised by universities that professional accreditation was very important as it raised the employability of graduates, ensured that content of programmes remained relevant and in line with industry best practice.

Employer Engagement and Universities

Competitive funding programmes, to facilitate the channelling of investment in prioritised areas is now a feature of the higher education landscape. A number of competitive funding streams currently exist such as

Springboard, which requires education-industry collaboration and is open to both public and private higher education providers. The springboard upskilling initiative in higher education offers free courses at certificate, degree and masters level leading to qualifications in areas where there are employment opportunities in the economy. It is co-funded by the Irish government and the European Social Fund as part of the ESF programme for employability, inclusion and learning 2014–2020. Springboard is acknowledged as a model of how competitive funding can be used by government adopting a market forces approach to direct policy.

Enhancing employer engagement and alignment has been a key priority in the programme of education and training reform (DES, 2017). The current economic climate is a significant challenge to employer engagement. Different industrial, business and community sectors take different approaches to working with the education sector. Some sectors actively engage e.g. through professional, trade and/or representative bodies, others do not and are more dependent on the education sector to supply their skill needs (QQI, 2014).

The National Employers Survey (hereafter NES) is published annually and reflects national and foreign employer satisfaction with graduate recruits. In 2015, it was reported that employers were very satisfied with graduate recruits across a range of workplace and personal attributes. These included ICT skills; teamwork; communication; adaptability and flexibility; positive attitude and energy. However, concern was expressed in relation to the lack of foreign language skills, entrepreneurial skills and business acumen/awareness (NES, 2015). Skills identified as currently not available, but which would be required over the next five years included engineering, languages, ICT and specific quantitative skills. These are viewed as key areas of workforce development. The report also suggested that higher educational institutions could improve collaboration with enterprises by liaising, collaborating and by being less bureaucratic and inflexible. It was suggested that practical components should be implemented on programmes and that higher education institutions should proactively seek (long-term) placements and internships for their students and update companies on progress being made and/or changes to the curriculum. Employers were also of the view that there was a misalignment of course content to requirements of industry and that courses should be specifically designed where demand was high (NES, 2015). The Department of Education and Skills has suggested that based on future reforms of the higher education sector that employers can be confident that they can influence the direction of higher education, that providers will be responsive to their emerging needs, and that the required skills will be delivered in an efficient and effective manner (DES, 2017). A new feature of university achievement in this area will include more employer-relevant metrics and indicators (DES, 2017).

Conclusions and Implications

The impact of austerity on the Irish economy and Irish universities had a number of implications for policy development, quality assurance and professional accreditation. The onset of the 'Great Recession', impacted negatively on the employment opportunities of professionals and resulted in reduced salaries for new entrants to professions. Cuts in funding, resulted in successive governments seeking more accountability from universities. The accompanying restructuring efforts highlighted a more centralised approach than had previously been the case. Successive Irish governments during this period have adopted what Hood (2004) described as a direct regulatory approach employing considerable oversight through the introduction of performance funding and contracts. As this approach became more embedded university performance is now explicitly linked to other government policies especially in relation to skills development and employment needs.

The funding of universities is a critical issue in the Irish context. The terms core or block grant funding masks the performance and competitive dimensions that successive governments have built into the allocation of funding to the sector. The Department of Education and Skills will through future reforms of the system ensure that employers can influence the direction of higher education and that universities will respond to employers' needs. The employer contribution to the funding of higher education through the National Training Fund (NTF) where the government will monitor how these funds are channelled into skills development areas is another example of increased regulation and control. It also represents an effort on the part of government to ensure that key areas of economic development are addressed.

The cuts to resources in Irish universities also impacted on quality assurance and accreditation processes. QQI has pointed to a number of issues in their analysis of the sector including the gaps in funding for capital maintenance, upgrades and developments; the tensions between reducing costs and enhancing income generation and the challenges of delivering current programmes within a reduced resource environment in the context of reduced staffing levels, increased student numbers and increased workloads. In this context, many universities have had to increase resources for accreditation due to new programmes, increased fees, increased student numbers, and changes in accrediting body requirements. Professional body accreditation requirements changed regularly which also increased the level of resources required. The insights emerging from the Irish context during a period of austerity highlights the challenges posed for universities in relation to government policies, quality assurance and professional accreditation. For countries that are seeking to reduce financial support for the higher education sector numerous lessons can be learned from the Irish context.

References

Arora, B. (2015). A Gramscian analysis of the employability agenda. *British Journal of Sociology of Education, 36*(4), 635–648.

Artess, J., Hooley, T., & Mellors-Bourne, R. (2016). *Employability: A review of the literature 2012–16. A report for the Higher Education Academy*. Higher Education Academy.

Boland, T. (2015). *Speech at Royal Irish Academy. A dialogue on higher education funding*. Royal Irish Academy, 23 September 2015. Retrieved from http://www.hea.ie/sites/default/files/ria_tb_funding_speech_v2_002.pdf

Bridgstock, R., & Cunningham, S. (2016). Creative labour and graduate outcomes: Implications for higher education and cultural policy. *International Journal of Cultural Policy, 22*(1), 10–26.

Calhoun, C. (2006). The university and the public good. *Thesis Eleven, 84*, 7–43. https://doi.org/10.1177/0725513606060516

Cave, M., Hanney, S., Henkel, M., & Kogan, M. (1997). *The use of performance indicators in higher education: The challenge of the quality movement* (3rd ed.). London: Jessica Kingsley.

Cerdeira, L., Machado-Taylor, M., Cabrito, B., Patrocínio, T., Brites, R., Gomes, R., ... Ganga, R. (2016). Brain drain and the disenchantment of being a higher education student in Portugal. *Journal of Higher Education Policy and Management, 38*(1), 68–77.

Clarke, M., Drennan, J., Harmon, D., Hyde, A., & Politis, Y. (2015). *The academic profession in Ireland*. Dublin: University College Dublin.

Coles, M. (2015). *National qualifications frameworks: Reflections and trajectories. Qualifications policies insights*. Quality and Qualifications Ireland.

Cranmer, S. (2006). Enhancing graduate employability: Best intentions and mixed outcomes. *Studies in Higher Education, 31*(2), 169–184.

Davies, H., & O'Callaghan, C. (2014). All in this together? Feminisms, academia, austerity. *Journal of Gender Studies, 23*(3), 227–232.

Department of Education and Skills. (2017). *Proposed Exchequer—Employer investment mechanism for higher education and future education and training*. Consultation Paper. Retrieved from https://www.education.ie/en/Publications/Education-Reports/pub_ed_proposed_exchequer_employer_investment_higher_further_training_2017.pdf

Dill, D. D. (2007). Are public research universities effective communities of learning?: The collective action dilemma of assuring academic standards. In R. L. Geiger, C. L. Colbeck, R. L. Williams, & C. K. Anderson (Eds.), *Future of the American Public Research University* (pp. 187–203). Rotterdam: Sense Publishers.

Dill, D. D., & Beerkens, M. (2013). Designing the framework conditions for assuring academic standards: Lessons learned about professional, market, and government regulation of academic quality. *Higher Education, 65*(3), 341–357.

Dill, D. D., & Soo, M. (2005). Academic quality, league tables, and public policy: A cross-national analysis of university ranking systems. *Higher Education, 49*(4), 495–533.

East, L., Stokes, R., & Walker, M. (2014). Universities, the public good and professional education in the UK. *Studies in Higher Education., 39*(9), 1617–1633.

Eaton, J. S. (2012). The future of accreditation? *Planning for Higher Education, 40*(3), 8–15.

El-Khawas, E. (2000). The impetus for organisational change: An exploration. *Tertiary Education and Management, 6*(1), 37–46.

Engineers Ireland. (2017). Budget submission 2017. Retrieved from https://www.engineersireland.ie/EngineersIreland/media/SiteMedia/communications/publications/Engineers-Ireland-2017-Budget-Submission-b.pdf

ENQA. (2003). *Quality procedures in European higher education*. ENQA Occasional Papers 5, Helsinki.

Eraut, M. (1994). *Developing professional knowledge and competence*. London and Washington, DC: The Falmer Press.

Ewell, P. T. (1999). Linking performance measures to resource allocation: Exploring unmapped terrain. *Quality in Higher Education, 5*(3), 191–209.

Friedman, A., Hogg, K., Nadarajah, K., & Pitts, R. (2017). *Professional body accreditation in higher education institutions in Ireland*. Quality and Qualifications Ireland.

Gibbs, G. (2010). *Dimensions of quality*. York, UK: The Higher Education Academy.

Harvey, L., Locke, W., & Morey, A. (2002). *Enhancing employability, recognising diversity: Making links between higher education and the world of work*. London: Universities UK.

Hassel, A. (2015). Public policy. In J. Wright (Ed.), *International encyclopedia of the social and behavioral science* (2nd ed.). Amsterdam and Boston: Elsevier.

Hays. (2010). *Accountancy practices Ireland Employment Report 2010*. Hays Recruiting Experts in Accountancy and Finance.

Heery, E., & Salmon, J. (Eds.). (2000). *The insecure workforce*. London: RoutledgeFalmer.

Higher Education Authority. (2016). *Higher education system performance 2014–2016*. Dublin.

Higher Education Authority. (2017). *Review of the allocation model for funding of higher education institutions. Working Paper 1: The higher education sector in Ireland*. Dublin.

Hood, C. (2004). Conclusion: Making sense of controls over government. In C. Hood, O. James, B. G. Peters, & C. Scott (Eds.), *Controlling modern government: Variety, commonality, and change* (pp. 185–205). Cheltenham, UK: Edward Elgar.

Howieson, B., Hancock, P., Segal, N., Kavanagh, M., Tempone, I., & Kent, J. (2014). Who should teach what? Australian perceptions of the roles of universities and practice in the education of professional accountants. *Journal of Accountancy Education, 32,* 259–275.

Humphries, N., McAleese, S., Matthews, A., & Brugha, R. (2015). Emigration is a matter of self-preservation. The working conditions … are killing us slowly': Qualitative insights into health professional emigration from Ireland. *Human Resources Health, 13*(35). Retrieved October 15, 2017, from https://www.ncbi.nlm.nih.gov/pmc/articles/PMC4437248/

Irish Medical Organisation. (2017). *IMO Pre-Budget Submission 2018*. Retrieved from http://www.imo.ie/news-media/news-press-releases/2017/imo-budget-submission-201/index.xml

Irish Survey of Student Engagement [ISSE]. (2016). *HEA, IUA, THEA and USI: Dublin*. Retrieved October 16, 2017, from www.studentsurvey.ie

Jarvis, C., & Gouthro, P. (2013). The role of the arts in professional education; making the invisible, visible. In *Research in work and learning*, 18–21 June 2013, University of Stirling. Retrieved October 16, 2017, from http://eprints.hud.ac.uk/id/eprint/18339/

Kis, V. (2005). *Quality assurance in tertiary education: Current practices in OECD countries and literature review on potential effects*. Paper contribution to the OECD Thematic Review of Tertiary Education. Retrieved from www.oecd.org/edu/tertiary/review

Law Society of Ireland. (2014). *The Solicitors' profession: Contribution to the Irish economy*. Fitzpatrick Associates Economic Consultants.

Levi, H. E. (1972). The place of professional education in the life of the university. *Ohio State Law Journal, 32,* 229–239.

Liu, S. (2016). Higher education quality assessment and university change: A theoretical approach. In S. Liu (Ed.), *Quality assurance and institutional transformation, the Chinese experience* (pp. 15–46). Singapore: Springer.

Lowi, T. J. (1972). Four systems of policy, politics and choice. *Public Administration Review, 32*(4), 314–325.

Lynch, S. (2017). *European policy on teaching and learning in higher education*. Presentation to EUA 1st European Learning and Teaching Forum. Pierre and Marie Curie University, Paris.

Martin, M., & Stella, A. (2007). *External quality assurance in higher education: Making choices*. France: UNESCO, International Institute for Educational Planning.

McInnis, C. (2005). *The Australia qualifications framework. Public policy for academic quality research program*. Chapel Hill: University of North Carolina. Retrieved from http://www.unc.edu

Mizikaci, F. (2006). A systems approach to program evaluation model for quality in higher education. *Quality Assurance in Education, 14*(1), 37–53.

Morley, L. (2001). Producing new workers: Quality, equality and employability in higher education. *Quality in Higher Education, 7*(2), 131–138.

National Employer Survey. (2015). *Employers' views on Irish further and higher education and training outcomes*. Higher Education Authority, SOLAS, QQI, Department of Education and Skills, Dublin.

Nicholson, N. (2002). Policy choices and the uses of state power: The work of Theodore J. Lowi. *Policy Sciences, 35*(2), 163–177.

OECD. (2004). *Review of national policies for education: Review of higher education in Ireland examiners' report*. OECD. Retrieved from http://www.hea.ie/sites/default/files/oecd_review_of_higher_education_2004.pdf

Patrick, J. P., & Stanley, E. C. (1998). Teaching and research quality indicators and the shaping of higher education. *Research in Higher Education, 39*(1), 19–41.

Quality and Qualifications Ireland. (2014). *Education and employers: Joining forces to promote quality and innovation across further and higher education and training. A strategic approach to employer engagement*. Retrieved October 14, 2017, from www.qqi.ie

Quality and Qualifications Ireland. (2016). *Quality in an era of diminishing resources' Irish higher education 2008–15. An analysis of published institutionally—Organised quality review reports of academic departments, schools and programmes in Irish public higher education institutions*. Retrieved September 15, 2017, from www.qqi.ie

Rich, J. (2015). *Employability: Degrees of value*. London: HEPI.

Schwarz, S., & Westerheijden, D. F. (2004). Accreditation in the framework of evaluation activities: A comparative study in the European higher education area. In S. Schwarz & D. F. Westerheijden (Eds.), *Accreditation and evaluation in the European higher education area*. Dordrecht: Kluwer.

Smith, J., McKnight, A., & Naylor, R. (2000). Graduate employability: Policy and performance in higher education in the UK. *The Economic Journal, 110*(464), 382–411.

The Teaching Council. (2017). *Striking the balance. Teacher supply in Ireland: Technical Working Group report*. Dublin: Teaching Council of Ireland and Department of Education and Skills.

Wächter, B., Kelo, M., Lam, Q. K. H., Effertz, P., Jost, C., & Kottowski, S. (2015). *University quality indicators: A critical assessment.* European Union: Directorate General for Internal Policy: Policy Department B: Structural and Cohesion Policies Culture and Education.

Young, M. F. D. (2003). National qualifications frameworks as a global phenomenon: A comparative perspective. *Journal of Education and Work, 16*(3), 223–237.

4

Accessing Expert Understanding: The Value of Visualising Knowledge Structures in Professional Education

Ian M. Kinchin

Introduction

At the outset of my own academic career, if asked, I would have identified myself as a Biologist. My interest was focused on invertebrate zoology and on one group of animals in particular—the Tardigrades (Kinchin, 1994). The main challenge with studying Tardigrades is that they are very small, typically less than 0.1 mm in length. A lot of effort has to be made to actually see the animals and the structures within them. So, I invested a lot of time and energy working with various types of microscopes and tissue stains in order to reveal the details that allowed me to make observations to add to the body of knowledge about these animals. When my disciplinary gaze shifted, and my professional identity moved from Biology to Education, my desire to see what was going on accompanied me as part of my 'disciplinary baggage'. However, the instruments available to visualise learning are not as well established as the instruments used to observe physical structures in the life sciences. I

I. M. Kinchin (✉)
University of Surrey, Guildford, UK
e-mail: i.kinchin@surrey.ac.uk

© The Author(s) 2019
K. Trimmer et al. (eds.), *Ensuring Quality in Professional Education Volume II*,
https://doi.org/10.1007/978-3-030-01084-3_4

found that research in the social sciences was much more concerned with developing tools and methods—things that are often accepted as 'givens' in the life sciences. One of the most powerful tools that I have discovered to visualise learning is concept mapping (Novak & Cañas, 2006, 2007). These diagrammatic representations of knowledge are simple to use and can help to reveal so much detail of the understanding that underpins expert practice that they have become my 'microscope of choice'.

My current academic role is described variously in the literature as educational development, academic development, faculty development or professional development of university teachers and is now an accepted part of the university landscape in the UK (e.g. Gosling, 2009). Academic development has evolved since its introduction, becoming increasingly scholarly, professional and discipline-sensitive over the years (Gibbs, 2013), with a number of identifiable factors being shown to elicit positive responses from engaged participants (Steinert et al., 2006). Inevitably, participants in professional development courses exhibit a diversity of backgrounds and experiences that make it difficult to determine universally suitable entry points for discussion about how to develop as teachers. As a starting point for teacher development prior knowledge can be used to raise awareness of assumptions about teaching that are often hidden, and that can be used to encourage self-reflection (Taylor, 2000). However, it is not only *what* is known, but *how* such understanding is organised that is an important factor that can impede or facilitate further professional learning. In addition, the unfamiliar language of teaching may provide a barrier for colleagues who are already experts in one discipline, to accessing and using prior knowledge about teaching and learning, and acknowledging their novice status as teachers (Green, 2009). For colleagues who work in professional areas such as medicine and dentistry, the observable separation of clinical practice from the underpinning science can be particularly problematic when reflecting upon their teaching practice (e.g. Kinchin, Cabot, & Hay, 2008b). The application of concept mapping can be used to help overcome these barriers.

Concept Mapping

A key characteristic of experts in any domain is that they possess an extensive and highly integrated body of knowledge related to their disciplinary area (Patel, Arocha, & Kaufman, 1999). This is coupled with the ability to recognise patterns within complex sets of information and to use this to identify quick and accurate responses. Concept mapping has been used as a tool to illustrate the nature of this expert understanding (Hoffman & Lintern, 2006). Whilst concept mapping (Novak, 2010) has been used extensively to record what has been learnt previously (*i.e.* accepted knowledge), it is being used increasingly as a tool to chart a way towards new understanding (Kinchin, 2014), or to gain access to the yet-to-be-known (*sensu* Bernstein, 2000). For example:

> *concept mapping may not only be a way of visualising existing theory to enable verification and dialogue, but it may also help new theoretical perspectives to emerge. This is often as a result of identifying links between ideas that had not been previously made, or by viewing known links from a different perspective.* (Kinchin, 2016, p. 88)

Whilst on the surface concept maps appear to be very simple, they should not be viewed as diagrams that just summarise previous learning, but as tools in the exploration of the relationship between ideas that are represented and as a stimulus for further dialogue. Excellent maps are dynamic constructs rather than static representations, providing an artefact to aid examination of beliefs and allow personal, private views to be externalised for analysis and/or discussion. As explained by Wilson, Mandich, and Magalhães (2015, p. 4):

> *Concept mapping is a medium through which people come to understand more about an event and about themselves. This change of self, re-shapes the meaning of the phenomenon that is being studied, and offers the participants an opportunity to "re-see" the significance the experience and the mapping process offer them. Through this process of "re-seeing," participants develop an artistic expression of self-discovery (the concept map) and their voice resonates on both an individual and a social level.*

The application of concept mapping helps to develop reflective practice whilst constructing knowledge structures that support the evolution of adaptive expertise (Bohle Carbonell, Stalmeijer, Könings, Segers, & van Merriënboer, 2014; Salmon & Kelly, 2015).

In practice, concept maps are diagrammatic representations of understanding in which concepts are drawn in boxes that are linked with arrows that carry explanatory linking phrases (Fig. 4.1). Some of the literature on concept mapping has made the assumption that increasing the size of maps to contain a greater number of concepts is an indicator of greater understanding. This has represented a misconception on the part of many researchers and has resulted in an unhelpful, diversionary focus on methods of scoring that has been a feature of the literature for some time (e.g. Stuart, 1985). Concept maps drawn by experts are often smaller than those drawn by novices as expert understanding is organised more efficiently than novice knowledge structures, using key concepts and explanatory linking phrases that often include the use of specialist, disciplinary terminology. By selecting what to include within a concept map, the expert is also selecting what *not* to include. The novice mapper finds

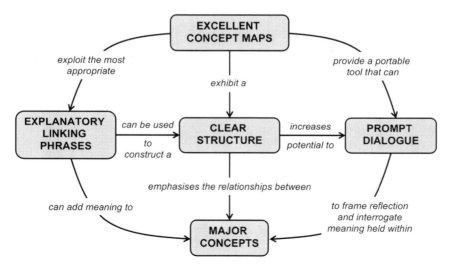

Fig. 4.1 A concept map to emphasise the key features of excellent concept maps

decisions regarding the exclusion of information difficult and there is a tendency for novices to include all related information—whether it is pertinent to the context or not. The ability to be concise within a concept map is regarded as one of the criteria for excellence (Cañas, Novak, & Reiska, 2015). This phenomenon has also been recognised in other areas of academic endeavour where diagrams are an essential element of the practitioner's toolkit. For example, it has been demonstrated in the sciences that expert neuroscientists often do not draw detailed or complex representations of the neurone within their research. Their diagrams show only the essential elements, often in a stylised form to emphasise the key characteristics under investigation (e.g. Hay, Williams, Stahl, & Wingate, 2013; Wingate & Kwint, 2006). A concise concept map that emphasises the key characteristics of excellent concept maps is given in Fig. 4.1.

Linking Tools with Theories

One of the most well-developed conceptual frameworks for the generic consideration of the variation in knowledge structures is that based on Bernstein's sociology of education (Bernstein, 1999, 2000). Bernstein describes '*horizontal knowledge structures*' and '*hierarchical knowledge structures*'. When elaborating upon horizontal knowledge, Bernstein (2000, p. 159) refers to a '*segmental organisation*' in which '*there is no necessary relation between what is learned in different segments*'. This resonates with the recognition of rote learning of content without understanding (Novak, 2010), where isolated assemblages of meaning can co-exist without interacting with each other. In contrast, Bernstein (2000, p. 161) sees hierarchical knowledge structures as attempting '*to create very general propositions and theories, which integrate knowledge at lower levels and in this way show underlying uniformities across an expanding range of apparently different phenomena*'. This resonates with the view of integrated expert knowledge structures that are often hierarchical in structure (Bradley, Paul, & Seeman, 2006).

Bernstein's work has been developed by Maton (2009, p. 44) to consider how 'curriculum structures play a role in creating conditions for students to experience cumulative learning, where their understandings integrate and subsume previous knowledge, or segmented learning, where new ideas or skills are accumulated alongside rather than build on past knowledge'. The segmented learning described by Maton equates to a surface approach that on its own would result from the serial acquisition of knowledge chains, ultimately leading to cycles of non-learning (Kinchin, Lygo-Baker, & Hay, 2008). The cumulative learning that is described by Maton equates to the meaningful learning espoused by Novak (2010) that is typically represented by integrated knowledge networks. The combining of hierarchical and linear knowledge structures has been described as a fundamental problem in education (Novak & Symington, 1982) and is considered necessary to develop expertise (Kinchin & Cabot, 2010). Making explicit links between these complementary knowledge structures is therefore a major issue in curriculum design and delivery.

Within this Bernsteinian framework, Maton (2014) has developed the concepts of semantic gravity and semantic density which resonate with the knowledge structures approach. Semantic gravity (SG) refers to the '*degree to which meaning relates to its context*' (*ibid*, p. 129). This may be seen to be relatively stronger (+) or weaker (−) along a continuum from theoretical to practical knowledge. Therefore, a concrete example of something tied to a particular context may be seen to exhibit a stronger semantic gravity (SG+) than a more abstract generalisation that may be derived from it (SG−). Importantly, the dynamic nature of semantic gravity needs to be acknowledged so that oscillations between theory and practice, or between principles and examples, can be referred to in terms of weakening (SG↓) or strengthening (SG↑) semantic gravity, depending on the direction of travel. So, for example, analysis of political theory followed by description of the practicalities of voting in local elections would be an example of SG↑, whilst fieldwork looking at patterns of banding in snail shells followed by a lecture on the principles of natural selection would be an example of SG↓. Repeated oscillations back and forth in this way are described by Maton as semantic waves.

The concept of semantic density (SD) refers to '*the condensation of meaning*' (Maton, 2014, p. 129) that may be determined by socio-cultural practices, symbols, terms, concepts, phrases, gestures, actions etc. Within specialist texts or practices of a discipline, there are highly nuanced and detailed meanings that are embedded. These are recognised by 'insiders' but may be overlooked by novices who fail to pick up on the appropriate cues from what they may see as 'heavy' text. For novices to start to gain access to the richness of understanding, some 'unpacking' is often necessary so that students can make links to at least some parts of the wider body of disciplinary knowledge. This is also complicated where some terms cross into everyday discourses. So, from an ecological analogy, the everyday use of 'plant food' has a low semantic density, however, in the more scientific context of photosynthesis, 'plant food' can be further unpacked to reveal understanding about soluble minerals and their active transport across cell membranes that allows them to fulfil their role in the biochemical processes of photosynthesis. So, in the right context, the term has greater semantic density. Professionals often try to reduce semantic density when talking to lay persons by avoiding jargon and using simplifications or analogies.

The relative strengths of semantic gravity and semantic density can vary independently along continua of strengths to form what Maton refers to as a semantic plane (Fig. 4.2). Here the semantic plane has been annotated to suggest the types of knowledge (represented by morphological types of concept map) that might be plotted within each quadrant. Practical knowledge (SD− SG+) relates to the competencies that are often described within the disciplines that are tied to a given context (when you see x, you do y) and can be summarized by a linear protocol. This is often the kind of knowledge that is learned in practical exercises that students are then required to link to the theoretical knowledge, (SD+ SG−) that they have obtained from their books and lectures. The successful combination of conceptual and procedural (SD+ SG+), may be seen as the hallmark of professional knowledge in which the links between theory and practice become second nature to the disciplinary expert. The stages of expertise development have been traced against the semantic plane by Shay and Steyn (2016), who see the novice-beginner occupying the top left quadrant and the expert-master occupying the bottom right quadrant of the plane. As a teaching tool within the knowledge structures approach, this becomes more useful if we can visualise the structural arrangements of knowledge that are likely to be found populating the quadrants, as indicated in Fig. 4.2.

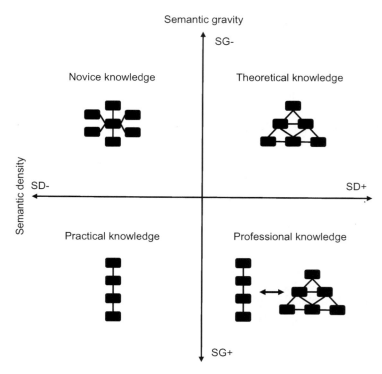

Fig. 4.2 The semantic plane indicating the typical knowledge structures that are likely to populate the quadrants (modified from Kinchin, 2016)

Extending the applicability of this tool beyond its sociological origins, Blackie (2014, p. 468) has applied the use of the semantic plane to the teaching of Chemistry. By applying the knowledge needed to understand examples such as the dissolution of sodium chloride in water, she has been able to increase her consciousness of the '*kinds of complexity that different sections of chemistry require*' and the '*extent of the leap required by the students at any particular stage*'. The process emphasises the importance to the teacher of moving from the comfort of the top right quadrant of the plane (SG− SD+), which may be a comfortable place for the subject expert, but an intimidating arena for the subject novice. Navigating the semantic plane in this way provides teachers with a '*way to make the organising principles of knowledge visible to students through explicitly teaching discipline-specific language resources that create and shape the knowledge of their disciplines*' (Macnaught, Maton, Martin, & Matruglio, 2013, p. 61). As such, it may provide a route for the navigation of threshold concepts within a discipline.

Practical knowledge is often dominated by chains of action (protocols and procedures), whereas theoretical knowledge is more likely to be structured as an integrated network of understanding. The professional knowledge that is needed to function as an expert in many fields requires the individual to oscillate between the chains and networks, allowing an apparently simultaneous access to theory and practice (Kinchin & Cabot, 2010). It may therefore be more 'correct' to say that these expert individuals oscillate between the practical and theoretical quadrants (i.e. repeatedly traversing the zone that appears as a theory-practice gap to the novice), but as structural shorthand here, it makes practical sense to consider the professional knowledge to exhibit high semantic density and high semantic gravity, as appropriate. The region of the plane that describes low semantic density (relatively little information held), and low semantic gravity (not linked with a particular context) to describe the novice who has not yet gained any degree of competence in the discipline. This is most likely to be depicted by a spoke–type concept map. I have to acknowledge that these are extreme structural types and most of the maps that are observed will tend to offer mixtures of the extreme morphological types shown here. The importance of these complementary knowledge structures in the development of expertise is emphasised by Maton (2014, p. 181) who states, '*Powerful knowledge comprises not one kind of knowledge but rather mastery of how different knowledges are brought together and changed through semantic waving and weaving*', by which he means navigating back and forth between the quadrants of the semantic plane, shown Fig. 4.2.

Adaptive Expertise and Pedagogic Frailty

Bohle Carbonell et al. (2014, p. 26) have commented on how 'The frequent changes in the current work environment driven by task and knowledge volatility calls for experts who possess the required domain expertise and can quickly overcome changes. Such experts are known as possessing adaptive expertise'. Whilst it clearly makes sense to have experts teaching within universities, some attributes of expertise can create problems within the teaching arena. Many experts (who possess complex theoretical knowledge) find it difficult to remember the novice state of mind (indicated by the simple spoke structure in the top left quadrant of Fig. 4.2) to pitch their teaching at the appropriate level (e.g. Fontaine, 2002), and process information and solve problems so quickly that their actions are not visible to students who are trying to emulate their expertise.

Salmon and Kelly (2015, p. 5) offer a very clear explanation of how adaptive expertise can be developed among teachers by using concept mapping. They state:

> *Adaptive experts are distinguished by a metacognitive learning orientation that enables them to continually learn from what they do. When teachers approach their practice with a metacognitive awareness, they can better adapt their teaching in relation to student learning. Concept mapping for instructional planning promotes this metacognitive orientation by making thinking visible and providing a process for its critique.*

Concept maps are rarely 'excellent' on first draft. They have to be revised and reflected upon over time. These map revisions are aimed at increasing the conceptual coherence of the map, developing from simple spokes and chains towards more complex networks that exhibit greater explanatory power (Kinchin, 2016). Salmon & Kelly (2015, p. 134) consider *'the generative nature of the network structure [to be] one of the characteristics that aligns with the knowledge bases and thinking of adaptive experts.'*

Lack of adaptive expertise is likely to prevent the professional from undertaking the *necessary waving and weaving* (*sensu* Maton, 2014, p. 181) that would enable progression from the lower left quadrant of Fig. 4.2 (practical knowledge) towards the lower right-hand quadrant (professional knowledge). This is why maintenance of professional standing often requires the undertaking of regular professional development (CPD) activities to refresh and enhance theoretical knowledge and practical skills. In addition, resistance to change through the maintenance of rigid chains of practice is likely to result in the development of pedagogic frailty (Kinchin et al., 2016; Kinchin & Winstone, 2017) and an unreflective maintenance of conservative teaching strategies (e.g. Bailey, 2014). Trying to maintain an illusory stable state within the professional environment (e.g. Schon, 1971) can manifest itself in continued professional activity that employs comfortable, well-rehearsed chains of practice—even when these have become out-dated. This occurs when the chains of practice have become detached from underpinning networks of understanding to form what Stronach, Corbin, McNamara, Stark, and Warne (2002) have referred to as 'broken stories' that lack the capacity to evolve. When this happens in professional education, it can result in the conservative maintenance of 'traditional teaching practices' that emphasise efficiency over innovation and convenience over evidence (Kinchin, 2016; Salmon & Kelly, 2015).

Different Structures for Different Audiences

Professional language is full of technical terminology (jargon) and acronyms that provide a short-hand way of discussing complex ideas within a community of experts. When professionals need to discuss areas of their practice with non-professionals (e.g. clients or patients) then this level of detail and precision is often not required. In the example illustrated in Fig. 4.3, the clinician has a detailed networked understanding of the theory that underpins his actions. This includes alternative procedures and information about likely success rates and possible complications (often accompanied by a level of uncertainty that might accompany some actions exemplified by comments such as "I can't be sure until I see the x-rays"). The young patient in this scenario may not want to know all this detail and may be anxious about the procedure. In this case he wants to know that he won't feel any pain and that he will leave the clinic feeling better (a simple chain of certainties that may deliberately ignore uncertainties). In addition, the adaptive expertise that accompanies expert professional practice may be viewed by the professional as a route to further learning. However, the patient probably does not want to share in the idea that the clinician is learning *on* him. Confidence in the professional

Fig. 4.3 The expert clinician's complex network of understanding may contain all sorts of uncertainties that are not passed on to the patient—who is *left* with a simplified and 'certain' chain of practice (from Kinchin, Cabot, & Hay, 2008a)

is based on the belief that he has the accumulated knowledge and experience to perform the task without problem.

The important distinction between procedural and conceptual knowledge has been explored by Schneider and Stern (2010) who have analysed the various theoretical viewpoints on the relationships between these types of knowledge. Conceptual knowledge is usually viewed as general and abstract whilst procedural knowledge is seen as practical knowledge that is often automated and tied to specific problem types. Figure 4.4 shows how details of the procedural and conceptual components may be illustrated using concept maps. Here the chain of practice is clear. This is what can be viewed externally by the novice (patient or student). The decisions taken about which chain of practice to proceed with are more

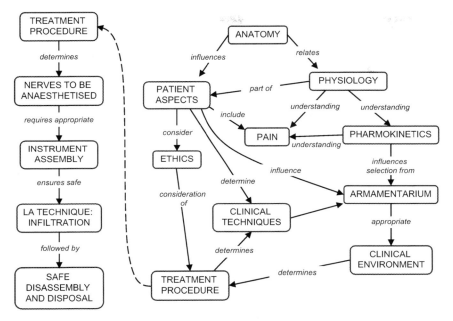

Fig. 4.4 An expert's knowledge structure of the application of local anaesthesia (LA) in dentistry (after Clarke, 2011), indicating the chain of practice (to the *left*) that is informed by the network of understanding (to the *right*)

opaque to the novice observer, and are dependent upon an appreciation of the network of understanding that underpins this practice. The expert practitioner will move between the chain and the network seamlessly and repeatedly whilst working (Kinchin & Cabot, 2010). As this is rarely articulated during practice, it is often considered as tacit knowledge. Patel et al. (1999, p. 89) have explained that *'an effective clinical teacher needs to be able to articulate knowledge that would normally be tacit for the practitioner not normally engaged in instruction'*. It is precisely this articulation, *expressing the inexpressible* (Elvira, Imants, Dankbaar, & Segers, 2017, p. 195), that can be facilitated by the concept mapping tool, providing students with a window into professional practice that they require for the development of their emergent expertise (Kinchin, Baysan, & Cabot, 2008).

Within the expert's knowledge structure in Fig. 4.4, the well-developed chain of practice and network of understanding are quite separate, connected by a single robust link that moves the 'treatment procedure' from theory into practice. The chain of practice is simple, with no deviations. Development of such an efficient chain is required in order to develop agreed clinical protocols that can be understood by a clinical team who may be holding different levels of theoretical understanding (e.g. between nurses and doctors or dentists), and quickly put into action in an emergency situation. Competence frameworks (e.g. Talbot, 2004) therefore have a place in clinical education where the student is concerned with developing efficient chains of practice. However, such chains are only efficient within a largely predictable environment that presents the same problem over and over again. In such cases, routinized expertise may be seen as a justifiable goal. But where the environment is less predictable or changing rapidly in a certain direction, the routinized chain may not remain fit for purpose for long. In such cases, expert understanding of the theory is needed in order to provide the knowledge that allows the chain of practice to evolve. This is when the expert is able to select or adapt to the most appropriate chain for an unusual instance by reference to the related theory. Expertise, therefore, requires the purposeful oscillation between the chain of practice and the network of understanding (Kinchin & Cabot, 2010). The fluidity of this linkage makes the expert knowledge powerful (*sensu* Young & Muller, 2013). Individuals who are excluded from the underpinning theory will be denied access to the powerful knowledge of expertise (Wheelahan, 2007), and will be reliant on others to identify to most appropriate chain of practice—highlighting a distinction between technical competence and professional expertise.

In Conclusion

The tacit knowledge that needs to be placed explicitly into the teaching arena is found connecting the chains of practice that are found in the expert's actions (that are visible to the student) with the underlying network of understanding that is usually held privately (Kinchin, Cabot, &

Hay, 2008a). The tacit nature of this knowledge and the difficulty that experts traditionally exhibit in verbalising the nuances of their professional activity may simply reflect the lack of appropriate tools to reveal to students what it is they are doing, or a vocabulary to articulate it. (McLeod, Meagher, Steinert, Schuwirth, & McLeod, 2004). Students need to gain experience in converting between complementary chains and networks and such structural transformations can be modelled for the student, once the teacher has recognised them. Such structural transformation has been suggested to operate as a threshold concept for teaching (Kinchin & Miller, 2012). If framed in terms of semantic codes, the expert will be able to move deftly between all four quadrants (Fig. 4.2). The expert teacher will also be able to support the movement of his/her students across the semantic plane, a process that can be enhanced by the active inclusion of students in the teaching process through peer instruction (e.g. Blackie, 2017). Engagement in concept mapping activities allows the teacher and students to recognise the existence of the structures, slowing down the movement between theory and practice during teaching episodes to allow examination of the process. This represents a shift in emphasis of the transactions between teachers and students, from a focus on fixed end-points of instruction, to a renewed examination of the activities that link knowledge structures. Increased familiarity with the fluid nature of knowledge structures and how they are related will also result in the acquisition of greater adaptive expertise, rather than the routinised expertise that accompanies acquisition of fixed knowledge. Adaptive expertise will leave students better equipped to maintain their learning within a changing professional context.

References

Bailey, G. (2014). Accountability and the rise of 'play safe' pedagogical practices. *Education + Training, 56*(7), 663–674.

Bernstein, B. (1999). Vertical and horizontal discourse: An essay. *British Journal of Sociology of Education, 20*(2), 157–173.

Bernstein, B. (2000). *Pedagogy, symbolic control and identity*. Oxford: Rowman & Littlefield.

Blackie, M. A. L. (2014). Creating semantic waves: Using legitimation code theory as a tool to aid the teaching of chemistry. *Chemistry Education Research and Practice, 15*(4), 462–469.

Blackie, M. (2017). Semantic waves and pedagogic frailty. In I. M. Kinchin & N. E. Winstone (Eds.), *Pedagogic frailty and resilience in the university* (pp. 49–61). Rotterdam: Sense Publishers.

Bohle Carbonell, K., Stalmeijer, R. E., Könings, K. D., Segers, M., & van Merriënboer, J. J. G. (2014). How experts deal with novel situations: A review of adaptive expertise. *Educational Research Review, 12*, 14–29.

Bradley, J. H., Paul, R., & Seeman, E. (2006). Analyzing the structure of expert knowledge. *Information Management, 43*, 77–91.

Cañas, A. J., Novak, J. D., & Reiska, P. (2015). How good is my concept map? Am I a good Cmapper? *Knowledge Management & E-Learning, An International Journal, 7*(1), 6–19.

Clarke, F. (2011). Injecting expertise: Developing an expertise-based pedagogy for teaching local anaesthesia in dentistry. *Higher Education Network Journal, 2*, 29–43.

Elvira, Q., Imants, J., Dankbaar, B., & Segers, M. (2017). Designing education for professional expertise development. *Scandinavian Journal of Educational Research, 61*(12), 187–204. https://doi.org/10.1080/00313831.2015.1119729

Fontaine, S. I. (2002). Teaching with the beginner's mind: Notes from my karate journal. *College Composition and Communication, 54*(2), 208–221.

Gibbs, G. (2013). Reflections on the changing nature of educational development. *International Journal for Academic Development, 18*(1), 4–14.

Gosling, D. (2009). Educational development in the UK: A complex and contradictory reality. *International Journal for Academic Development, 14*(1), 5–18.

Green, D. A. (2009). New academics' perceptions of the language of teaching and learning: Identifying and overcoming linguistic barriers. *International Journal for Academic Development, 14*(1), 33–45.

Hay, D. B., Williams, D., Stahl, D., & Wingate, R. (2013). Using drawings of the brain cell to exhibit expertise in neuroscience: Exploring the boundaries of experimental culture. *Science Education, 97*(3), 468–491.

Hoffman, R. R., & Lintern, G. (2006). Eliciting and representing the knowledge of experts. In K. A. Ericsson, N. Charness, P. J. Feltovich, & R. R. Hoffman (Eds.), *The Cambridge handbook of expertise and expert performance* (pp. 203–222). Cambridge, UK: Cambridge University Press.

Kinchin, I. M. (1994). *The biology of Tardigrades*. London: Portland Press.

Kinchin, I. M. (2014). Concept mapping as a learning tool in higher education: A critical analysis of recent reviews. *The Journal of Continuing Higher Education, 62*(1), 39–49.

Kinchin, I. M. (2016). *Visualising powerful knowledge: A knowledge structures perspective on teaching and learning at university*. Rotterdam: Sense Publishers.

Kinchin, I. M., Alpay, E., Curtis, K., Franklin, J., Rivers, C., & Winstone, N. E. (2016). Charting the elements of pedagogic frailty. *Educational Research, 58*(1), 1–23.

Kinchin, I. M., Baysan, A., & Cabot, L. B. (2008). Towards a pedagogy for clinical education: Beyond individual learning differences. *Journal of Further and Higher Education, 32*(4), 373–387.

Kinchin, I. M., & Cabot, L. B. (2010). Reconsidering the dimensions of expertise: From linear stages towards dual processing. *London Review of Education, 8*(2), 153–166.

Kinchin, I. M., Cabot, L. B., & Hay, D. B. (2008a). Visualising expertise: Towards an authentic pedagogy for higher education. *Teaching in Higher Education, 13*(3), 315–326.

Kinchin, I. M., Cabot, L. B., & Hay, D. B. (2008b). Using concept mapping to locate the tacit dimension of clinical expertise: Towards a theoretical framework to support critical reflection on teaching. *Learning in Health and Social Care, 7*(2), 93–104.

Kinchin, I. M., Lygo-Baker, S., & Hay, D. B. (2008). Universities as centres of non-learning. *Studies in Higher Education, 33*(1), 89–103.

Kinchin, I. M., & Miller, N. L. (2012). 'Structural transformation' as a threshold concept in university teaching. *Innovations in Education and Teaching International, 49*(2), 207–222.

Kinchin, I. M., & Winstone, N. E. (2017). *Pedagogic frailty and resilience in the university*. Rotterdam: Sense Publishers.

Macnaught, L., Maton, K., Martin, J. R., & Matruglio, E. (2013). Jointly constructing semantic waves: Implications for teacher training. *Linguistics and Education, 24*, 50–63.

Maton, K. (2009). Cumulative and segmented learning: Exploring the role of curriculum structures in knowledge building. *British Journal of Sociology of Education, 31*(1), 43–57.

Maton, K. (2014). *Knowledge and knowers: Towards a realist sociology of education*. London: Routledge.

McLeod, P. J., Meagher, T., Steinert, Y., Schuwirth, L., & McLeod, A. H. (2004). Clinical teachers' tacit knowledge of basic pedagogic principles. *Medical Teacher, 26*, 23–27.

Novak, J. D. (2010). *Learning, creating, and using knowledge: Concept maps as facilitative tools in schools and corporations* (2nd ed.). Oxford: Routledge.

Novak, J. D., & Cañas, A. J. (2006). The origins of concept maps and the continuing evolution of the tool. *Information Visualization Journal, 5*(3), 175–184.

Novak, J. D., & Cañas, A. J. (2007). Theoretical origins of concept maps, how to construct them, and uses in education. *Reflecting Education, 3*(1), 29–42.

Novak, J. D., & Symington, D. J. (1982). Concept mapping for curriculum development. *Victoria Institute for Educational Research Bulletin, 48*, 3–11.

Patel, V. L., Arocha, J. F., & Kaufman, D. R. (1999). Expertise and tacit knowledge in medicine. In R. J. Sternberg & J. A. Horvath (Eds.), *Tacit knowledge in professional practice: Researcher and practitioner perspectives* (pp. 75–99). Mahwah, NJ: Lawrence Erlbaum.

Salmon, D., & Kelly, M. (2015). *Using concept mapping to foster adaptive expertise: Enhancing teacher metacognitive learning to improve student academic performance.* New York: Peter Lang.

Schneider, M., & Stern, E. (2010). The developmental relations between conceptual and procedural knowledge: A multimethod approach. *Developmental Psychology, 46*(1), 178–192.

Schon, D. (1971). *Beyond the stable state.* New York: W.W. Norton & Co.

Shay, S., & Steyn, D. (2016). Enabling knowledge progression in vocational curricula: Design as a case study. In K. Maton, S. Hood, & S. Shay (Eds.), *Knowledge-building: Educational studies in legitimation code theory.* London: Routledge.

Steinert, Y., Mann, K., Centeno, A., Dolmans, D., Spencer, J., Gelula, M., & Prideaux, D. (2006). A systematic review of faculty development initiatives designed to improve teaching effectiveness in medical education, BEME Guide No. 8. *Medical Teacher, 28*(6), 497–526.

Stronach, I., Corbin, B., McNamara, O., Stark, S., & Warne, T. (2002). Towards an uncertain politics of professionalism: Teacher and nurse identities in flux. *Journal of Education Policy, 17*(1), 109–138.

Stuart, H. A. (1985). Should concept maps be scored numerically. *The European Journal of Science Education, 7*(1), 73–81.

Talbot, M. (2004). Monkey see, monkey do: A critique of the competency model in graduate medical education. *Medical Education, 38*, 587–592.

Taylor, K. (2000). Teaching with developmental intention. In J. Mezirow & Associates (Eds.), *Learning as transformation: Critical perspectives on a theory in progress* (pp. 151–180). San Francisco, CA: Jossey-Bass.

Wheelahan, L. (2007). How competency-based training locks the working class out of powerful knowledge: A modified Bernsteinian analysis. *British Journal of Sociology of Education, 28*(5), 637–651.

Wilson, J., Mandich, A., & Magalhães, L. (2015). Concept mapping: A dynamic, individualized and qualitative method for eliciting meaning. *Qualitative Health Research, 26*(8), 1151–1161.

Wingate, R., & Kwint, M. (2006). Imagining the brain cell: The neuron in visual culture. *Nature Reviews Neuroscience, 7*, 745–752.

Young, M., & Muller, J. (2013). On the powers of powerful knowledge. *Review of Education, 1*(3), 229–250.

5

Serving Ethically: A Developing Country Perspective on Quality Education for Professional Practice

Jeanette Baird

Introduction

Developing and emerging nations encounter particular challenges in providing quality education for professional practice, particularly those that are small island states (UNESCO, 2016). Underlying assumptions about the system and societal dynamics of professions in developed countries usually do not apply. Frequently, in developing nations, significant emphasis is placed on 'knowledge transfer' from highly developed nations, that is, on generalised international technical knowledge, skills and competencies as ends in themselves. I suggest, however, that the value of such training is limited unless it is accompanied by a multi-faceted approach to the ethics of professional education for graduates who will practice in very specific national and regional contexts.

Ethical professional education in this sense goes beyond ensuring that students learn to act with integrity and to make moral decisions so as to avoid actions regarded as corrupt. Rather, it includes a consideration of the dilemmas in providing an education that attuned to local societal

J. Baird (✉)
Divine Word University, Madang, Papua New Guinea

rhythms and sustainable development based on local knowledge. It also includes an education that sensitises professionals to the national purposes that their privileged position must serve. Further, ethical professional education, in this broad interpretation, requires those providing the teaching to have the skills effectively to support learners in deliberative reflection (McEwen & Trede, 2016).

Consequently, developing country educators themselves must engage with the ethical responsibilities inherent in the tangible circumstances of the nation. Many of these responsibilities are common to all professional educators but it is only in developing countries that certain ethical and moral dilemmas come into sharp relief. While financial integrity and avoidance of corrupt conduct are very significant behaviours for professional practice in developing countries, supporting the wider 'social good' can be seen as equally important. In this regard, the challenges for professional education in lower-income, developing countries are starting to be documented in a body of literature on professional education for the public good, especially in post-colonial development (McLean & Walker, 2016). In particular, the 'Public-Good Professional Capabilities Index' of Walker and McLean (2009, 2015) provides an enhanced framework for educating socially-focused and committed professionals in emerging nations.

The title of this chapter is deliberate: professional practice with a spirit of service is likely to reinforce ethical conduct, while ethically acceptable decisions help to meet national needs for integrity in society, so important to each country on a journey of international validation.

Models for professional learning in developing countries therefore, in my view, need to address at least three elements: (1) build students' capabilities for resilient, ethical conduct as independent actors in fraught situations; (2) help students reflexively to balance local and global skills to serve national needs; and (3) equip educators with the skills to be effective facilitators of learning in an environment where the higher education infrastructure is somewhat immature.

In this chapter, I present a perspective on professional education in developing nations drawn primarily from experiences at my faith-based university in Papua New Guinea (PNG). After describing common impediments to appropriate professional education and practice in developing countries, I outline the PNG environment for professional education. Micro case study examples are provided of the three specific topics identified above in fashioning fit-for-purpose professional education at Divine Word University, taken from the human client and enterprise/production fields (Stark, 1998). In my concluding comments, I suggest that elements of a capabilities-based framework (Walker & McLean, 2013) can be used to foster an ethos of service and given practical effect. Other suggestions are offered for improving the quality of learning and teaching practice in education for the professions in developing countries.

Opportunities and Challenges in Education for Professional Practice in Developing Countries

The opportunities and challenges for education of professionals in developing countries often differ in degree rather than in kind from those of developed nations. Particular features of geography, history, population size and culture, however, affect the ways in which professions are viewed and professional practice is performed.

Developing nations have well-defined and urgent national needs for human capital formation, including the need for professionals in many fields. While importing expertise is one option, many post-colonial nations have placed a significant emphasis on 'nation-building' and self-sustaining expertise through education of their citizens for professional leadership (in PNG, as in some other countries, this approach is referred to as 'localisation'). Establishment of viable education and health sectors, and skills for economic and social development, are crucial first priorities for newer states. The production of graduates capable of participating in global labour markets is another priority, despite concerns over brain drain (Beine, Docquier, & Rapoport, 2008). For all these reasons, government policy usually, and helpfully, gives some priority to the education of professionals.

Development partners also recognise the likely beneficial impacts for human well-being of cadres of skilled professionals and tend to fund significant investments in national capacity building, in health, education and law and justice (Department of Foreign Affairs and Trade, Australia, 2015), including substantial scholarship programs for international studies. Indeed, there is now a well-trodden path established by donor agencies that facilitates internationally-normed education for professional practice in selected professions. As I note later, uneven support for education across professional fields is an area that development partners might do well to review.

Similarly, most developing nations have ready access to assistance from professionals internationally, through non-government organisations and higher education institutions, to augment the skills of local practitioners (Sopoaga et al., 2015). Both these groups and international aid agencies highlight the importance of cultural relevance and local ownership in professional education.

For some developing nations, the emergence of small groups of professionals across a range of fields can be a source of strength, as the new professional elites know each other and their ready networking can exert a steady shaping influence on professional conduct. Of course, this strength can easily become a weakness if it produces an incestuous culture that imposes unreasonably restrictive barriers to new entrants or if a concern for the standing of the profession as a whole fails to materialise.

Developing nations also offer sites for unique professional practice and innovative use of local knowledge. The practice of professional skills in diverse settings offers the promise of vastly extended and more nuanced exercise of professional responsibilities, for better outcomes, an expansion of international professional knowledge and frames of reference, and more reflexive approaches to professional education.

At the same time, many developing nations struggle to emerge from a pervasive culture of poor governance, political instability and corrupt practices in public services, including higher education (Robinson, 2015; Task Force on Higher Education and Society, 2000). In such an environment, the pressures can be intense for professionals to act unethically or against their own best professional judgement.

Challenges for the education of professionals tend to be magnified in lower income environments, where social and physical infrastructure is highly patchy. Students may be very under-prepared for tertiary studies due to weak school systems. Tertiary education systems are likely to be under-funded and academics under-skilled, even where higher education remains elite rather than mass. The use of pedagogies based on transmission of ideas rather than on engaged learning is common. Academics in professional fields such as teaching and law do not always provide good role models for their students, as academic absenteeism appears to be tolerated in some institutions (Namaliu & Garnaut, 2010, p. 20). There may be requirements to admit more students than the post-secondary education system can realistically support, resulting in a downwards spiral of ever-more students experiencing an ever-diminishing quality of learning.

Competitive entry into tertiary profession programs may be significantly gender-biased, due in part to boys' preferential access to school-level education (Asian Development Bank, 2014). Small numbers of tertiary institutions may provide few opportunities for collaborative competition (Snow, 2015) or experiencing alternate models of learning. Conferences and other national networking meetings may simply not be affordable, let alone regular attendance at international conferences. Weak internet links, limited access to fee-paying journals, and an absence of requirements for continuing professional development similarly are likely to limit access to new modes of practice or professional education.

In some national systems, the establishment of highly specialised universities and colleges—rather than broadly-based tertiary institutions—may mean that all the graduates in a profession are produced by a single institution, with corresponding difficulties in establishing credible professional licensing or accreditation bodies. The environment for professional self-regulation may be weak for other reasons, including a lack of coordinated government action, a small number of professionals, and an unwillingness on the part of professionals to be seen to be exercising quasi-regulatory functions.

Moreover, the structural arrangement of tertiary specialisation may also limit the extent of cross-disciplinary fertilisation, making it difficult for broader elements of professional practice, including management and communication skills, readily to be embedded within the professional programs taught in single-discipline institutions.

In lower income countries, sites for practice-based education, like hospitals and health centres in human services professions, can be desperately under-resourced, lacking even basic equipment, let alone advanced technologies that would be routinely available in developed nations. The advantages of modern ICT tools, including software for business and accounting applications, may simply not be available to students.

Given national needs for active practitioners in fields such as medicine, nursing, health sciences, and engineering, academic professional educators in some of these fields may be in short supply, while demand for business, accounting and legal skills may generate higher incomes in professional practice than tertiary institutions ever can afford to offer. Those professionals who join tertiary institutions to teach skills may not have strong supports to develop their identities as 'educators', with academic professional responsibilities over and above classroom teaching. Conversely, expatriate academics often start with little understanding of local cultures and of the systemic weaknesses that have produced poorly-prepared students.

Less obviously, understandably ambiguous attitudes of people in developing and post-colonial nations to well-intentioned 'assistance' from developed countries—with their comparatively abundant material wealth and quality services—may exacerbate rather than ameliorate international efforts to strengthen professional education. Hidden and undiscussed resentment of the situation of people living in developed nations, and demands for rapid localisation, may not help academics in tertiary education institutions in lower income countries to achieve a balanced critical view of the advantages and disadvantages of professional competencies that are 'transferred in' (van Bilzen, 2015).

In human services professions especially, academics in developing countries face competing demands when developing and structuring their teaching. Professional curricula copied from international norms may not be localised or even feasible yet there is an ever-increasing demand by higher education regulatory bodies for international comparability. The exploration of effective local practices thus is overshadowed by an emphasis on normative internationalised professional standards.

Underlying these structural and economic challenges in education for professional practice lie a range of cultural and social factors that influence the ways in which professional practice and the education of professionals are constructed and able to be undertaken. High community expectations of service delivery can be accompanied by naivety around elements of acceptable conduct, making it difficult to reinforce messages about privacy, appropriate communication and professional ethics that would be standard in developed countries. For example, litigation on matters of professional standards may not be a feature of the societal landscape in developing countries. Although this may seem a blessing, it adds to an environment where there is limited public discussion over the expected conduct of professionals and thus limited societal reinforcement of expectations.

The Situation in Papua New Guinea

Papua New Guinea (PNG) looks both west, to Asia, and east to the Pacific, where it is the largest Pacific Island state. The country is located north of Australia and its main island shares a border with Indonesia. In 1975 PNG gained its independence from Australia, having been an administered territory.

The nation has a population of around 8 million, with abundant natural resources and beauty, from its mountainous highlands to its tropical islands. The terrain is often rugged, and roads are limited, much travel being undertaken by air or ship. Cultural diversity is possibly the country's most striking characteristic: around 850 languages are spoken. English is the primary language of government and of educational instruction but the most commonly used shared languages are Tok Pisin and Motu.

Despite great richness in natural resources, from minerals to fisheries, economic development is very uneven. The formal employment sector is small, and most people continue to live in villages as subsistence farmers. At the same time, there is a pronounced movement of younger people to larger cities and towns, where new informal settlements are expanding.

PNG is aspirational: its national Vision 2050 aims to achieve a "smart, wise, fair, healthy and happy society" (GoPNG, 2010).

While the national Constitution establishes PNG as a Christian country, the nation's diverse social structures and cultural values are rooted in the Melanesian tradition, which emphasises collective consensual action and respect for established hierarchy but allows for status mobility through 'bigmanship' (Kavanamur & Okole, 2004). There are well-established clans and tribes throughout the 22 provinces and 89 districts: the strength of these locally-based networks, which underpin the 'wantok' social welfare system, contrasts with a weak culture of observance of Western-style rules, under-employment and fragmented social ties across clan groups.

PNG has six established universities, all small, together with numbers of single-discipline nursing and teachers' colleges. The two longest-established universities were established in the 1960s and modelled on Australian universities of the time. Two of the six universities are faith-based private institutions. There are public technical colleges and a number of private providers of higher education and technical and vocational education and training (TVET). While other tertiary institutions are coming on stream, including a projected open university, rapidly expanding numbers of Grade 12 school-leavers cannot all find a place in further or higher education or employment.

Quality assurance of higher education and TVET by government regulation is improving slowly. There is a small number of active professional associations, in addition to State-based bodies such as the PNG Medical Board and the PNG Nursing Council, which accredit programs and register graduates. These professional associations include CPA PNG, Institute of Engineers, Law Society, PNG Computer Society and the PNG Human Resources Institute.

The non-government professional associations provide codes of conduct or values statements and some, such as CPA PNG, register graduates. Most are not yet set up to impose peer review or sanctions other than removal of membership. Their influence on ethical conduct, which could be profound, is yet to be fully realised.

PNG receives significant support from development partners, through the foreign aid programs of countries such as Australia, Japan and several other nations, as well as from non-government organisations.

The Crucial Matter of Ethical Conduct

Among many issues, the need for ethical conduct stands out as a professional and personal competence that requires customised nurturing in many lower income, emerging or developing nations, in view of widespread concerns over corruption in all its many forms and interpretations (Ayius & May, 2007; Larmour, 2012).

A strong case can be made for highlighting ethical conduct in professional education in Papua New Guinea, which as a nation in 2016 is rated at 136 of 176 countries on a well-known corruption perceptions index (Transparency International, 2017). While many other developing nations share concerns over corrupt activity, the anguish caused by a collapse of integrity in the political system and public sector seems particularly acute in PNG (Institute of National Affairs, 2016). An earlier 'nation-building' fervour in Papua New Guinea has been replaced by goals of individual advancement and personal gain. If this situation is to be addressed, for societal well-being as well as economic development, the professions as well as the private sector, churches and NGOs, will need to contribute to creating a bulwark against further declines in ethical standards.

In Papua New Guinea, those in formal employment and professionals of all kinds routinely negotiate many and varied frames of reference (or codes) for 'right conduct', many of which are not fully analysed or translated into lived experience. Recent work aimed at re-establishing appropriate conduct among leaders in the PNG public sector (Department of Personnel Management, 2014) has sought to build on commonalities across multiple sets of values (cultural; religious; personal; workplace) but also to sensitise managers to the need appropriately to apply their value sets in specific environments. This model recognises that individuals often hold competing values, for example, loyalty to clan members or loyalty to an employer, and that many Papua New Guineans are not certain which unwritten rules to apply in a particular situation.

In PNG higher education, the amount of attention given to teaching professional ethics varies by institution (cf. Simpson, Onumah, & Oppong-Nkrumah, 2016) and by discipline. Health professions, particularly medicine and nursing, have well-established codes of conduct that are routinely taught to students, as do some other professional associations such as CPA PNG. Other professions may have placed more emphasis on technical competence:

> *Interest in engineering ethics education has developed significant momentum in almost all advanced countries. The developing countries have not yet paid enough attention to such critical issues and Papua New Guinea is no different. This is probably the reason why corruption activities have become part of the normal activities of politicians, senior public servants and many other higher office holders as reported in the daily news media.* (Pumwa, 2010, Abstract)

Ethical challenges and pressure points also vary by discipline: accounting professionals are likely to face tensions over financial controls, auditing measures and fraudulent transactions; primary teachers and health workers in PNG may not accept the burden of trying to manage largely on their own in a remote and unfamiliar school or aid post; engineers may be asked to inflate contract bids or use shoddy materials; doctors and nurses have choices over which patients to prioritise when medicines are extremely scarce.

Turning now to my university, Divine Word University (DWU) is "a national university, open to all, serving society through its quality of research, teaching, learning and community engagement in a Christian environment" (DWU, 2016a). The University, which is multi-campus, aims to serve national objectives simultaneously with Church purposes, based on core disciplines such as health sciences, education, business and ICT and development-related studies.

The University's approach to ethics education is grounded naturally in its Catholic heritage and the concept of virtue ethics, or ethics shaped by character (McCarthy, 2006; Rae & Wong, 2012). Christian ethics, including equity, compassion and a concern for social justice, are given prominence in teaching and in student life and are believed from employer feedback to exert a positive influence on the ethical sense of graduates. Recently, however, staff of the University have started to reflect on whether there are better or more sustained ways in which to engender robust moral and ethical values and behaviours among staff and students, not least because of an increase in secularisation and student disciplinary problems.

All students must take a compulsory subject on ethics but it is possible that this subject dwells more on teaching 'about' various ethical theories than on supporting students to find ways to reflect on and address ethical problems in their personal and professional life. We may run the risk identified by Raes: "All too often, ethics is seen as an 'external'—if not alienated—point of view, a 'view from nowhere'." (1997, p. 244). While acknowledging the difficulties of purely context-based ethical education, we can agree that questions of 'whose ethics?', 'which contexts', are not explored to their full extent in a PNG environment.

There are additional subjects on professional ethics in most professional disciplines but, similarly, a view has been expressed that our teaching may not enable students to negotiate competing moral frameworks, especially if teaching foregrounds learning about a specific 'code of conduct' that is separate to students' authentic experiences. As with many institutions in PNG, professional education at DWU infrequently asks students to reflect on the values they bring to their professional careers, usually being more concerned with the uncritical transmission of a body of expert knowledge.

Given this situation, when an opportunity arose in 2016 for external funding (by the Australian Government) to carry out a quality improvement project, the University decided to augment a scheduled review of business and accounting programs by concentrating on the development of new approaches to teaching ethics in these programs. (Entrepreneurship is a second theme, given a national need for rapid development of small and medium enterprises in PNG.)

Working with one of our well-established international partners with expertise in professional and Christian ethics, the Australian Catholic University, the review of our professional business and accounting programs is now in progress in 2017. We trust that the funding, which we use primarily to enable face to face exchanges, will lead to sustained discussions of preferred models for teaching professional ethics, particularly within accounting programs.

We recognise that it is very difficult to assess the outcomes of ethics education or even to decide which learning approaches are most effective (see for example, Serodio, Kopelman, & Bataglia, 2016; Crigger & Godfrey, 2014; and for an overview, Avci, 2017). It is likely that, in keeping with some recommended practices (IFAC Education Committee, 2005), we will aim to embed ethical topics into all subjects, while keeping a separate introductory unit. Areas for improvement in teaching include the introduction of more reflective sessions and practice in gaining 'moral competence' (Lind, 2008). Without resiling from ethics as grounded in character, we would like to make extended use of cases drawn from typical situations in PNG, "for it is only in confrontation with all the complexities of a concrete case wherein various values conflict, that ethics as an encompassing viewpoint can be made clear" (Raes, 1997, p. 245). One useful line of enquiry is in crafting techniques to help students to discover the strategies they can use to evade or neutralise requests made to them for unethical behavior in plausible situations, i.e. strategies that do not cause parties to lose face, but which help an accountant, for example, to avoid poor conduct or fraud.

Balancing the Local and the Global to Meet National Needs

Most people accept that professional education in developing countries must take account of local situations and available resources, and also acknowledge established traditional practices. How to achieve these ends while still claiming international comparability of standards is a recurrent challenge, particularly in health sciences disciplines. Questions raised some years ago remain relevant:

> *Can one be a first-class practitioner of a type of medical practice that accepts compromises due to resource constraints? A developing country that trains its health professionals to the world's highest standards might justifiably be proud, but surely not if this comes at the cost of providing training on the health problems that are most pressing in that country.* (Cash, 2005, p. 281)

In real life, in PNG as elsewhere, professions operate with the resources, advantages and constraints to hand. Resource constraints are not always a weakness: the test of quality surely must be cost-effective outcomes for clients or patients. Many practitioners are, in fact, superbly adapted to be effective in local circumstances, using situated knowledge and skills. And it is difficult to train a student to use sophisticated equipment if the equipment is not present in-country. Nonetheless, all universities in PNG have to engage with these issues of curricular balance in a conceptual as well as a practical way, by considering firstly where and how they expect professional graduates to practice.

At DWU, a recent sustained experience in tackling these issues is provided by the medical program for rural doctors that started in 2016. The University has significant programs in health sciences, including nursing, health extension, physiotherapy, and advanced training in eye care. The impetus for the medical program was a desire to produce more 'public good professionals' (Walker & McLean, 2013) and to reduce inequalities in access to expert medical care, consistent with the University's Vision and the principles of social justice.

The stated aim of the DWU medical program is: "To produce competent medical professionals imbued with Christian ethical values and sensitivity to the needs of the least privileged rural populations of PNG" (DWU, 2016b). There is an urgent need for more doctors in PNG (World Bank, 2011; Radio New Zealand, 2014), but there is an even more urgent 'social good' need to provide medical graduates committed to working in rural areas. Some time ago, most districts had a medical officer or at least a regular visiting medical officer but a drift to towns and cities—combined with a very limited supply of new medical graduates—has resulted in an estimated 90% of doctors working in urban areas, although at least three-quarters of the population lives in rural areas.

To achieve the delicate balance between local and international in designing the program, the DWU curriculum committee, which included medical staff of the local hospital, engaged extensively with all in-country stakeholders. In doing so, of course, the University has had to take account of beliefs, desires and practices of many rural and remote communities. The curriculum committee sought to learn from strategies that had worked in other nations, including developed countries such as Australia and Canada. For example, there is good evidence that a rural upbringing and sustained rural clinical exposure is more likely to produce graduates committed to rural practice (Farmer, Kenny, McKinstry, & Huysmans, 2015; Kawan, Kondalsamy-Chennakesavan, Ranmuthugala, Toombs, & Nicholson, 2017; Tate & Aoki, 2012), so these aspects are reflected in the design of the DWU program. Resilience and courage are requirements of professional practice in rural PNG so practice of these qualities has to be designed in as well.

The University works in partnership with the University of Naples Federico II in Italy, which has experience in organising and running a successful medical program in Uganda, and Australian partners: James Cook University, which emphasises rural medicine; Cabrini Institute of Clinical Education; and the Australian Catholic University, a longstanding twinning partner of DWU with extensive experience in health programs.

Although no one in PNG argues with the need for more doctors, the DWU medical program has faced hurdles in gaining professional recognition, as it could be viewed as a competitor to the one other medical program run by the University of Papua New Guinea (UPNG). Members of the Medical Board are from UPNG and not all were convinced that a small private university had the resources to run such a program. There were no written standards for medical education, presumably because the prospect of another university offering a medical program had not been entertained. In the absence of local contextualised standards, the University is using the World Foundation for Medical Education (WFME) standards for Basic Medical Education as its benchmark (WFME, 2015), with specific adaptations of curriculum elements for the PNG context.

Our engagement with the global principles-based WFME standards has provoked helpful reflection on how better to give voice to Melanesian practices and ethical codes in a medical school curriculum, to enable students to respect and engage with local socio-cultural understandings. For now, we believe that our medical curriculum, which highlights PNG health status indicators and ethics in rural health as well as rurally-based practice, assists students reflexively to balance local and global learning to serve national needs.

Supporting Practitioners to be Effective Academics and Facilitators of Learning

As noted elsewhere in this book, educators of professionals need to employ quality teaching practices, but many sets of professional standards are silent on approaches to effective teaching and practice-based supervision. In developing countries, practicing professionals frequently are called on to teach, as there may be too few professionals in the field to allow for full-time academic professional educators. This situation is not unique to developing countries but in disciplines where the number of professionals is very limited, practitioners may themselves face an ethical dilemma over whether to serve the public directly or to support the next generation of practitioners.

Further, in becoming an academic professional educator, professionals must adopt an additional set of ethical values and responsibilities—the moral code of academia—incorporating the values of integrity, a search for truth, valid and reliable assessment, genuine student learning and respect for knowledge in all forms. Even more expansive conceptions of academic ethics, including a concern for sustainability and learning for all, are becoming accepted (Stückelberger, 2017). Not all practitioners who teach will have had previous opportunities to become 'deliberate professionals', able to discuss and reflect on the "social and moral aspects of collective professional judgement and decision-making" (McEwen & Trede, 2016, p. 224).

At Divine Word University, these considerations were brought into sharp focus when in 2016 a request came from our recently-amalgamated school of nursing in Rabaul (a separate campus) for teaching staff to learn more about good teaching practices. All new staff at DWU (academics and administrators also) who do not have a formal teaching qualification are required to undertake the University's Postgraduate Certificate in Higher Education Teaching and Learning yet we had somehow overlooked staff who joined through an institutional amalgamation. The program is taught by academics in the Faculty of Education and includes numerous activities to promote reflective practice (Schön, 1983). It was agreed to offer the program in-situ to the small cadre of nursing and midwifery educators based at Rabaul, to be taken in intensive mode in 2016. The program was regarded as highly successful and helped to reinforce an implicit identity of the academics not as nurses but as 'nurse educators' committed to reflecting on their teaching as well as their practice. We have discussed making the program available to teachers of nursing at the stand-alone nursing colleges in PNG, to bring knowledge of quality teaching methods, and reflective practice, to a wider group of professional educators.

Two key points emerge from this brief example. The first is that professional educators in developing countries, especially those in single-discipline institutions, need to engage with others to develop their skills in academic teaching and reflection, and to develop techniques to promote reflexivity and questioning in students about ethical and moral questions (Trede & McEwen, 2016). Arguably, institutions have an ethical responsibility to ensure that professional educators have the skills to be effective facilitators of learning that promotes an ethos of service. The second point, relevant to developing countries, is that skills in good teaching and reflective practice are likely to be available in-country, through established teacher education programs.

Conclusions

Divine Word University is gradually embracing opportunities to provide a more 'public good' education for professional practice, grounded in an appreciation of the types of ethical choices young professionals will need to make and the skills required of educators. The somewhat nascent activities at DWU described above obviously need integrating, to provide a holistic model of ethical education for professional programs. With experience from these examples, and reinforcement of our values-based and socially responsible approach through a new Office of Mission and Identity, we hope over the next few years to draw together such disparate threads into a coherent fabric of broadly-based professional education in the service of a stronger, more capable and resilient Papua New Guinean society.

From these examples at Divine Word University, it is evident that educators and students need reflexive and deliberative capabilities, to explore and give voice to the complex adaptive behaviours required to respect and observe both Western professional norms and Melanesian cultural knowledge, skills and behaviours in ways that are ethical, and which promote a well-functioning just society. Expanding a capacity for reflexive interrogation of professional actions could be a useful starting point for many academics in PNG.

In this regard, the 'human capabilities' approach developed by Walker and McLean in South Africa, drawn from the work of Amartya Sen (2009), would appear to have much to offer a country like PNG. Elements of a 'Public Good Professional Capabilities Index' (Walker & McLean, 2013) are reflected in the examples above: reinforcing integrity (and courage); deliberately aiming for a certain kind of professional for a specific context; identifying with disadvantaged communities; promoting resilience; and respecting different forms of knowledge. These elements could be given practical effect through scenarios and rehearsing strategies for the specific type of ethical dilemmas likely to be experienced by different professions, approaches that complement the virtue ethics taught at institutions such as DWU. Issues around Melanesian, Christian, Western and Eastern value systems can be discussed within a broader framework of imagining of the 'good' professional in context.

There are recent calls in both developed and emerging nations to 'decolonise' curricula and universities in both general and professional education (for example, Hennessy, 2016), not least to avoid the reproduction of established social inequalities. These calls express the frustration and disempowerment experienced by many groups in post-colonial nations and resentment at 'deficit' models that privilege Western knowledge and epistemologies over traditional and under-explored alternatives. At DWU, we have ongoing conversations about Melanesian values in academic life and teaching (Kula-Semos, 2009, 2014), although we would be the first to admit that these discussions need to be more sustained and systematic.

Of course, we continue to rely on generous international partners, both professional and academic, to assist us in our endeavours. Over time, we know that opportunities will expand to share experiences and ideas across the developing nations of the world. In the meantime, however, there are actions that governments and non-government agencies can take in order to scaffold strong PNG professional cultures rooted in moral and ethical values, despite political and social constraints.

For example, governments and development partners can help to expand social and community dialogue on appropriate professional conduct guided by different ethical domains. There are clear opportunities for professional associations to inform the public about professional practice and showcase examples of 'public good' professionals. They can encourage the use of social media, already widespread in developing countries such as PNG, to highlight rules and norms of appropriate conduct such as client or patient confidentiality or give awards for public good actions.

Governments and development partners can also assist by fostering the establishment and authority of professional associations, including the authority of these associations to impose meaningful sanctions on members who behave inappropriately. The provision of small amounts of support for better self-regulation across a wider range of professions than at present may be a strategy worth piloting.

In higher education, the Department of Higher Education, Research, Science and Technology, could do much to promote the effective teaching of ethics, firstly by including requirements for training in ethics in its quality assurance standards for academic programs and by working more closely with credible professional associations. Sponsorship of cross-institutional profession-specific forums (or conferences on public good professionals) would not require significant funding but, again, could augment both teaching and peer-inspired ethical conduct. The Department might also ensure that stand-alone professional education institutions have access to advice and mentoring on good practices in learning and teaching, especially in regard to assessment and workplace supervised practice. Identifying and gradually building cadres of experienced educators in a range of professional disciplines may be one way forward.

As educators of professionals, and whether we are national or expatriate, we do our students a disservice if we do not test ourselves by seeking to make student learning more relevant and appropriate for national circumstances and needs. In each generation and in each place, we constantly re-make professional knowledge and skills, in our own human, imperfect, limited way. As professionals in a global world, perhaps our greatest strength is an ability to tolerate diversity in professional practice where such practice demonstrably contributes to the overarching goal of ethical service to individual societies.

References

Asian Development Bank. (2014). Country partnership strategy: Papua New Guinea, 2016–2020. Gender Analysis Strategy. Retrieved from https://www.adb.org/sites/default/files/linked-documents/cps-png-2016-2020-ga.pdf

Avci, E. (2017). Learning from experiences to determine quality in ethics education. *International Journal of Ethics Education, 2*, 3–16. https://doi.org/10.1007/s40889-016-0027-6

Ayius, A., & May, R. J. (Eds.). (2007). *Corruption in Papua New Guinea: Towards an understanding of issues*. NRI Special Publication No. 47. The National Research Institute, Port Moresby, PNG.

Beine, M., Docquier, F., & Rapoport, H. (2008). Brain drain and human capital formation in developing countries: Winners and losers. *The Economic Journal, 118*, 631–652. https://doi.org/10.1111/j.1468-0297.2008.02135.x

Cash, R. (2005). Ethical issues in health workforce development. *Bulletin of the World Health Organization, 83*(4), 280–284.

Crigger, N., & Godfrey, N. (2014). From the inside out: A new approach to teaching professional identity formation and professional ethics. *Journal of Professional Nursing, 30*(5), 376–382. https://doi.org/10.1016/j.profnurs.2014.03.004

Department of Foreign Affairs and Trade, Australia. (2015, September 30). Aid investment plan Papua New Guinea: 2015–16 to 2017–18. Retrieved from http://dfat.gov.au/about-us/publications/Pages/aid-investment-plan-aip-papua-new-guinea-2015-16-to-2017-18.aspx

Department of Personnel Management, PNG. (2014). *Public sector ethics and values based executive leadership and management capability framework*. Port Moresby, PNG: DPM.

DWU. (2016a). Vision statement. Retrieved March 10, 2017, from http://www.dwu.ac.pg/en/index.php/vision-mission-core-values

DWU. (2016b). MBBS program specification document.

Farmer, J., Kenny, A., McKinstry, C., & Huysmans, R. D. (2015). A scoping review of the association between rural medical education and rural practice location. *Human Resources for Health, 13*, 27. https://doi.org/10.1186/s12960-015-0017-3

GoPNG [Government of Papua New Guinea]. (2010). Vision 2050. Retrieved from http://www.treasury.gov.pg/html/publications/files/pub_files/2011/2011.png.vision.2050.pdf

Hennessy, B. (2016, October 7). Decolonising the university: Lessons from Oceania. *Demos*. Retrieved from http://www.demosproject.net/decolonising-the-university-lessons-from-oceania/

IFAC Education Committee. (2005). Professional ethics for accountants: Approaches to the development and maintenance of professional values, ethics and attitudes in accounting education programs. Retrieved from https://www.iaesb.org/system/files/meetings/files/1625.pdf

Institute of National Affairs. (2016). *PNG at 40 symposium: Learning from the past and engaging with the future, papers from Alotau symposium, 1–3 March 2016*. Institute of National Affairs, Port Moresby, PNG. Retrieved from www.inapng.com/pdf_files/PNG%20at%2040%20Symposium%20ReportPB.pdf

Kavanamur, D., & Okole, H. (2004). *Understanding reform in Papua New Guinea: An analytical evaluation*. Port Moresby, PNG: Institute of National Affairs.

Kawan, M. M. S., Kondalsamy-Chennakesavan, S., Ranmuthugala, G., Toombs, M. R., & Nicholson, G. C. (2017, July 7). The rural pipeline to longer-term rural practice: General practitioners and specialists. *PLoS One, 12*(7), e0180394. https://doi.org/10.1371/journal.pone.0180394

Kula-Semos, M. A. (2009). *Seeking transformative partnerships: Schools, university and the practicum in Papua New Guinea*. PhD thesis, James Cook University.

Kula-Semos, M. A. (2014). An interpretation of the competing values framework in PNG's multicultural higher education landscape. *Contemporary PNG Studies, 21*, 29–43.

Larmour, P. (2012). *Interpreting corruption: Culture and politics in the Pacific Islands*. Honolulu: University of Hawaii Press.

Lind, G. (2008). The meaning and measurement of moral judgment competence: A dual-aspect model. In D. Fasko Jr. & W. Willis (Eds.), *Contemporary philosophical and psychological perspectives on moral development and education* (pp. 185–220). Creskill: Hampton Press. Retrieved from https://www.uni-konstanz.de/ag-moral/pdf/Lind-2008_Meaning_measurement.pdf

McCarthy, W. (2006). Ethics in education—Which ethics? *Contemporary PNG Studies, 5*, 96–108.

McEwen, C., & Trede, F. (2016). Educating deliberate professionals: Beyond reflective and deliberative practitioners. In F. Trede & C. McEwen (Eds.), *Educating the deliberate professional: Preparing for future practices* (pp. 223–230). New York: Springer.

McLean, M., & Walker, M. (2016). A capabilities approach to educating the deliberate professional: Theory and practice. In F. Trede & C. McEwen (Eds.), *Educating the deliberate professional: Preparing for future practices* (pp. 141–155). New York: Springer.

Namaliu, R., & Garnaut, R. (2010). PNG universities review: Report to Prime Ministers Somare and Rudd. Retrieved from dfat.gov.au/about-us/publications/documents/png-universities-review.doc

Pumwa, J. (2010, November 12–18). Engineering ethics: A necessary attribute for Papua New Guinea engineers. In *ASME 2010 International Mechanical Engineering Congress and Exposition, Volume 6: Engineering Education and Professional Development* (pp. 23–231). https://doi.org/10.1115/IMECE 2010-37023

Radio New Zealand. (2014, July 9). 'Critical shortage' of rural doctors in PNG. *Dateline Pacific*. Retrieved from http://www.radionz.co.nz/international/programmes/datelinepacific/audio/20140917/'critical-shortage'-of-rural-doctors-in-png-doctor

Rae, S. B., & Wong, K. L. (2012). *Beyond integrity: A Judeo-Christian approach to business ethics* (3rd ed.). Grand Rapids, MI: Zondervan.

Raes, K. (1997). Teaching professional ethics: A remark on method. *Ethical Perspectives, 4*(2), 243–245.

Robinson, M. (2015). *From old public administration to the new public service implications for public sector reform in developing countries*. Singapore: UNDP Global Centre for Public Service Excellence. Retrieved from http://www.undp.org/content/undp/en/home/librarypage/capacity-building/global-centre-for-public-service-excellence/PS-Reform.html

Schön, D. A. (1983). *The reflective practitioner: How professionals think in action*. New York: Basic Books.

Sen, A. (2009). *The idea of justice*. London: Allen Lane.

Serodio, A., Kopelman, B. I., & Bataglia, P. U. R. (2016). The promotion of medical students' moral development: A comparison between a traditional course on bioethics and a course complemented with the Konstanz method of dilemma discussion. *International Journal of Ethics Education, 1*, 81–89. https://doi.org/10.1007/s40889-016-0009-8

Simpson, N. Y., Onumah, J. M., & Oppong-Nkrumah, A. (2016). Ethics education and accounting programmes in Ghana: Does university ownership and affiliation status matter? *International Journal of Ethics Education, 1,* 43–56. https://doi.org/10.1007/s40889-015-0005-4

Snow, C. (2015). Organizing in the age of competition, cooperation, and collaboration. *Journal of Leadership and Organizational Studies, 22*(4), 433–442.

Sopoaga, F., Crampton, P., Ekeroma, A., Perez, D., Maoate, K., Watson, B., … Blattner, K. (2015). The role of New Zealand health professional training institutions in capacity building in the Pacific region. *NZMJ, 128*(1420), 6–9.

Stark, J. S. (1998). Classifying professional preparation programs. *The Journal of Higher Education, 69*(4), 353–383.

Stückelberger, C. (2017). The significant role of higher education in developing a global ethical culture. In D. Singh & C. Stückelberger (Eds.), *Ethics in higher education* (pp. 31–52). Education Ethics No. 1. Geneva: Globalethics.net. Retrieved from http://www.globethics.net/publications

Task Force on Higher Education and Society. (2000). *Higher education in developing countries: Peril and promise*. Washington, DC: World Bank. Retrieved from http://documents.worldbank.org/curated/en/345111467989458740/Higher-education-in-developing-countries-peril-and-promise

Tate, R. B., & Aoki, F. Y. (2012). Rural practice and the personal and educational characteristics of medical students. *Canadian Family Physician, 58*(11), e641–e648.

Transparency International. (2017). Corruption Perceptions Index 2016. Retrieved from https://www.transparency.org/news/feature/corruption_perceptions_index_2016#regional

Trede, F., & McEwen, C. (Eds.). (2016). *Educating the deliberate professional: Preparing for future practices*. New York: Springer.

UNESCO. (2016). *Small Island developing states: UNESCO's Action Plan*. Paris, France: UNESCO. Retrieved from unesdoc.unesco.org/images/0024/002460/246082E.pdf

Van Bilzen, G. (2015). *The development of aid*. Newcastle Upon Tyne: Cambridge Scholars Publishing.

Walker, M., & McLean, M. (2009, December 8). *A public good professional capability index for university-based professional education in South Africa*. Presentation to Society for Research in Higher Education, UK. Retrieved from http://www.nottingham.ac.uk/educationresearchprojects/developmentdiscourses/conferencesandpresentations.aspx

Walker, M., & McLean, M. (2013). *Professional education, capabilities and the public good: The role of universities in promoting human development.* London: Routledge.

Walker, M., & McLean, M. (2015). Professionals and public-good capabilities. *Critical Studies in Teaching and Learning (CriSTaL), 3*(2), 60–82. Retrieved from http://eprints.nottingham.ac.uk/32146/1/Prof%20and%20Pub%20good.pdf

WFME [World Foundation for Medical Education]. (2015). Final 2015 revision of 2012 basic medical education standards. Retrieved from http://wfme.org/standards/bme

World Bank. (2011). *PNG health workforce crisis: A call to action.* Washington, DC: World Bank.

6

Interrogating the Value of Learning by Extension in Enhancing Professional Quality: The Case of Australian and Venezuelan Engineers

David Thorpe, Emilio A. Anteliz, and P. A. Danaher

Introduction

The contemporary character of professions is complex, diverse and increasingly politicised (Corey, Schneider Corey, Corey, & Callinan, 2014). Formerly accepted certainties have faded and previously accepted knowledge claims on behalf of presumed professions are now contested (Collins, 2014). Assertions of professional autonomy and social

---

D. Thorpe (✉)
University of Southern Queensland, Toowoomba, QLD, Australia
e-mail: david.thorpe@usq.edu.au

E. A. Anteliz
Central University of Venezuela, Caracas, Venezuela

P. A. Danaher
University of Southern Queensland, Toowoomba, QLD, Australia

Central Queensland University, Rockhampton, QLD, Australia

University of Helsinki, Helsinki, Finland

© The Author(s) 2019
K. Trimmer et al. (eds.), *Ensuring Quality in Professional Education Volume II*,
https://doi.org/10.1007/978-3-030-01084-3_6

separateness are subjected to enhanced public scrutiny and media attention (Noordegraaf, 2011). It is therefore timely to redirect scholarly attention to current professions, to whom and what they are for, and to their effects and ongoing impact.

More specifically, these developments highlight the particular timeliness of this volume's focus on the interplay among contemporary professions, higher education and the enactment of quality practice. Like professions, universities are increasingly under question about their purposes and relevance (Brady, 2012). Similarly, the notion of quality has been deployed as a conceptual lens for analysing the intentions and actions of members of professions (Jonnergård & Erlingsdóttir, 2012) and of universities (Boni & Gasper, 2012) alike.

The authors of this chapter take up this intersection among contemporary professions, higher education and quality practice by considering the cases of Australian and Venezuelan engineers and their access to and take-up of opportunities for continuing professional development. The chapter interrogates two sites of this development. The first site is the provision of postgraduate engineering education with a sustainability focus by the University of Southern Queensland (USQ), an Australian regional university, where the first-named author enacts a leadership role in conceptualising and implementing such postgraduate education. The second site is a program of extension learning provided for working engineers by the Central University of Venezuela (Universidad Central de Venezuela) (UCV), the country's oldest and largest higher education institution. This program has been until recently coordinated and facilitated by the chapter's second-named author, himself an engineering graduate from the same university.

The authors use the analysis of these two sites of continuing professional development to explore three themes of quality practice in engineering in Australia and Venezuela as well as internationally. At the same time, the authors highlight the enduring significance of the globally, regionally, nationally and locally constituted contexts within which individual programs of professional renewal are designed and enacted and against which their effectiveness needs to be evaluated.

Interrogating the Value of Learning by Extension in Enhancing... 117

The chapter consists of the following four sections:

* A combined literature review, conceptual framework and research design
* An analysis of the identified provision of extension learning for Australian engineers
* An analysis of the equivalent provision for Venezuelan engineers
* Distilling three themes of quality practice in Australian and Venezuelan engineering professional education.

Literature Review, Conceptual Framework and Research Design

Professions, professionals and professionalisms have all undergone considerable change in the late 20th and early 21st centuries. Three key dimensions have been articulated by previous scholars as being central to defining what a profession is and what its members do: a specialised body of knowledge (Saks, 2012); recognised autonomy to apply that knowledge (Singer, 2007); and accompanying ethical principles and standards (Grace, 2014). These dimensions have contributed directly to the constructions of professions as high-status occupations with associated higher rates of remuneration than other forms of work (Ingersoll & Perda, 2008). A direct corollary of this high status and higher remuneration was the perceived importance of gatekeeping perceived professional norms and exercising quality control over who was permitted to enter each profession and who was not (Coffee, 2006; Sturdy & Wright, 2011).

Changes to the high status of contemporary professions have paralleled challenges to the definition, understanding and relative valuing of different forms of knowledge. These dramatic developments included a fundamental shift from profession as a coherent, consensually accepted, largely homogeneous set of specialised practices to knowledge-based work that is fluid, heterogeneous and often contested by rival claims about specific expertise (Gorman & Sandelfur, 2011). This shift has been accompanied by particular critiques of professions, including a perceived decline in public trust in occupants of professions (Tait, 2011), a potential for professions to replicate patriarchy (Chamberlain, 2012), and an ambivalent connection between professional membership and the sociocultural identities of various minority groups (Slay & Smith, 2011).

Some of these broader shifts have taken distinctive forms in the engineering profession. Davis (2015) contended that focusing excessively on the functions of what engineers do in practice as a way of defining their profession restricts understandings of their wider contributions to society. Similarly from this perspective, "Engineers themselves can fail to see their work in its fuller social context," and "The challenges of a complex, increasingly connected world demand that the engineering profession renew itself continuously, highlight and promote its accomplishments, and cultivate a future generation of engineers" (Russell, 2013, p. 654). For instance, the ethical dimension that helps to define professions is manifested in particular ways in engineering (Basart & Serra, 2013). Indeed, this dimension has recently expanded, in line with broader sociocultural changes. According to Nasser and Romanowski (2016), a previously "technical[,] trivialized education" (p. 409) with an excessive focus on practical processes has given way to a growing openness to "a new language and discourse in engineering education, widening the ethical education of engineers" (p. 409), arising from an explicit focus on "the significance of social justice" (p. 409) in engineering education.

Moreover, and from a related viewpoint:

> Most traditional engineering ethics has focused on the prevention of harm to the public.... [However, d]uring the past few years, scholars in engineering ethics have emphasized that engineering ethics should have a more positive dimension: encouragement of engineers to promote human welfare through technology. (Harris, Pritchard, Rabins, James, & Englehardt, 2014, p. xvi)

These debates encapsulate more general considerations of engineering's claimed contributions to economic growth and sociocultural progress, as well as discussions of the interplay between engineering education and engineers' work practices (Jørgensen & Valderrama, 2016).

Extension learning refers to diverse manifestations of adult, community-oriented educational provision for practitioners working in fields such as agriculture, engineering and science and taking multiple forms, ranging from longer, formally credentialled programs to shorter, non-credentialled courses. A widely encompassing definition of "extension" referred to:

> ...any advisory, consulting, technology transfer, research, training, marketing, industry development, learning, change, communication, education, attitude change, collection and dissemination of information, human resource development, facilitation, or self-development activities that are undertaken with the aim of bringing out positive change on farms and in agriculture. (Fulton et al., 2003, p. v)

This is clearly a very comprehensive definition of extension learning, and from some perspectives excessively so. A more specific interpretation was provided by Davis (2008): "Extension originally was conceived as a service to 'extend' research-based knowledge to the rural sector to improve the lives of farmers" (p. 16). Considered in this worldview, extension learning is expected to contribute directly to tangible outcomes such as production volumes and net incomes (Wu, Lin, & Chang, 2011), depending on the exigencies of the respective sectors in which it is enacted, thereby accentuating "the changing roles of extension agents, underlining their current roles as learning–innovation–change facilitators and knowledge brokers" (Cristóvão, Koutsouris, & Kügler, 2012, p. 201). At the same time, the effectiveness of extension learning depends on factors like the alignment between the training provided and the participants' learning needs. When these factors are in place, extension learning is crucial for upskilling participants and for maximising their professional growth. Moreover, extension learning has been posited as potentially promoting transformative education, and as "bring[ing] about deep change in individuals, families, and communities" (Franz, Garst, Baughman, Smith, & Peters, 2009, n.p.).

Given the aforementioned expectation of the role of engineers from a primarily technical function to one in which they are the recipients of considerable societal expectations, such as the exercise of ethical judgment, incorporating the principles of sustainability into their design and practice, and an increased expectation of social responsibility, and given also the developments in extension education noted above, the research question that is addressed by this chapter is: "How can engineering professional quality be enhanced through extension learning in Australia and Venezuela?"

This chapter explores this question, using postgraduate education and extension learning provided by two universities, one in Australia and the other in Venezuela, as examples of broader themes of quality extension learning. Figure 6.1 presents the conceptual framework that guides and underpins this exploration.

As was noted above, the chapter's research design mobilises selected elements of a dual site case study (Yin, 2012), comparing the extension of extension learning by USQ and UCV. This approach to case study highlights its constructivist (Boblin, Ireland, Kirkpatrick, & Robertson, 2013), exploratory (Yin, 2014) and qualitative (Stake, 2005) affordances, by being attentive to diverse and potentially conflicting perspectives related to the phenomenon under review. This approach also emphasises the capacity of case study to contribute to theory building by deploying both abductive and inductive strategies of data collection and data analy-

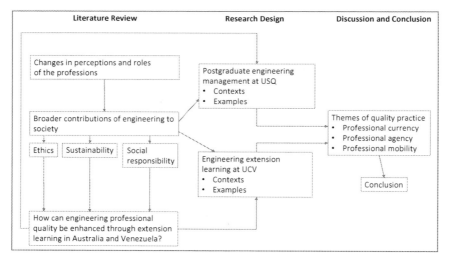

Fig. 6.1 Conceptual framework for chapter discussion

sis (Thomas, 2016). The chapter's data analysis technique focuses on thematic analysis as a comprehensive and systematic yet responsive and nuanced means of coding and interpreting qualitative data (Braun & Clarke, 2014; Clarke & Braun, 2014, 2017), and as helping to distil the three themes articulated in the final section of the chapter. The study's research design appeals to the claims to credibility, dependability, confirmability and transferability associated with qualitative research (Lincoln & Guba, 1985; see also Marshall & Rossman, 2016). Finally, although the chapter has drawn on the first- and second-named authors' reflections on their selected experiences in facilitating extension learning in their respective universities, and hence has not required formal ethics approval, the authors have been mindful of the importance of the ethical principles of beneficence and reciprocity (Resnik, 2017) in presenting this comparative account of those experiences (for instance, by keeping in mind the interests of colleagues and program participants as legitimate stakeholders in program outcomes being relevant and enabling).

Data Analysis: Australian Engineers' Extension Learning

Contexts

The main professional association for engineers in Australia, Engineers Australia (2017), recognises three levels of Australian engineering graduates: Engineering Associate; Engineering Technologist; and Professional Engineer. Graduates in these grades of membership complete programs consisting of the equivalent of two years, three years and four years of full-time study, or the part-time equivalent, respectively. The four-year program at USQ is an honours program that includes a significant research project (University of Southern Queensland, 2017c).

While some graduates remain satisfied with their academic level of achievement, other graduates desire to articulate to a higher level or to obtain additional skills. Their motivation for doing so might include increased pay, improved job satisfaction, a desire to succeed at the highest possible level in their profession, the potential to make an increased contribution to society at a higher professional level or other reasons.

One approach that graduates at a particular level follow to increase their professional qualification level is articulation between levels through completing additional undergraduate studies. An alternative means of articulating to a higher degree by Engineering Technologists, who at USQ graduate with a Bachelor of Engineering Science degree after a program of study of the equivalent of three years in length, is to undertake an extension postgraduate program. USQ offers two such programs: the Master of Engineering Science; and the Master of Engineering Practice. The Master of Engineering Science program is equivalent to two years' full-time study, and it is aimed primarily at newer graduates from a three-year Bachelor of Engineering Science degree or equivalent, or alternatively Professional Engineers wishing to qualify in a second discipline. Students undertaking the Master of Engineering Practice degree, which has a duration of one-and-a-half years of equivalent full-time study, are typically experienced Engineering Technologists (University of Southern Queensland, 2017c).

A further approach, which tends to be focused on qualified Professional Engineers who have completed a four-year engineering program or equivalent, is an extension into other engineering skills or to a different field of engineering. For example, the University of Technology Sydney offers a formal Master of Engineering (Extension) degree. This program aims to develop engineering graduates or to provide them with the opportunity to study a discipline at a sub-major level different from their own (University of Technology Sydney, 2017). Similarly, USQ's Master of Advanced Engineering degree is an extension program for qualified Professional Engineers. It is equivalent to one year of full-time study in duration and includes an industry project, and it can be taken in engineering management, engineering project management and advanced structural design majors.

Finally, there are USQ research programs available to suitably qualified Professional Engineers, including the Master of Engineering by Research degree (equivalent to 18 months of full-time study), a Doctorate of Professional Engineering, which consists of a combination of coursework and research, and the Doctorate of Philosophy (University of Southern Queensland, 2017c).

All of these USQ programs are available in full-time or part-time study mode, and they may be studied either on-campus or in online study mode. Online students are also expected to attend the university's main campus at Toowoomba, Queensland, Australia for practice classes, such as laboratory work, presentations and exposure to the engineering profession. In a very real sense, the external and online offerings of these programs constitute an important form of extension learning by affording opportunities for such learning by practising members of the engineering profession to extend and build on their current knowledge and skills.

Examples

The extension engineering programs taught by USQ consist of a range of advanced undergraduate courses, courses in the Master of Engineering Practice degree that take account of professional experience and specialised postgraduate engineering courses, including engineering management. Typical engineering management courses include ENG8101 Technological Impact and Its Management, ENG8103 Management of Technological Risk, ENG8104 Asset Management in an Engineering Environment and ENG8208 Advanced Engineering Project Management (University of Southern Queensland, 2017c). The most popular of these courses are ENG8104 and ENG8208, which are core courses in a number of extension programs.

ENG8104 Asset Management in an Engineering Environment aims to provide engineering and technology managers with the skills to make better decisions about infrastructure asset management, particularly from the point of view of engineering economics and finance. Students completing this course are assisted to improve their understanding of asset management, be able to apply whole of life financial planning to engineering and technological assets, develop and implement options for asset replacement, rehabilitation or upgrading, and evaluate and manage computer-based asset management systems (University of Southern Queensland, 2017a).

ENG8208 Advanced Engineering Project Management takes students through the historical background of project management and the project management environment, and then discusses a number of topics in advanced project management. These topics include the project life cycle, project documentation and management knowledge areas, professional issues and program management. This course includes a discussion of some specialised topics, including sustainability aspects of project management, and current and future issues in this field (University of Southern Queensland, 2017b).

These courses aim at transforming the thinking of learners, and in particular developing their sustainable strategic thinking skills. While traditional methods such as transmissive teaching are used to impart information, more advanced methods are utilised to encourage deep learning (Biggs, 2012). For example, student-centred approaches like reflective practice, constructive alignment and a problem-solving approach in assignments (Biggs, 2012) are adopted to encourage students' exploration and improved understanding of the course material. Other approaches followed in these courses include authentic assessment (Gulikers, Bastiaens, & Kirschner, 2004; Litchfield & Dempsey, 2015) and experiential learning principles (Kolb, 1984; Thorpe, 2016).

For instance, in ENG8104, learners are set an assignment in which the main question, worth 30 per cent of the course assessment, requires the learner to articulate a strategy to change an underperforming engineering asset network (such as a network of roads) and to implement contemporary practices to achieve best industry practice within five years, and a national leadership position within 10 years, by considering topics like stakeholder requirements, network performance, and likely benefits and costs. Because of the wide variety of backgrounds and the diversity of engineering disciplines of the learners in this course, learners nominate the asset network about which they undertake the assignment. They are then challenged, within the parameters of the course material, to develop their own strategy to change an underperforming asset network into a high performing one, and to write this strategy in the form of a report to their organisation's chief executive. Allowing the learners to select an asset network and giving them the freedom to develop a strategy enable them to construct their own solution to the problem. Writing the strategy in the form of a report to their chief executive provides them with a real-life challenge that they need to address authentically.

Data Analysis: Venezuelan Engineers' Extension Learning

Contexts

Like USQ, UCV provides a range of accredited undergraduate and postgraduate programs for engineers, including the five-year full-time equivalent Bachelor of Engineering program that has been prescribed in Venezuela since 1970. By contrast, the second-named author has had almost 20 years of experience in facilitating the provision of non-credentialled extension learning by Venezuelan engineers and related professionals, including architects, earth scientists, information technology specialists and technicians, among others. This particular form of continuing professional development entails short training courses that are separate from the programs in UCV's undergraduate and postgraduate engineering curricula. Examples of such courses include the inspection and supervision of civil works, instrumentation, metrology, solar technology design and unit price analysis. For instance, these courses highlight the context-specific elements related to labour, machines and materials as separate but interrelated elements of building construction.

This kind of learning by extension values situated knowledge and professional competence that are developed and enacted in particular and complex contexts—or, as Gherardi (2008) asserted, "knowing in practice is always a practical accomplishment" (p. 517). This approach emphasises "learning by doing" and "just in time learning", both of which are crucial in all professions but have a distinctive resonance in engineering education: please see respectively Bot, Gossiaux, Rauch, and Tabiou (2005), Felder and Brent (2003) and Goggins (2012); and Prince and Felder (2006). For example, as a country rich in oil deposits, Venezuela needs its engineers employed in its oil industry to have a working knowledge of different legal, technical and/or administrative aspects of that industry, including the organic hydrocarbon law (Fry & Ibrahim, 2013), as well as of the various value chain steps that compose that industry.

This type of professionally contextualised and nuanced knowledge is difficult to include in full curricula, not only because they are already crowded with the content mandated by accrediting bodies but also because they are almost by definition often segregated from the settings and sites of practice-based action where such knowledge is required and enacted. From that perspective, practising engineers might choose to develop this knowledge through self-study and/or informal learning from and with their industry peers. However, self-study is not always feasible or successful, depending on the circumstances in which it is attempted. Accordingly, targeted short training courses such as those provided by UCV constitute a crucial form of continuing professional development for Venezuelan engineers employed in a wide range of industries and workforces.

These courses are designed to enable Venezuelan engineers to acquire specific knowledge relatively quickly and on a "just in time" and "need to know" basis. On this basis, extension learning is predicated on being accurate, current and flexible. For instance, courses are tailored to the distinctive needs of engineers who do not have the time to attend a university campus during the working week, or who are working long distances from Caracas, Venezuela's capital city. These courses can be provided on-campus during weekends or in distance, e-learning and online study modes, with the materials being downloadable at home or in the workplace. Relatively recent developments include course lecturers using electronic mail, Skype and the instant messaging service WhatsApp as contemporary means of communicating with students. Course participants include Venezuelan engineers working abroad in countries such as Argentina, Chile, Spain and the United States.

More broadly, Venezuela is facing continuing economic, political and social challenges related to declining world oil prices (Cerra, 2017) and concerns about democratic governance (De Corte, 2017) and human rights (Gill, 2017). These challenges have been encapsulated in the politicisation of the Venezuelan oil industry (Kingsbury, 2016), which in turn has impacted directly on engineers and other professionals working in that industry. UCV's short courses are suited to this kind of occupational instability by virtue of their currency and flexibility, thereby contributing to these engineers' empowerment and helping to maximise their personal resilience and their capacity to sustain themselves as active members of their chosen profession.

This discussion of the diverse and sometimes conflicting influences on Venezuelan engineers highlights the situated and in certain respects politicised character of the occupational contexts in which their work is experienced. In these circumstances, extension learning emerges as an opportunity for alternative forms of continuing professional development that are relatively short-term, flexible and current, and that complement the formally accredited engineering curricula delivered by UCV and other Venezuelan universities.

Examples

Examples of the face-to-face short training courses provided by UCV for practising engineers range from NGSPICE (an electronic circuit simulation) based on GNU (an operating system based on free software) (requiring eight contact hours) and TCP/IP (Transmission Control Protocol/Internet Protocol) network operations (16 contact hours) to upgrading heavy and extra heavy crude oil (20 contact hours), introduction to statistical inference using R (24 contact hours) and water hammers/fluid hammers (24 contact hours) to the measurement and modelling of solar radiation (32 contact hours), risk and electrical safety (40 contact hours) and multivariate data analysis using R (45 contact hours). These courses include the completion of practical exercises (such as working with open source software models), spending time in laboratories and/or practical fieldwork.

Examples of e-learning courses include cryptography and electronic signatures (entailing six weeks of allocated study), network management and services (10 weeks) and security of information (11 weeks). These courses require the completion of continuous, on-course assessment (for instance, there are 17 units of homework/assessment in the security of information course), as well as interacting with an electronic platform to submit the online assessment items. The e-learning courses also mandate students' signing a code of ethics to act professionally in the courses.

All facilitators of both the face-to-face and the e-learning courses are staff members of the Faculty of Engineering at UCV. Ideas for new courses are sometimes suggested by these staff members; others emerge from the second-named author's extensive professional networks of Venezuelan companies and engineers. Sometimes courses are delivered exclusively to particular companies, in which case some of those courses require the signing of confidentiality agreements if commercial in confidence information is involved.

There is a formal evaluation of every course, with participants being asked to indicate their views about whether course objectives have been achieved, the performance of the facilitator, the logistics of the course and any suggestions for future improvements. While participants' opinions inevitably vary about specific aspects of certain courses, overall there is sufficient endorsement of the currency and effectiveness of the courses to justify their future delivery.

Themes of Quality Practice in Australian and Venezuelan Engineering Professional Education

As was noted above, the authors engaged in a targeted thematic analysis of the two cases of extension learning provision at USQ and UCV in order to address the research question framing the chapter: "How can engineering professional quality be enhanced through extension learning in Australia and Venezuela?". This analysis took account of the significant differences between the cases that contrasted USQ's delivery of accredited undergraduate and postgraduate programs with UCV's provision of short training courses. These contrasting approaches represented divergent but complementary approaches to learning by extension for engineers.

Despite these differences, the themes that emerged from the analysis of both cases presented here were clustered around the commonalities between the two sites of extension learning provision. The first of these themes was *professional currency*, understood as being enabled to keep up-to-date and familiar with the changing circumstances of professional practice (Ali, Pascoe, & Warne, 2002; Kaufman, 1972; Murray & Lawry, 2011). For the USQ undergraduate and postgraduate engineering programs, this currency was maximised through the program accreditation processes as well as through the first-named author's national and international networks of colleagues who like him were committed to enhancing engineering's contributions to ensuring global sustainability. Currency was also ensured by the case studies and assessment tasks in the courses being updated. For the UCV short training courses, professional currency was ensured through the close associations among the second-named author, the faculty academics who facilitated the courses and the industry contacts with whom they interacted.

The second theme that was analysed was *professional agency*, characterised as professionals' capacity to engage with high degrees of autonomy in their workplaces, with Eteläpelto, Vähäsantanen, Hökkä and Paloniemi (2013) advocating "a conceptualization of professional agency from a subject-centred socio-cultural perspective. This takes individual agency and social context to be analytically separate, but mutually constitutive, and in complex ways highly interdependent" (p. 45). This kind of agency was particularly relevant to engineers' confidence and self-efficacy about being able to discharge their professional responsibilities (Brown, Ashley, & Farrelly, 2011; Kastenhofer, Lansu, van Dam-Mieras, & Sotoudeh, 2010; Lent et al., 2008), as well as being linked more broadly with renegotiating professional identities (Hökkä, Eteläpelto, & Rasku-Puttonen, 2012). From the different perspectives of the USQ long-term programs and the UCV shorter-term courses, equipping students with the knowledge and skills attendant on increased professional agency was a key intended element of their learning by extension.

The third and final theme emerging from the analysis was *professional mobility*, referring to the affordance of formal learning in expanding the occupational opportunities and options available to practising engineers (Friesen, 2011; Guest, 2006; Heitmann, 2005). Both cases reviewed in this chapter demonstrated professional mobility as being among the motivations for students to engage in extension learning, as well as being among the planning considerations in both sites when designing and delivering that learning. From this perspective, professional mobility emerges as a form of learning mobility whereby practising engineers become increasingly familiar with and confident about their professional practice, which they embrace as an ongoing series of facilitated learning experiences from which they continue to learn and develop.

These three themes help to constitute the authors' response to the research question guiding this chapter: "How can engineering professional quality be enhanced through extension learning in Australia and Venezuela?". That is, we contend that high quality extension learning entails ongoing attentiveness to professional currency, professional agency and professional mobility, and to effective strategies for enabling these attributes as learning goals and outcomes. Furthermore, we assert that, despite their considerable differences, both institutions analysed in the chapter were successful in identifying the importance of, and in laying the foundations for continuing experience in relation to, these themes. From this perspective, the generation of quality practice in extension learning for engineers can take multiple forms and with varying effects.

More broadly, extension learning for engineers is implemented in institutional, occupational, national, regional and global contexts that both frame and constrain the possibilities for those same engineers to experience and exhibit professional currency, professional agency and professional mobility. Moreover, those contexts accentuate engineering as an increasingly socially responsive and politicised profession that needs to acknowledge and contribute to complex and sometimes contentious public policy debates like those related to sustainability. It is against the grain of these contexts and often competing expectations that the individual programs and courses such as those delivered in the two cases analysed in this chapter need to be interrogated and evaluated.

Conclusion

Duderstadt (2010) argued in relation to contemporary and future engineering that "We live in a time of great change", and that "It is a time of challenge and contradiction", "Yet it is also a time of unusual opportunity and optimism" (p. 17). Given these asserted circumstances, high quality engineering education and practice are crucial if this "time of unusual opportunity and optimism" is to be mobilised successfully and sustainably.

A key element of that mobilisation is effective extension learning for engineers, including in relation to maximising engineers' professional currency, professional agency and professional mobility through such extension learning. Learning by extension thus emerges as distilling wider lessons for higher education in the professions, and for the character and value of quality practice.

Acknowledgments The authors are grateful for the inputs and insights afforded by their colleagues and the participants in the extension learning programs analysed in this chapter. The final version of the chapter has benefited from the constructive feedback of two anonymous peer reviewers. Professor Karen Trimmer has been an encouraging and facilitative editor.

References

Ali, I. M., Pascoe, C., & Warne, L. (2002, April). Interactions of organizational culture and collaboration in working and learning. *Journal of Educational Technology & Society, 5*(2), 60–68.

Basart, J. M., & Serra, M. (2013, March). Engineering ethics beyond engineers' ethics. *Science and Engineering Ethics, 19*(1), 179–187. https://doi.org/10.1007/s11948-011-9293-z

Biggs, J. (2012). What the student does: Teaching for enhanced learning. *Higher Education Research and Development, 31*(1), 39–55. https://doi.org/10.1080/07294360.2012.642839

Boblin, S. L., Ireland, S., Kirkpatrick, H., & Robertson, K. (2013). Using Stake's qualitative case study approach to explore implementation of evidence-based practice. *Qualitative Health Research, 23*(9), 1267–1275. https://doi.org/10.1177/1049732313502128

Boni, A., & Gasper, D. (2012). Rethinking the quality of universities: How can human development thinking contribute? *Journal of Human Development and Capabilities: A Multi-disciplinary Journal for People-Centred Development, 13*(3), 451–470. https://doi.org/10.1080/19452829.2012.679647

Bot, L., Gossiaux, P.-B., Rauch, C.-P., & Tabiou, S. (2005). "Learning by doing": A teaching method for active learning in scientific graduate education. *European Journal of Engineering Education, 30*(1), 105–119. https://doi.org/10.1080/03043790512331313868

Brady, N. (2012). From "moral loss" to "moral reconstruction"? A critique of ethical perspectives on challenging the neoliberal hegemony in UK universities in the 21st century. *Oxford Review of Education, 38*(3), 343–355. https://doi.org/10.1080/03054985.2012.698987

Braun, V., & Clarke, V. (2014). What can "thematic analysis" offer health and wellbeing researchers? *International Journal of Qualitative Studies in Health and Well-being, 9*(1). https://doi.org/10.3402/qhw.v9.26152

Brown, R., Ashley, R., & Farrelly, M. (2011, December). Political and professional agency entrapment: An agenda for urban water research. *Water Resources Management, 25*(15), 4037–4050. https://doi.org/10.1007/s11269-011-9886-y

Cerra, V. (2017). How can a strong currency or drop in oil prices raise inflation and the black-market premium? *Economic Modelling.* https://doi.org/10.1016/j.econmod.2017.05.015

Chamberlain, J. M. (2012). *The sociology of medical regulation: An introduction.* Dordrecht, The Netherlands: Springer.

Clarke, V., & Braun, V. (2014). Thematic analysis. In T. Teo (Ed.), *Encyclopedia of critical psychology* (pp. 1947–1952). New York, NY: Springer.

Clarke, V., & Braun, V. (2017). Thematic analysis. *The Journal of Positive Psychology, 12*(3), 297–298. https://doi.org/10.1080/17439760.2016.1262613

Coffee, J. C. (2006). *Gatekeepers: The professions and corporate governance.* Oxford, UK: Oxford University Press.

Collins, H. (2014, October). Rejecting knowledge claims inside and outside science. *Social Studies of Science, 44*(5), 722–735. https://doi.org/10.1177/0306312714536011

Corey, G., Schneider Corey, M., Corey, C., & Callinan, P. (2014). *Issues and ethics in the helping professions* (9th ed.). Stamford, CT: Cengage Learning.

Cristóvão, A., Koutsouris, A., & Kügler, M. (2012). Extension systems and change facilitation for agricultural and rural development. In L. Darnhofer, D. Gibbon, & B. Dedieu (Eds.), *Farming systems research into the 21st century: The new dynamic* (pp. 201–227). Dordrecht, The Netherlands: Springer.

Davis, K. E. (2008, Fall). Extension in sub-Saharan Africa: Overview and assessment of past and current models, and future prospects. *Journal of International Agricultural and Extension Education, 15*(3), 15–28. Retrieved from https://www.aiaee.org/attachments/article/111/Davis-Vol-15.3-2.pdf

Davis, M. (2015). Engineering as profession: Some methodological problems in its study. In S. H. Christensen, C. Didier, A. Jamison, M. Meganck, C. Mitcham, & B. Newberry (Eds.), *Engineering identities, epistemologies and values: Engineering education and practice in context (Philosophy of Engineering and Technology Vol. 21)* (Vol. 2, pp. 65–79). Zug, Switzerland: Springer International Publishing.

De Corte, J. (2017, November 21). Locked in a stalemate: The Organization of American States and the Venezuelan democratic crisis. Retrieved from https://papers.ssrn.com/sol3/papers.cfm?abstract_id=3073692

Duderstadt, J. J. (2010). Engineering for a changing world: A roadmap to the future of American engineering practice, research, and education. In D. Grasso & M. B. Burkins (Eds.), *Holistic engineering education* (pp. 17–35). New York, NY: Springer.

Engineers Australia. (2017). Apply for membership. Retrieved from https://www.engineersaustralia.org.au/Membership

Eteläpelto, A., Vähäsantanen, K., Hökkä, P., & Paloniemi, S. (2013, December). What is agency? Conceptualizing professional agency at work. *Educational Research Review, 10*, 45–65. https://doi.org/10.1016/j.edurev.2013.05.001

Felder, R. M., & Brent, R. (2003, Fall). Learning by doing. *Chemical Engineering Education, 37*(4), 282–283.

Franz, N., Garst, B. A., Baughman, S., Smith, C., & Peters, B. (2009, August). Catalyzing transformation: Conditions in extension educational environments that promote change. *Journal of Extension, 47*(4). Retrieved from https://www.joe.org/joe/2009august/rb1.php

Friesen, M. R. (2011). Immigrants' integration and career development in the professional engineering workplace in the context of social and cultural capital. *Engineering Studies, 3*(2), 79–100. https://doi.org/10.1080/19378629.2011.571260

Fry, J. D., & Ibrahim, E. (2013, September). Reassessing Venezuela's organic hydrocarbon law: A balance between sovereignty and efficiency. *Journal of World Energy Law & Business, 6*(3), 234–259. https://doi.org/10.1093/jwelb/jwt005

Fulton, A., Fulton, D., Tabart, T., Ball, P., Champion, S., Weatherley, J., & Heinjus, D. (2003, May). *Agricultural extension, learning and change: A report for the Rural Industries Research and Development Corporation.* Barton, ACT: Rural Industries Research and Development Corporation.

Gherardi, S. (2008). Situated knowledge and situated action: What do practice-based studies promise? In D. Barry & H. Hansen (Eds.), *The Sage handbook of new approaches to management and organization* (pp. 516–525). London, UK: Sage Publications.

Gill, T. M. (2017). Unpacking the world cultural toolkit in socialist Venezuela: National sovereignty, human rights and anti-NGO legislation. *Third World Quarterly, 38*(3), 621–635. https://doi.org/10.1080/01436597.2016.119925

Goggins, J. (2012). Engineering in communities: Learning by doing. *Campus-Wide Information Systems, 29*(4), 238–250. https://doi.org/10.1108/10650741211253831

Gorman, E. H., & Sandelfur, R. L. (2011, August). "Golden age", quiescence, and revival: How the sociology of professions became the study of knowledge-based work. *Work and Occupations, 38*(3), 275–302. https://doi.org/10.1177/0730888411417565

Grace, P. J. (2014). Philosophical foundations of applied and professional ethics. In P. J. Grace (Ed.), *Nursing ethics and professional responsibility in advanced practice* (2nd ed., pp. 1–43). Burlington, MA: Jones & Bartlett Learning.

Guest, G. (2006). Lifelong learning for engineers: A global perspective. *European Journal of Engineering Education, 31*(3), 273–281. https://doi.org/10.1080/03043790600644396

Gulikers, J. T. M., Bastiaens, T. J., & Kirschner, P. A. (2004). A five-dimensional framework for authentic assessment. *Educational Technology Research and Development, 52*(3), 67–86.

Harris, C. E., Pritchard, M. S., Rabins, M. J., James, R., & Englehardt, E. (2014). *Engineering ethics: Concepts and cases* (5th ed.). Boston, MA: Wadsworth/Cengage Learning.

Heitmann, G. (2005). Challenges of engineering education and curriculum development in the context of the Bologna process. *European Journal of Engineering Education, 30*(4), 447–458. https://doi.org/10.1080/03043790500213136

Hökkä, P., Eteläpelto, A., & Rasku-Puttonen, H. (2012). The professional agency of teacher educators amid academic discourses. *Journal of Education for Teaching: International Research & Pedagogy, 38*(1), 83–102.

Ingersoll, R. M., & Perda, D. (2008). The status of teaching as a profession. In J. H. Ballantine & J. Z. Spade (Eds.), *Schools and society: A sociological approach to education* (3rd ed., pp. 106–118). Thousand Oaks, CA: Sage Publications.

Jonnergård, K., & Erlingsdóttir, G. (2012, September). Variations in professions' adaption of quality reforms: The cases of doctors and auditors in Sweden. *Current Sociology, 60*(5), 672–689. https://doi.org/10.1177/0011392112440440

Jørgensen, U., & Valderrama, A. (2016). The politics of engineering professionalism and education. In U. Jørgensen & S. Brodersen (Eds.), *Engineering professionalism (Professional practice and education: A diversity of voices)* (pp. 283–309). Rotterdam, The Netherlands: Sense Publishers.

Kastenhofer, K., Lansu, A., van Dam-Mieras, R., & Sotoudeh, M. (2010, March). The contribution of university curricula to engineering education for sustainable development. *GAIA—Ecological Perspectives for Science and Society, 19*(1), 44–51. https://doi.org/10.14512/gaia.19.1.10

Kaufman, H. G. (1972). Relations of ability and interest to currency of professional knowledge among engineers. *Journal of Applied Psychology, 56*(6), 495–499. https://doi.org/10.1037/h0033751

Kingsbury, D. V. (2016, October). Oil's colonial residues: Geopolitics, identity, and resistance in Venezuela. *Bulletin of Latin American Research, 35*(4), 423–436. https://doi.org/10.1111/blar.12477

Kolb, D. A. (1984). *Experiential learning: Experience as the source of learning and development.* Englewood Cliffs, NJ: Prentice-Hall/Harris.

Lent, R. W., Sheu, H.-B., Singley, D., Schmidt, J. A., Schmidt, L. C., & Gloster, C. S. (2008, October). Longitudinal relations of self-efficacy to outcome expectations, interests, and major choice goals in engineering students. *Journal of Vocational Behavior, 73*(2), 328–335. https://doi.org/10.1016/j.jvb.2008.07.005

Lincoln, Y. S., & Guba, E. (1985). *Naturalistic inquiry.* Beverly Hills, CA: Sage Publications.

Litchfield, B. C., & Dempsey, J. V. (2015, Summer). Authentic assessment of knowledge, skills, and attitudes. *New Directions for Teaching & Learning, 2015*(142), 65–80. https://doi.org/10.1002/tl.20130

Marshall, C., & Rossman, G. B. (2016). *Designing qualitative research* (6th ed.). Thousand Oaks, CA: Sage Publications.

Murray, C., & Lawry, J. (2011, August). Maintenance of professional currency: Perceptions of occupational therapists. *Australian Occupational Therapy Journal, 58*(4), 261–269. https://doi.org/10.1111/j.1440-1630.2011.00927.x

Nasser, R. N., & Romanowski, M. H. (2016). Social justice and the engineering profession: Challenging engineering education to move beyond the technical. In M. Abdulwahed, M. O. Hasna, & J. E. Froyd (Eds.), *Advances in engineering education in the Middle East and North Africa: Current status, and future insights* (pp. 409–428). Zug, Switzerland: Springer International Publishing.

Noordegraaf, M. (2011, October). Risky business: How professionals and professional fields (must) deal with organizational issues. *Organization Studies, 32*(10), 1349–1371. https://doi.org/10.1177/0170840611416748

Prince, M. J., & Felder, R. M. (2006, April). Inductive teaching and learning methods: Definitions, comparisons, and research bases. *Journal of Engineering Education, 95*(2), 123–138. https://doi.org/10.1002/j.2168-9830.2006.tb00884.x

Resnik, D. B. (2017). Examining the social benefits principle in research with human participants. *Health Care Analysis, 26*(1), 66–80. https://doi.org/10.1007/s10728-016-0326-2

Russell, J. S. (2013, June). Shaping the future of the civil engineering profession. *Journal of Construction Engineering and Management, 139*(6), 654–664. https://doi.org/10.1061/(ASCE)CO.1943-7862.0000600. Retrieved from http://ascelibrary.org/doi/10.1061/(ASCE)CO.1943-7862.0000600

Saks, M. (2012). Defining a profession: The role of knowledge and expertise. *Professions and Professionalism, 2*(1). https://doi.org/10.7577/pp.v2i1.151 Retrieved from https://journals.hioa.no/index.php/pp/article/view/151

Singer, J. B. (2007). Contested autonomy: Professional and popular claims on journalistic norms. *Journalism Studies, 8*(1), 79–95. https://doi.org/10.1080/14616700601056866

Slay, H. S., & Smith, D. A. (2011, January). Professional identity construction: Using narrative to understand the negotiation of professional and stigmatized cultural identities. *Human Relations, 64*(1), 85–107. https://doi.org/10.1177/0018726710384290

Stake, R. E. (2005). Qualitative case studies. In N. K. Denzin & Y. S. Lincoln (Eds.), *The Sage handbook of qualitative research* (3rd ed., pp. 443–466). Thousand Oaks, CA: Sage Publications.

Sturdy, A., & Wright, C. (2011, November). The active client: The boundary-spanning roles of internal consultants as gatekeepers, brokers and partners of their external counterparts. *Management Learning, 42*(5), 485–503. https://doi.org/10.1177/1350507611401536

Tait, M. (2011, June). Trust and the public interest in the micropolitics of planning practice. *Journal of Planning Education and Research, 31*(2), 157–171. https://doi.org/10.1177/0739456X11402628

Thomas, G. (2016). *How to do your case study* (2nd ed.). London, UK: Sage Publications.

Thorpe, D. S. (2016). Experiential learning approaches for developing professional skills in postgraduate engineering students. In A. Rahman & V. Ilic

(Eds.), *Proceedings of international conference on engineering education and research 21–24 November 2017 Western Sydney University, Parramatta Campus, Sydney, Australia*. Sydney, NSW: School of Computing, Engineering and Mathematics, Western Sydney University. Retrieved from https://www.westernsydney.edu.au/__data/assets/pdf_file/0005/1176746/iCEER2016_Conference_Proceedings_official.pdf

University of Southern Queensland. (2017a). *Course specification: ENG8104 Asset Management in an Engineering Environment*. Toowoomba, QLD: Author.

University of Southern Queensland. (2017b). *Course specification: ENG8208 Advanced Engineering Project Management*. Toowoomba, QLD: Author.

University of Southern Queensland. (2017c). *USQ handbook: Engineering and built environment*. Retrieved from https://usq.edu.au/handbook/current/engineering-built-environment/engineering-built-environment.html

University of Technology Sydney. (2017). Master of Engineering (Extension). Retrieved from https://www.masterstudies.com/Master-of-Engineering-(Extension)/Australia/UTS/

Wu, H.-Y., Lin, Y.-K., & Chang, C.-H. (2011, February). Performance evaluation of extension education centers in universities based on the balanced scorecard. *Evaluation and Program Planning, 34*(1), 37–50. https://doi.org/10.1016/j.evalprogplan.2010.06.001

Yin, R. K. (2012). *Applications of case study research* (3rd ed.). Thousand Oaks, CA: Sage Publications.

Yin, R. K. (2014). *Case study research: Design and methods* (5th ed.). Thousand Oaks, CA: Sage Publications.

7

Developing Engineering Knowledge and Skills: The Advanced Engineering Project Management Course at USQ

David Thorpe

Introduction

Although projects have been delivered for many thousands of years, the development of standard professional concepts and practices have tended to occur since the 1930's (Garel, 2013). Since then, project management has developed from good management practices such as those used to plan, control and coordinate the construction of the Hoover Dam (Kwak, 2005) to quite sophisticated project management methodologies. Over this period, project management has developed from a focus on time and cost management of a specific project to a complex methodology, which is based on a trade-off between time, cost, quality and scope (Stretton, 2007), and considers both the project life cycle and a range of management functions. The application of project management has also expanded to include many areas of business activity (Project Management Institute, 2013).

While project management principles and practice have delivered many positive results, there are also significant issues, particularly with

D. Thorpe (✉)
University of Southern Queensland, Toowoomba, QLD, Australia
e-mail: david.thorpe@usq.edu.au

larger and more complex projects. Thus, engineering projects—and particularly larger projects in uncertain environments—have the potential to fail. For example, there may be failure for project results to be delivered on time or within budget, and with predicted performance, safety, or reliability (Trevelyan, 2014, p. 328). There are consequently challenges in dealing with areas like risk management, stakeholder interaction and management, and sustainability. In addition, some authors have questioned whether traditional measures (primarily project time, cost and performance) are sufficient to describe project success and should be extended by other measures (Ramos & Mota, 2014; Shenhar et al., 2001). Therefore, it is desirable that project managers are equipped with the knowledge and skills that assist them to deliver these projects successfully, and to be able to effectively measure that success.

This chapter outlines the development of project management as a discipline and discusses the issues in the achievement of project management success. It then briefly discusses the role of professionally qualified engineers in delivering project success and how the Advanced Engineering Project Management course can aid this success. This discussion is followed by a description of the objectives of this course, its content and how this content has been designed to enhance the understanding of project management, using a more strategic viewpoint, by learners studying postgraduate engineering management. This section is followed by a description of the course development and delivery process, and an evaluation of how well the course has met its objectives, how challenges in developing the course have been addressed, and a reflection on the success of delivery of the course with respect to achieving its goals. Enhancements that have been made to the course as at the date of writing as a result of these considerations a conclusion complete the chapter.

Development of Project Management as a Discipline

The practice and theory of the management of projects has developed over time, firstly into a managerial practice, then from about the 1930s into a rationalised approach and finally, starting in the 1950s, into a standard management model, with the first edition of a formal project body of knowledge (PMBOK) being developed by the Project Management Institute in 1987 (Garel, 2013).

Kwak (2005) has divided the recent development of project management into four stages, during each of which project management has developed both as a practice and a theoretical discipline. The stages that he has identified are application of the craft system to human relations administration (prior to 1958), the application of management science between (1958 to 1979), a production centre with a focus on human resource management and the use of modern computer systems (1980 to 1994), and finally, from 1995 onwards, creating a new environment using modern systems like the Internet (Kwak, 2005).

This latest period has also seen the growth of other initiatives such as project management maturity models, the advent of a range of sophisticated project management methodologies and the globalisation of project management. Project management has also been more closely integrated with the business activities of the organisation, leading to a portfolio management approach for prioritising and managing projects (Larson & Gray, 2011, pp. 10–16). Two of the project management methodologies that are representative of the current period of project management development are the fifth edition of the PMBOK methodology (Project Management Institute, 2013) and Projects in Controlled Environments, or PRINCE2 (The Stationery Office, 2009).

Achieving Project Success

A major challenge in project management has been to manage projects successfully in an increasingly challenging environment. As observed in the Introduction, projects are required to meet time, cost and performance objectives. Performance objectives were initially focused on quality, with the later addition of scope (Stretton, 2007). Research and practice have extended these performance objectives to include items such as safety and reliability (Trevelyan, 2014, p. 328), and to other factors such as client, communication, team, and planning (Ramos & Mota, 2014). Stretton (2007) reinforces the planning aspect of project success when he discusses the increasing emphasis on the "front end" of projects. A similar view has been stated by Merrow (2011), who emphasises the importance of front-end loading, or stage gating the project definition phase through steps like developing the business case, scope development and preparation to execute the project (Merrow, 2011, pp. 202–215).

Further aspects of managing projects successfully include stakeholder considerations (Trevelyan, 2014, pp. 340–347) and the management and negotiation of sustainability issues. (Trevelyan, 2014, pp. 423–438) cites the 1984 Bhopal (India) chemical explosion, the BP Horizon explosion and fire that caused considerable environmental and economic damage in the Gulf of Mexico in 2010 and the more recent (2011) Fukushima nuclear power plant failure in the wake of an earthquake and tsunami, as significant contributors to community sensitisation about engineering projects.

A number of other authors have also investigated project success. For example, de Carvalho, Patah, and de Souza Bido (2015) tested a number of hypotheses related to project success measured against the three criteria of cost variation, schedule variation and margin variation (a longer-term objective that relates to the success of ongoing projects in a company) across Argentina, Brazil and Chile, in a range of industries. They found that the national environment played a key role in project performance. Project management skills and training were factors in the success of project schedule variation.

Armstrong (2015), who has authored an International review of construction project success from the point of view of project owners for KPMG International Cooperative, interviewed, from the point of view of maturity in managing the project dynamics of power, responsibility and control executives from 100 organisations that carried out considerable construction activity. Of the projects reviewed in this process, 53 per cent failed, primarily from the point of view of budget and time. In addition, only 31 per cent of projects in the previous three years were delivered within 10 per cent of budget, and only 25 per cent were completed within 10 per cent of their original deadlines. The research found that while planning and prioritising appeared to be rigorous, that talent shortages remain a challenge, project management information systems were not yet ubiquitous, and that contracts continued to emphasise the divide between contractors and owners.

Shenhar et al. (2001) investigated project success from the premise that projects are part of the strategic activity of an organisation and asked the question: "What does project success mean?" In addressing this question, the researchers cited the Sydney Opera House as an example of a project that took three times longer than anticipated and cost five times the anticipated amount, and yet can be considered a long-term success as it is a national icon that draws many tourists. They identified four distinct project and business success dimensions—project efficiency, impact on the customer, business and organisational success, and preparing for the future—the importance of which varied with the time and the level of technological uncertainty involved in the project. Lower technology projects tended to be more focused on shorter time dimensions, with higher technology projects being more focused on business success and the preparing for the future dimensions.

With respect to the complexity of project management, Trevelyan (2014, pp. 321–330) notes that engineers manage projects in uncertain environments and have the task of bringing predictability through managing risk, including that resulting from human behaviour, through good project management. He further states that managing a project is a three-stage process—managing and organisation, monitoring progress and completing the project. It was noted that successfully managing a project is a combination of the traditional constraints of scope, time, cost and quality, and that cost depends on a range of policy factors (Trevelyan, 2014, pp. 394–395). He cites the case of a multi-national mining company that, through seeing an opportunity to use newly discovered natural gas reserves to convert less valuable nickel ores into a higher grade product that could be more easily sold, which built a nickel processing plant in Central Asia that, through poor project management practice, became a major business failure, resulting in deaths and injuries to some workers, and a very high cost to the organisation, amounting to several billion dollars (Trevelyan, 2014, pp. 411–416).

According to Merrow (2011, pp. 1–8), the main reasons for the failure of such megaprojects tend to be greed, schedule pressure, the business arrangement being made without due consideration for the project, concern about spending money up front, cost reduction without sufficient consideration, asking contractors with limited resources to carry the risk and blaming project managers for cost overruns. He suggests that project sponsors should address the business-technical divide, formalise and institutionalise the opportunity shaping process, develop a team staffing strategy, use a stage-gated front-end loading to ensure that projects are well prepared and restore professionalism to the owner-contractor relationship (Merrow, 2011, pp. 332–340).

Armstrong (2015) has stated that, as project owners climb the project management maturity curve, they should consider the issues of talent management, use integrated project management information systems, demand practical targets from contractors based on realistic expectations of what can go wrong, adopt prudent cost management and invest in relationships with contractors to build mutual trust and discuss problems or shortcomings.

Geraldi et al. (2008) have provided a further perspective on the nature of the academic discipline of project management and have observed that there is continuing research interest in this field from a range of disciplines other than project management, and that there is probably no one complete project management model. As well, some of the traditional tools of project management may not represent the reality of projects. However, it can be said that there is a traditional discipline of project management and that it should be about striving for order by recognising the chaos inherent in projects and managing this chaos in a structured way.

In summary, the project management environment is often both uncertain and complex. Achieving successful project performance in such an environment requires a strategic approach that requires well executed risk management and attention not only to traditional project performance factors such as time and budget, but also gives close attention to other project factors. Such factors include the business aspects of the project, the project operating environment, safety, reliability, stakeholder needs, sustainability issues, staffing, information systems, communication and the extended project management team. Good project management also benefits from spending a significant period of time in planning the project, and properly financing it. At the same time, the use of sound engineering project management principles that link with the business environment and that are appropriate for the technology used can reduce the risk involved and aid engineers managing projects to achieve a successful result for both the project itself and its long-term success.

Meeting Project Success from an Engineering Viewpoint

Professional Engineers have a significant role in managing and delivering successful projects. They may be involved in any phases of the project life cycle; can operate at any level of management within a project or a program of projects; and may represent any of the major participants in the project management process, such as financiers, owners, contractors and sub-contractors. Professionally, engineers have responsibility for engineering projects and programs, including the reliable functioning of all materials, components, sub-systems and technologies used and their integration to form a complete, sustainable and self-consistent system. They are also responsible for ensuring that costs, risks and limitations are properly understood in the context of the desirable outcomes, and for managing risks as well as sustainability issues. Engineers have a particular responsibility for ensuring that all aspects of a project are soundly based in theory and fundamental principle, and for understanding clearly how new developments relate to established practice, experience and to other disciplines with which they may interact (Engineers Australia, 2013).

These responsibilities can be linked with many of the requirements for project success, including successful project planning, project delivery, stakeholder involvement, achieving project goals, and managing both risk and sustainability. In addition to meeting these requirements, experienced engineers who have achieved Chartered Professional Engineer status are expected to practice independently or unsupervised and are responsible for a number of project management related functions (Engineers Australia, 2012).

To achieve these objectives and other professional practice requirements, Chartered Professional Engineers are expected to meet 16 elements of competency, grouped under the headings of personal commitment, obligation to community, value in the workplace and technical proficiency. Examples of such competencies that are related to successful project management include dealing with ethical issues; developing safe and sustainable solutions; engaging with the relevant community and stakeholders; identifying, assessing and managing risks, meeting legal and regulatory requirements; communication; taking action; and problem analysis and evaluation (Engineers Australia, 2012).

While the achievement of these competencies is primarily practice based, an essential understanding of them can be achieved through formal study. A well-designed and well-structured course in advanced engineering project management course can aid engineering professionals to better understand and apply the Engineers Australia requirements in project management through providing the theory, background and knowledge of professional project management, and at the same time better equip them to deliver successful projects in uncertain environments.

As a result of these considerations, the Advanced Engineering Project Management course was developed as a postgraduate coursework engineering management course to teach successful project management skills in engineering at the project level, the program level and the wider business level. This course is a core course in the Master of Engineering Science (University of Southern Queensland, 2016a) program, and an alternative core course in the Master of Engineering Practice (University of Southern Queensland, 2016b). These programs are accredited by Engineers Australia to enable Engineering Technologists to qualify as graduate professional engineers. This course is also offered in other postgraduate programs. It is complementary to, and links with, other engineering management courses at the University of Southern Queensland, such as Asset Management in an Engineering Environment (University of Southern Queensland, 2016c) and the Management of Technological Risk (University of Southern Queensland, 2016d) at the University of Southern Queensland.

Description of the Advanced Engineering Project Management Course

The Advanced Engineering Project Management course has been designed to meet a number of objectives aimed at the successful planning and delivery of delivery of projects in a range of engineering disciplines. These objectives can be summarised as:

* Know and understand the project management life cycle and knowledge areas.
* Understand and assess the environment and context of a project.
* Apply the project management process to the delivery of an engineering project.
* Evaluate the effectiveness of applying project management to the delivery of outcomes.
* Understand the challenges of complex projects and how to deal with them.
* Develop, deliver and evaluate the delivery of a program of engineering projects.
* Understand and apply the importance of special focus areas in project management. (University of Southern Queensland, 2016e).

In achieving these objectives, this course aims to address a number of aspects of project success, including not only successfully delivering a project, but also recognising that project management is becoming a standard approach to undertaking business, and will increasingly play a role in the development of the strategic direction of business (Larson & Gray, 2011).

The course is divided into two main sections. The first section considers traditional aspects of engineering project management, such as the engineering project life cycle and project management knowledge areas, which are primarily based on the PMBOK project management methodology (Project Management Institute, 2013) and, to a lesser extent, those of PRINCE2 (The Stationery Office, 2009), and also draws on other literature. The balance of the course discusses a range of more advanced topics.

In order to address the objectives of the course, its contents have been grouped as follows:

* Introduction to engineering project management and the engineering project life cycle.
* Project management knowledge areas, including project integration, meeting project objectives, managing risk, project communication management, and stakeholder management.
* Advanced topics—management of project sustainability, attributes of an effective engineering project manager, managing complex engineering projects, engineering program management
* Current and future issues in engineering project management.

It is offered in two study modes. The first of these modes is an on-campus study mode at the Toowoomba campus of the University, in which, over a 13-week semester, learners attend a two hour lecture and a one hour tutorial, which is structured around reflective questions that challenge those attending to think about the theory, practice and application of advanced engineering project management. This course is also offered in a distance education mode, which is attractive to learners engaged in engineering practice or those who cannot attend the on-campus lectures. This mode is delivered on-line through a Study Desk that is also available to on-campus learners,

Because of the strong relevance of this course to professional practice, a significant challenge in course development has been the achievement of assessment that matches, as closely as possible, situations that professional engineers encounter in practice. From a pedagogical point of view, there has therefore been a strong focus, as much as is possible in a course of this nature, on utilising the principles of authentic assessment (Gulikers, Bastiaens, & Kirschner, 2004; Thorpe, 2013) to relate course material to good project management practice, and to use experiential learning principles (Kolb, 1984) to enable lessons learnt from a first assignment to be applied to a second, more complex assignment.

Assessment for this course consists of two assignments—one aimed at rectifying issues at the project level (worth 40%) and the second focused on developing a strategy to align a program of projects with corporate strategic direction (60%)—that have been designed to test the learner's understanding of course material, assess how and where such material and information gained from the literature can be applied to professional practice, and evaluate and comment on options.

The first assignment has two questions—a numerical question on Earned Value Management and a more complex question that places the learner in the role of a new project manager who has just taken over an engineering project that is lagging behind the required rate of progress to be completed on time and is not meeting other targets such as cost and quality. In this question, learners are asked to develop a project plan to achieve project requirements within given time constraints and write a report on their plan to company management. They are able to nominate the project, provided it fits within a small set of project management parameters.

The main question in the second assignment asks learners to assume the role of manager of a program of six projects, three of which are progressing satisfactorily and three of which have issues that require addressing. The three projects are of quite different cost and type. In this question, learners are asked to define the key characteristics of each of the projects, review them with respect to their alignment with the principles of advanced project management and develop a plan to manage each of the projects to successfully achieve project objectives. This question is designed to encourage learners to apply the feedback from the first assignment to a more complex problem related to program management, through using experiential learning approaches, thus utilising the experiential principles of Kolb (1984) to enable application of feedback from the first assignment in the execution of the second assignment.

Development and Delivery of the Course

The development of the Advanced Engineering Project Management course was undertaken by a team of three academics, who shared considerable industry experience between them. The development process therefore drew on considerable academic rigour and industry knowledge. It was based on the development of a sound business case for the course and was founded on a previous project management course delivered to a local government organisation. Because the course was being developed to a tight timetable, its initial offer was developed as the course was being delivered. This process allowed ongoing consideration of the learning experiences of the learners in the course, who were all experienced engineers actively engaged in project management.

A key consideration in developing this course was to equip professional engineers with the knowledge and skills to manage engineering projects, and programs of projects, successfully. It was also recognised that, as professional engineers are closely linked with the practice of successful project management, the focus of the course, while including project management delivery principles, should be primarily strategic to facilitate the enhancement by learners of their existing project management knowledge with advanced concepts.

Accordingly, it was decided to offer a more strategically focused course than most existing project management courses. To enhance the relevance of this course to the practising engineer, the course addresses not only the factors for project success, but also contemporary project management issues, such as innovation management and knowledge management, and the requirements of engineers to manage both programs (groups of projects) and portfolios (groups of programs and projects). Human factors like the attributes of a good project manager were also considered an important consideration in success at the strategic level of project and program management, as were emerging issues in project management.

Another factor in the development of the course was that it should be written so that engineers in all disciplines, including civil engineering, mechanical engineering, and electrical engineering; plus, professionals from related disciplines such as construction, surveying and town planning; could benefit from studying it. Therefore, the course has used examples of practice drawn from engineering projects and programs.

A number of existing courses were reviewed, and principles drawn from them. An example of such courses was the Advanced Engineering Project Management course offered at Florida International University

(Chen, 2013). This course considers project management from an organisational point of view, discusses the main principles in project management, and considers modern project management concepts like leadership, outsourcing and project closure, which are considered in modern project management.

The strong focus on strategic and other higher-level project management skills of project management distinguish this course from undergraduate courses, which tend to be more focused on the operational aspects of project delivery. This aspect of the course strongly contributes to the professional development of learners from the point of view of the competencies required of independently practicing engineers (Engineers Australia, 2012), better addresses the long-term success factors of projects, provides a better platform for managing project risk, and has the potential to be a significant factor in the continual improvement of professionals from graduate to leading professional.

The course material was designed to meet the meet a combination of academic, learner and industry needs. It was also required to meet the specification objectives of the Australian Qualifications Framework Second Edition (Department of Education and Training, 2013) for a Masters Degree (AQF Level 9). A further consideration was that the course had to be sufficiently flexible to accommodate the requirements of a wide range of learners, ranging from learners with little or no professional experience who were undertaking a postgraduate qualification to achieve professional engineer status to experienced professional engineers.

A further consideration in developing this course was for it to use good pedagogical principles to promote deep learning and a thorough understanding of the course material. Thus, student-centred learning principles (Biggs, 2001), the prompting of learning (Boud, 1998), and constructive alignment (Biggs, 1999; Gulikers et al., 2004) have been used in developing course material through the use of assignments that require learners to nominate the projects that they are using to address assignment questions, and through reflective questions in both the text of courses and tutorial material. These principles have been augmented with other principles like authentic assessment (Gulikers et al., 2004; Thorpe, 2013) and experiential learning principles (Kolb, 1984) that were, as previously discussed, used in developing course assessment.

This course was developed and delivered for the first time in Semester 1, 2014 by distance education to three learners who were studying postgraduate engineering management programs. This enrolment number increased to 87 learners (58 on-campus and 65 external) for the 2015 offer of this course, and 158 learners (93 on-campus and 65 external) for its 2016 offer. These enrolments have included a number of International students undertaking the Master of Engineering Science.

Evaluation of the Course in Achieving Learning Outcomes

An evaluation of the delivery of this course in achieving its learning outcomes was made against the following criteria, which are modified from those used for an interactive program evaluation criteria (Owen, 2007, p. 45). It is focused on the evaluations and perceived needs of the learners, who are the primary stakeholders.

The evaluation criteria selected are:

- How well the course met its development objectives.
- How well the course was delivered (student evaluations)
- Course development and delivery against progress plan
- Potential enhancements to the course to make it more effective.

The first three evaluation criteria, which primarily utilise student evaluation scores and comments, are discussed in this section. They are shown in Table 7.1. Possible future enhancements to the course are discussed in the next section.

Evaluation of Course Against Development Objectives

The Advanced Engineering Project Management course was developed to provide engineers with the knowledge and skills to deliver successful

Table 7.1 Evaluation of course against desired development objectives

Desired objectives for development	Criteria	Comment
Project success criteria	Project control (time, cost, quality, scope)	Addressed. Includes Earned Value Management
	Communication	Addressed
	Team	Addressed
	Clients/Stakeholders	Addressed
	Sustainability	Addressed
	Project planning	Addressed—possible future enhancement
	Project life cycle including long-term success	Addressed—possible future enhancement
	Risk management	Addressed—possible future enhancement
	Business factors	Addressed—possible future enhancement
Meet Project Management requirements of Engineers Australia—Role Description for Mature Professional Engineer	Take responsibility for engineering projects and programs	Addressed
	Ensure that costs, risks and limitations are properly understood in the context of the desirable outcomes, and for managing risks as well as sustainability issues	Addressed
	Have a particular responsibility of ensuring that all aspects of a project are soundly based in theory and fundamental principle	Addressed
Experienced Professional Engineer Competencies	Meet project management competencies of Experienced Professional Engineer	Addressed

(continued)

Table 7.1 (continued)

Desired objectives for development	Criteria	Comment
Australian Qualifications Framework Second Edition Level 9 criteria (Masters Degree) applied at the course level	Specialised knowledge and skills	Addressed
	Advanced and integrated understanding of a complex body of knowledge	Addressed
	Expert, specialised cognitive and technical skills in a body of knowledge or practice	Addressed
	Apply knowledge and skills to demonstrate autonomy, expert judgment, adaptability and responsibility	Addressed

projects, and to meet the project management requirements of Engineers Australia for the mature professional engineering and the Australian Qualifications Framework (AQF) (second edition) Level 9 criteria (Department of Education and Training, 2013) (Masters Degree), applied at the course level. The evaluation of the course against these development objectives is shown in Table 7.1.

Overall, it is considered that the course meets the evaluation criteria in Table 7.1. Possible future enhancements could be made to strengthen the areas of project planning, the project life cycle, risk management and business factors, with a particular focus on the success of engineering projects.

How Well Course Was Delivered ("My Opinion") Student Surveys)

Student evaluations of learning and teaching are considered important guides to how courses can be improved. The University of Southern Queensland accordingly undertakes "My Opinion" surveys of student opinion for each course at the conclusion of delivery of the course.

The responses from student "My Opinion" surveys for the 2015 offer of the course are listed in Table 7.2.

Table 7.2 Learner responses to "My Opinion" survey for 2015 course delivery

No.	Criterion	Score (0–5)—external learners	Score (0–5)—on-campus learners
1	Overall, I am satisfied with this course	3.40	4.00
2	I had a clear idea of what was expected of me in this course	3.40	4.36
3	My learning was assisted by the way the course was structured	3.80	4.18
4	My learning was supported by the course resources	3.70	4.27
5	I found the assessment in this course reasonable	3.10	4.27
6	My learning was supported by the course feedback	3.60	4.30
7	My learning was supported by the teaching in this course	3.60	4.30
8	Overall, I was satisfied with how the course was taught	3.50	4.27

Scores are measured on a 0 to 5 scale, with a score of 5 being the highest level possible

Response rates for these surveys with respect to the 2015 offer of the Advanced Engineering Project Management course were reasonable, with 10 out of 29 external students (34%) responding to the questionnaire, and 11 out of 58 (19%) of on-campus students responding to all questions, except Questions 6 and 7, to which 10 students (17%) responded.

The scores received were good to very good, with the on-campus class receiving better scores than the class offered by external studies. This may possibly be the result of a special weekly tutorial session for on-campus learners. While the questions for the tutorial were placed on an on-line Study Desk available to all learners, they external learners would not have been present at their discussion.

Comments on delivery of the course were quite positive overall, with some minor improvements noted with respect to assessment and sharing of tutorial discussions with external students. These comments have been taken into account in the conduct of the 2016 offer of the course. Student undertaking this course on campus delivery of the course have the advantage of a weekly tutorial session, the content of which is provided on the course electronic Study Desk.

One issue found was that some learners had not previously been exposed to a project management course. This aspect has been addressed through enhancements to the course, expanding the lectures given early in the semester to include more information about basic project management, and including some material about basic project management concepts in the initial tutorials for the course.

Course Development and Delivery Against Progress Plan

Indications are the learners in this course, who are significant stakeholders in it, appear to be satisfied with it. Every endeavour has been made to address the relevant professional level requirements with respect to project management of Engineers Australia. The industry experience of the project development and delivery team, along with the lessons learnt during course development and delivery, and the feedback from learners working in industry, has been of considerable value in the ongoing course development and delivery process,

It is concluded that development and delivery of the course have to date been quite successful. As with all courses, however, it is being enhanced on a continual basis.

Enhancements to the Course as a Consequence of Its Delivery

As a result of a number of learners not initially having a sound knowledge of project management principles, there is now increased emphasis on the basic project management requirements of integration, scope, time, cost and quality management, which maintaining the strategic focus of the course. There is now also a specific section on project control through Earned Value Management (Larson & Gray, 2011, pp. 458–463).

Additional enhancements for the current (2016) offer of the course include discussions on knowledge management and the project management office. There has also been a stronger focus on experiential learning (Kolb, 1984) approaches in the assignments. The approach used is that feedback given to learners from the first assignment is an experience that aims to stimulate a process of review and thinking that encourages them to apply the lessons learnt from undertaking the first assignment to the second, more complex assignment.

Future changes are expected for the 2017 offer of the course and would consider better addressing those project success areas where possible future enhancements have been indicated in Table 7.2, and in particular in risk management and the application of business management principles in project management. There is also likely to be more integration between this course and complementary courses, and the possible future development of specialised courses.

A further step in the improvement of the course will be the development of a closer link between it and the requirements of industry and Engineers Australia, with a particular focus on enhancing the course to assist professional engineers to meet that organisation's Stage 2 competencies (Engineers Australia, 2012). Similarly, links are expected to be sought with other organisations that accredit professional engineers. It is envisaged that the linkages with these organisations will not only include theoretical aspects of the course, but also the way in which learners in the course can apply, in real project undertakings, the principles taught in the course.

Conclusion

While development and delivery of the Advanced Engineering Project Management course has been quite successful, a number of lessons have been learnt from its implementation. In particular, while the course has been well accepted by learners, it can be further enhanced to improve its quality and its ability to help Professional Engineers to continue to plan, manage and deliver successful projects of both low and high complexity, and to effectively manage project risks.

It is therefore concluded that while there are a number of improvements that can be made to the Advanced Engineering Project Management course, it has to date largely achieved its purpose of developing the project management knowledge and skills of graduate and experienced engineers with respect to delivering successful projects, and the knowledge component of the project management requirements of Professional Engineers.

Learner feedback with respect to this course as at the date of writing has been positive, and at the same time has provided suggestions for improvement. Other suggested improvements have resulted from the experience of personnel delivering the course, including the authors. Some of these suggestions have been put in place for the current offer of the course, and others will be considered for future offers of it.

A next step in improving the course will be to further consult with relevant professional organisations and industry, in order to better meet their requirements with respect to the project management skills and knowledge of professional engineers in delivering successful projects, particularly from a strategic management and complex project management point of view. The long-term objective for this course is for it to play a leading role in the development of the project management knowledge, skills and application of professional engineers. This objective will be achieved through close liaison with industry and the engineering profession, maintaining currency with developments in project management, taking account of learner comments, a commitment to ongoing improvement of the course, and ensuring its continued integration within the suite of Professional Engineering courses offered by the University.

References

Armstrong, G. (2015). *Global construction survey 2015: Climbing the curve*. Zug, Switzerland: KPMG International Cooperative.

Biggs, J. (1999). What the student does: Teaching for enhanced learning. *Higher Education Research and Development, 18*(1), 57–75.

Biggs, J. (2001). The reflective institution: Assuring and enhancing the quality of teaching and learning. *Higher Education, 41*(3), 221–238.

Boud, D. (1998). *Assessment and learning—Unlearning bad habits of assessment*. Presentation to the conference *Effective Assessment* at University, University of Queensland, 4–5 November 1998.

Chen, Chin-Sheng. (2013). *Advanced Engineering Project Management*. Syllabus. Florida International University. Retrieved from http://web.eng.fiu.edu/chen/Spring%202015/ESI%206455%20MSIT/ESI%6455%20Spring%202015%20Regular.html

de Carvalho, M., Patah, L., & de Souza Bido, D. (2015). Project management and its effects on project success: Cross-country and cross-industry comparisons. *International Journal of Project Management, 33*, 1509–1522.

Department of Education and Training. (2013). *Australian Qualifications Framework* (2nd ed.). Canberra: Australian Government.

Engineers Australia. (2012). *Australian engineering competency standards stage 2—Experienced Professional Engineer*. Canberra, ACT: Author.

Engineers Australia. (2013). *Guide to assessment of eligibility for membership (stage 1 competency)*. Canberra, ACT: Author.

Garel, G. (2013). A history of project management models: From pre-models to the standard models. *International Journal of Project Management, 31*, 663–669.

Geraldi, J., Turner, J., Maylor, H., Söderholm, A., Hobday, M., & Brady, T. (2008). Innovation in project management: Voices of researchers. *International Journal of Project Management, 26*(5), 586–589.

Gulikers, J. T. M., Bastiaens, Th. J., & Kirschner, P. A. (2004). Perceptions of authentic assessment: Five dimensions of authenticity. In *Proceedings, Second Biannual Northumbria/EARLI SIG assessment conference*, Bergen.

Kolb, D. A. (1984). *Experiential learning: Experience as the source of learning and development*. Englewood Cliffs, NJ: Prentice-Hall.

Kwak, Y. H. (2005). A brief history of Project Management. *The story of managing projects*. Retrieved from http://home.gwu.edu/~kwak/PM_History.pdf

Larson, E. W., & Gray, C. F. (2011). *Project management—The managerial process* (5th ed.). International Edition, NY: McGraw-Hill Irwin.

Merrow, E. W. (2011). *Industrial megaprojects—Concepts, strategies and practices for success*. Hoboken, NJ: Wiley.

Owen, J. M. (2007). *Program evaluation—Forms and approaches* (3rd ed.). New York: The Guildford Press.

Project Management Institute. (2013). In Project Management Institute (Ed.), *A guide to the project management body of knowledge* (5th ed.). Newtown Square, PA.

Ramos, P., & Mota, C. (2014). Perceptions of success and failure factors in information technology projects: A study from Brazilian companies. *Procedia—Social and Behavioral Sciences, 119*, 349–357.

Shenhar, A. J., et al. (2001). Project success: A multidimensional strategic concept. *Long Range Planning, 34*(6), 699–725.

Stretton, A. (2007). A short history of modern project management. *PM World Today, IX*(X), 1–18.

The Stationery Office. (2009). *Managing successful projects with PRINCE2*. Norwich, UK: The Stationery Office.

Thorpe, D. (2013). Reflections on assessment: Comparison of assessment processes for postgraduate engineering management courses. In *24th annual conference of the Australasian Association for Engineering Education (AAEE2013)*, 8–11 December 2013, Gold Coast, QLD, Australia.

Trevelyan, J. P. (2014). *The making of an expert engineer*. London: CRC Press/Balkema—Taylor & Francis.

University of Southern Queensland. (2016a). *Master of Engineering Science*. Retrieved from http://www.usq.edu.au/handbook/current/engineering-built-environment/MENS.html

University of Southern Queensland. (2016b*). Master of Engineering Practice*. Retrieved from http://www.usq.edu.au/handbook/current/engineering-built-environment/MEPR.html

University of Southern Queensland. (2016c). *Course specification, Asset Management in an Engineering Environment, on-campus offer*. Retrieved from http://www.usq.edu.au/course/specification/2016/ENG8104-S1-2016-ONC-TWMBA.html

University of Southern Queensland. (2016d). *Course specification, ENG8103 Management of Technological Risk, on-campus offer*. Retrieved from http://www.usq.edu.au/course/specification/2016/ENG8103-S2-2016-ONC-TWMBA.html

University of Southern Queensland. (2016e). *Course specification, ENG8208 Advanced Engineering Project Management, on-campus offer*. Retrieved from http://www.usq.edu.au/course/specification/2016/ENG8208-S1-2016-ONC-TWMBA.html

8

Designing Quality Engineering Curricula to Produce Industry Ready Graduates: A Whole of Course Approach

Neal Lake and Julienne Holt

Introduction

Within the engineering academic world educators need to ensure that students are provided with a solid theoretical grounding in engineering and the underpinning sciences. However the professional engineering industry also requires industry ready graduates, able to write, be self-sufficient and check their own work, be technically capable, and be able to communicate in a professional context. The challenge therefore is to develop engineering curricula that balances theoretic understanding and relevant, authentic practical application. Ideally this should be developed through a cohesive educational approach that meets the ultimate goal of producing professional engineering graduates who are capable and employable in the beginning stages of their careers but with sufficient theoretical grounding to evolve into high performing, experienced engineering professionals in the future.

N. Lake (✉) • J. Holt
Southern Cross University, Lismore, NSW, Australia
e-mail: neal.lake@scu.edu.au; julienne.holt@scu.edu.au

Historically engineering degrees have had a significant emphasis on knowledge content and have aimed to expose students to a multitude of engineering knowledge-based problems relevant to a particular discipline of engineering. Less focus was placed on professional and personal skills perhaps because engineering companies were willing to invest in training newly employed engineers after graduation, often in drawing offices or on site to gain additional understanding and experience of engineering projects. This early training by industry organisations focused particularly on how to think and act like an engineer, before taking on the specific roles and responsibilities of an engineer. Unfortunately, the pressures of the modern engineering industry have seen both education of students and company training post-graduation, rationalised. Companies require graduates to be immediately productive and typically cannot justify drawn out developmental phases which were common in the past. Spinks, Silburn, and Birchall (2006) report that current graduates lack work readiness and in particular lack the ability to apply knowledge to industry problems. In order to improve work readiness, Beder (1999) highlighted the need for engineering education to place focus on understanding the social context within which engineers will work, be able to make ethical decisions based on critical thinking and also be able to assess the long-term consequences of their work.

Engineering degrees were also rationalised in the early 2000s to have contact hours commensurate with other university disciplines, reducing the contact hours from around 26 hrs to more like 16 hrs per week. This significantly reduces the volume of content that can be taught in a degree and requires educators to re-think ways of learning and teaching. There has been a significant refocus within engineering education on a more encompassing approach to educating students with an emphasis on how an engineer thinks and behaves including knowledge development skills, application skills, real world engineering problem solving and importantly, personal and professional skills. These skills are essential to ensuring work readiness on graduation. Engineers Australia has also developed a more rounded view of engineering education through the Engineers Australia (EA) Stage 1 competency standards (Engineers Australia, n.d.) which is the framework used to accredit engineering bachelor degree programs in Australia. This accreditation from Engineers Australia is required for each individual engineering undergraduate course and is an important milestone for every university. Attainment provides an automatic recognition of a student's bachelor degree and establishes eligibility to join Engineers Australia at the level of a professional engineering graduate. Failure of institutional accreditation for a course would result in individual students needing to demonstrate competencies through a personal written application directly to Engineers Australia. There are 16 mandatory elements of competency within the EA Stage 1 framework (Appendix) which are categorised into three 3 broad areas including, knowledge and skill base, application skills and personal and professional skills.

Quality Assurance and Quality Enhancement

There are a number of frameworks and governing bodies that are in place in Australia to regulate and assure quality student outcomes such as Tertiary Education Quality Standards Agency (TEQSA, 2015) and the Australian Quality Framework (AQF, 2013). While these are important organisations and frameworks in the quality education equation, they tend to focus on broad institutional and course outcomes rather than what happens in the classroom (Biggs, 2014), and they are not discipline specific. The EA Stage 1 competency accreditation provides a strong discipline specific framework for specifying what an engineering graduate should be able to demonstrate to enter the profession at the level of a graduate engineer.

Constructive alignment as described by Biggs and Tang (2007) and Biggs (2014) is the typical quality assurance framework used to demonstrate that the student has developed the relevant EA Stage 1 competencies. Within this framework, intended learning outcomes are developed, teaching and learning activities are undertaken to activate the intended learning outcomes and then assessment tasks are set to determine how well the students' performance meets the intended learning outcome. Constructive alignment provides a solid quality assurance framework but like all quality assurance frameworks, it is possible to demonstrate compliance without fully engaging in the spirit of the framework. While such a framework is important, by itself it may not result in the intended outcomes for students.

It is the actualisation and expression of the quality assurance framework that actually produces quality outcomes for the students. This expression of the framework comes through the quality enhancement practices implemented by the teaching staff for students that encourage the higher-level engagement and understanding required to develop the relevant competencies for professional practice. However, the extent that the student engages with the competencies may be limited depending on the approach and skills of the individual teachers and the ability to coordinate this across the whole course.

Rationale Behind the Program Development

In order to produce graduates that are work ready, the Southern Cross University (SCU) Civil Engineering degree has been developed through a collaboration between the course coordinator as a discipline academic with significant industry experience, a teaching and learning academic and other discipline academics. Both the course coordinator and the teaching and learning academic have a key focus on developing pedagogy that embraces a whole of course approach, professionally relevant content and importantly the embedding of academic skills within the curriculum. The course development has specifically focused on ensuring that:

- students develop a strong theoretic scientific and engineering underpinning knowledge
- the program is balanced addressing all of the sub-disciplines of Civil Engineering adequately
- each sub-disciple has a good grounding in the theory but with sufficient experience in the industry application of this theory to ensure the development of professionally relevant skills including the commonly used software packages.
- holistic authentic assessment tasks are set that focus on commonly undertaken work in industry rather than assessing components of learning in isolation.

- students develop rounded competency that focuses on evenly developing underpinning knowledge, application skills and professional and personal skills.
- students develop an understanding of their skills, competencies, gaps in knowledge and have the capability to identify, adjust and rectify these aspects of their understanding.

In order to realise the goals of the program in an effective way it was essential that the course be developed with a whole of course approach rather than focusing on individual units alone. The pedagogical underpinning of the whole of course approach is primarily focused on developing students' capacity to think and act like an engineer.

Much focus has been placed on how engineers think and act in the engineering literature. Lucas, Hanson, and Claxton (2014) and Lucas and Hanson (2014) have researched how engineers think and act, drawing on the Habits of Mind (HoM) concept proposed by Resnick (1999) and developed by Costa and Kallick (2002) and Claxton (2009). Schon (1987) proposed more generically that students need to develop an understanding of the artistry of their profession with a focus on life-long learning and the importance of reflection-in-action. How engineers think and act, can also be explored through the generic and engineering specific competencies an engineer should have and be able to demonstrate on graduation (Male, Bush, & Chapman, 2011). While these aspects are all important, without considering the mechanisms of how students develop the relevant capabilities or competencies, the value of these important ideas may not be realized. Of critical importance is to find ways to engage students with the ideas of competency development and create a framework within which they can organise their understanding of their emerging competency over time.

To engage students in competency development they must first understand the relevance and importance of developing their competency. For students to see this relevance, any framework needs to be founded in a professional engineering context. The Stage 1 competency framework described by Engineers Australia and used to accredit degrees in Australia, is a suitable framework to seat competency development in an industry relevant context. This framework describes a range of essential competencies and indicators of attainment an engineer should possess on graduation (Appendix). Aside from assisting the university with the accreditation process, a key benefit of adopting the EA Stage 1 competency framework for competency development is the potential for training and preparation for gaining chartered engineering status. Chartered status is an important milestone in an engineer's early career, is usually applied for 3–5 years or more after graduation and is based on the EA Stage 2 competency standards. These standards are presented in a similar framework to the Stage 1 competency standards. Moreover, they also provide an opportunity for authentic training, preparing students for the processes of becoming a fully chartered engineer in the future. This provides a professionally relevant reason to engage with the idea of developing competencies.

While both the idea of developing competency and actually developing the competencies is important, if the student is not aware of their developing competency, many opportunities for learning, personal development and particularly developing a professional identity may be lost. Taking an approach where the student can explore and is made explicitly aware of their developing competencies results in many opportunities for learning and professional development through explicit teaching, reflective practice and opportunities for meta-learning (Biggs, 1985; Meyer et al., 2012). According to Biggs (1985), meta-learning, a sophisticated application and a subprocess of metacognition, 'refers specifically to learning and study processes in institutional settings and more particularly to students' awareness of their motives, and control over their strategy selection and deployment' (p. 192). Thus to aid the development of meta-learning capacity, it is necessary to provide students with opportunities that focus on supporting them to explore and understand their own learning processes and introduce learning activities that assist them to develop strategic control over their own study and personal development. We see this important underpinning concept as promoting learners' self-awareness and empowerment in order to regulate, change and improve learning behaviour (Meyer et al., 2012) and thus have made it a feature of the curriculum design. Importantly, meta-learning opportunities and a skills and knowledge narrative help to make the implicit and tacit, become explicit and articulated (Taffs & Holt, 2013).

Once a student is aware of their developing competency the final link is for students to be able to use their awareness to articulate their competency to others. Articulation of competency is very important to a professional engineer throughout their entire career. Particularly it can be used for writing resumes, addressing selection criteria, preparation for behavioural interviews and the promotion of ideas. Competency statements are also used to assess the EA Stage 2 competencies required for gaining chartered status so the importance of being able to articulate competency is clearly well founded in a professionally relevant context.

In order to articulate competency to others the student must fully understand the nature of their competency and have a strong understanding of the evolution of their competency over time. Competency is complex and personal in nature and the awareness of the evolution of a competency can often be far more significant to a student than the actual level of competency achieved. So, in order to understand competency development, articulate it and use it to expand future capabilities, it is essential the student develops a strong reflective approach to their studies across the course.

Developing a Whole of Course Approach

Scaffolding

Often courses are thought of as individual units of knowledge content that when added together provide sufficient knowledge for students to begin practising as an engineer. However, engineering is also about understanding and applying the processes, ways of thinking and skills required to solve problems. These aspects are difficult to develop in single units of study. According to Forneris and Peden-McAlpine (2006), the attributes of context, reflection, dialogue and time are essential to contextual thinking and critical thinking in practice. Therefore, in order to develop competency across knowledge, application and skills domains, these four important attributes are scaffolded across the program.

The scaffolding occurs in two major ways within the course, firstly from a discipline knowledge and application perspective and secondly from a professional engineering competencies development perspective. These are intrinsically linked and need to be considered together in curriculum development. From discipline knowledge and application point of view each sub discipline is scaffolded by carefully constructed units that sequentially take the student through the cycle of: exposure to underpinning engineering science knowledge; development of typical analysis, design and evaluation techniques; and the application of these techniques to real world authentic projects. The development of professional engineering competencies is also scaffolded throughout the course.

Scaffolding is critical to developing transition pedagogy (Kift, 2009), to enhance the first-year experience of our students. Thus the first year focuses on developing the EA Stage 1 teamwork competency with the aim of scaffolding experiences and reflective tasks over a number of units. This culminates in writing a single statement of competency on teamwork at the end of the year. As part of this process, the students are progressively introduced to increasingly complex critical reflective tasks which encourage them to be more aware of their own learning processes and develop their ability to critically evaluate, judge and improve the effectiveness of their own approaches to learning. This enables them to understand the evolution of their skill development which can then form the cornerstone of well-developed professional competency statements.

Participation in Authentic Projects

Participation in authentic and real-world projects is vital to gaining high levels of student engagement and contributes to creating a pedagogical framework that allows real world engineering issues to be interwoven into units as well as across the whole course. It also allows a more encompassing professional view of engineering to be explored which is more in keeping with the intentions of the EA Stage 1 competencies. Working on assessment tasks that closely resemble industry projects and/or can actually be implemented also creates potential for engagement and motivation amongst students and ensures a specific focus on how engineering is conducted in an industry context. Strong links with industry are fostered, resulting in guest lecturers, use of authentic project and workplace documentation and simulation of industry engineering projects involving clients and authentic project briefs. Such industry context builds student confidence and experience in producing high quality, industry appropriate outputs in a professional manner. This leads to students who are better prepared for industry and able to work on the difficult open-ended problems that they will experience in their professional life.

Self-Assessment, Reflective Practice and Critical Thinking

At the core of competency development is student self-assessment. Boud and Falchikov (2006) stress the importance of learning beyond the academy and the imperative of assisting students to develop sustainable self-assessment and judgement of their own current and potential learning behaviours. For a student to engage with competency development, self-assessment is critical to the evolution of competency. However self-assessment cannot effectively occur without students developing an attitude of reflective practice. Through critical reflection a student can identify and assess their understanding and practice of their skills. Students can also reflect on their competency development and identify gaps in their capabilities and explore areas for improvement. Both self-assessment and reflective practice rely on the development of critical thinking skills.

Hammer and Green (2011) contend that critical thinking needs to be conceptualised and articulated within a disciplinary context, linked closely with academic literacy and considered in the light of students' learning progression across an undergraduate program. They propose that the acquisition of critical thinking within a disciplinary context develops at different levels of learning across a program as the capabilities, proficiency and confidence of students improve. However, they also note the importance of critical thinking in a workplace context where graduates must demonstrate capacity to think critically as professionals

(Hammer & Green, 2011). Through self-assessment, reflection and critical thinking the student also has the opportunity to explore deeply the development of engineering competency. As students gain confidence in self-assessment, reflection and critical thinking they can develop awareness and control over their own learning processes and products and will be able to make judgements about their levels of competency and whether their approaches to date have been effective.

Competency Development and ePortfolios Across the Program

In order to realise the primary goal of students' developing professional competencies and ensuring articulation, an embedded competency development model (CDM) was designed to frame how a student evolves competency over time. The model, developed as part of the curriculum design process, is founded in experiential learning, reflective practice and the development of personal models of understanding. These are contextualised into a framework that allows continual evolution, evaluation and development of students' competency. The explicit emphasis on competency development within the course provides a logical and powerful focus to raise the concept of meta-learning with students in an accessible and professionally relevant way.

The primary mechanism for documenting a student's competency development over time is through the implementation of a course-wide ePortfolio. Kilgore, Sattler, and Turns (2012) note that the development of a portfolio provides opportunities for engineering students to critically reflect on their learning products, such as selected artifacts and their learning processes in preparation for professional work. Particularly they found that students valued their portfolio learning experience and developed awareness of their own level of preparedness for professional life and what additional experience was required. Interestingly, Kilgore et al. (2012) suggest that making metacognitive awareness explicit may provide more opportunities for students to identify themselves as lifelong learners. Students can thus recognise the transformative possibilities and the challenges arising within the context of engineering education and understand the link between learning experiences and future professional goals.

While ePortfolios in other programs or disciplines are often focused on the artifacts themselves and the presentation of an electronic folio, the ePortfolio at SCU is focused on collection, collation and synthesis of evidence that can be used to demonstrate the evolution of engineering competency over time, in particular the 16 EA Stage 1 competencies. The ePortfolio is implemented throughout the course with a strong experiential, scaffolded and modelled process in the first year to develop an understanding of what competency is and how to collect, collate and synthesise evidence that can be used to write a statement of competency. Through the middle years of the course, reflective assessment tasks are included in the final unit of the various sub-discipline streams to assist in the collection of evidence. The capstone unit bookends the course and brings the ePortfolio program together where 16 statements of competency addressing the EA Stage 1 competencies are written by each student. In addition, the students are required to write and present a CV with a selection criteria statement. Mock interviews are conducted to prepare students for the initial stages of entering professional life. This allows the students to employ the products of the ePortfolio developed across the whole of course in a contextually relevant setting.

Assessment for Learning

The whole of course approach developed at SCU relies on scaffolding, participation in authentic projects, self-assessment, reflective practice and critical thinking and the development of competency using an ePortfolio across the program. However, student engagement is driven by an assessment for learning philosophy. Assessment for learning plays an essential role in the design and development of professional skills and competency across units and across the whole of course, as it frames how and what students learn. Boud and Associates (2010) propose that assessment is most effective and sustainable (Boud, 2000) when it engages students in productive, authentic learning opportunities, that feedback is an integral part of promoting positive attitudes to improve students' future learning and that a dialogue about learning and critical thinking within disciplinary contexts is cultivated.

According to Tan's (2013) framework of assessment for learning, the integration and interplay between assessment standards, assessment design and assessment feedback are major requirements for student success. Enhancing learning opportunities by providing feedback supports students to improve their own work and to assist them to articulate the gaps between past performance and what can be achieved in the future. This future focus provides for 'longer-term learning beyond a programme of study' (Tan, 2013, p. 3).

Competency Development Model (CDM)

Competency is evolutionary in nature therefore the model has been developed based on a cyclic and developmental approach. The application of this model also acknowledges that some competencies are more complex than others and that activities that engage students with competency development need to be capacity building in nature and progressively scaffolded in terms of complexity. The model expresses the embedded nature of competency. Competency is not just an end product, it is embedded in everything that a student does or indeed an industry professional does. As such, the only way to keep the focus on competency development is to ensure it is embedded in curriculum in a whole of course approach (Fig. 8.1).

The model (Fig. 8.1) is founded on providing a range of different experiences that enable opportunities for students to develop competencies that will be relevant to both their current academic life and their future industry practice. The experiences need to be carefully designed such that the student has the opportunity to grow and develop but also be authentic enough that significant critical reflection is possible about what this means for their future engineering career. The key to making this work is to ensure such assessment tasks are scaffolded throughout the degree so that their knowledge, skills and experiences build on one another. Typically, technical tutorial questions will only lead to very limited competency development. Indeed, the EA Stage 1 competencies only have

Designing Quality Engineering Curricula to Produce Industry...

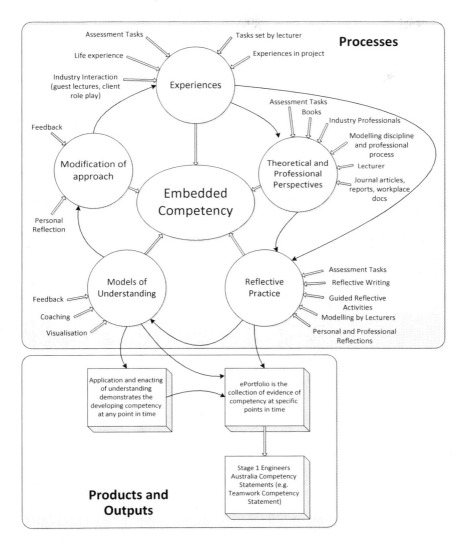

Fig. 8.1 Embedded competency development model

one or two competencies related to core technical engineering science capabilities. Engineering projects in industry occur in an environment of uncertain, open-ended and often technically and personally challenging environments. In order to give the students the opportunity to develop industry relevant engineering competency they need to be set challenging assessment tasks that are authentic, complex and related to the real world.

Examples of such experiences within the Civil Engineering course include community engaged learning with community partners and organisations such as Engineers Without Borders (Humanitarian Engineering projects), Coffs Harbour Student Association (Humanitarian projects in Nepal) and New Colombo Plan scholarships to undertake projects in Indonesia and Timor Leste. Projects in association with local councils include investigating emerging issues such as traffic impact assessment and transport planning strategies, tender development for council projects such as developing tenders for a bridge design including client site meetings, full tender documentation and use of the Tenderlink website. Industry based research projects as well as whole projects such as in the capstone unit and in the final unit in each discipline stream are also included.

Exposing students to theoretical and workplace perspectives is at the core of developing the students' ability to think and act like an engineer. In order for a student to make sense of their experiences they typically require some sort of reference point for whether or not their experiences are normalised or relevant to the discipline. These perspectives of what is normal for the discipline can come from many sources including the lecturer, guest lecturers, industry professionals, books, journals, industry magazines, the EA competencies and the experiences associated with authentic assessment. However, much of a student's development happens through mimicry (Cousin, 2006), thus the role of the lecturer as a coach or mentor is paramount to the student's development. Therefore, it is important to have a balanced academic teaching staff profile that includes academics with varied industry experience.

Reflective practice defined by Osterman and Kottkamp (2004, p. 2) is 'a means by which practitioners can develop a greater level of self-awareness about the nature and impact of their performance, an awareness that creates opportunities for professional growth and development'. Importantly reflective practice is not about the product rather it is about becoming aware of our own learning processes (Sonntag, 2006). This self-awareness is essential to developing a practitioner's professional competency but more importantly it assists students to develop their ability to articulate the breadth of their own knowledge, skills and understanding which make up their competency. Therefore, reflective practice is key to assisting students to develop a more professional identity and to remind them that they are student engineers rather than engineering students.

The role of the academic in supporting student reflections is similar to the role of a coach. The role of the coach is to convey, transmit and develop professional knowledge and importantly it is to make the implicit, explicit (Kinsella, 2007). Adam, Turns, and Atman (2003) and Sonntag (2006) highlighted the importance of timing and critical distance and the important role the academic must play by setting appropriate and timely reflective tasks. Critically the academic, in the role of coach, needs to model the process and provide opportunities for students to receive feedback from both the academic and their peers and importantly to integrate this feedback into future development activities.

For reflective practice to be effective and transformative it needs not only to be rational and cognitive but also embodied in action (Adams et al., 2003; Kinsella, 2007). Argyris and Schon (1974) also promote the idea that reflection is not just thinking, embodied reflection in action is about doing. This is very challenging in a student environment because students are often locked into their existing habit structures and they tend to focus on only what is assessed. To overcome this, it is important to focus on an assessment for learning centred approach.

With a significant scaffolded process, the students are progressively introduced to more challenging critical reflective tasks. Early reflections relate to observations within the classroom or based on personal experiences alone. Reflective tasks then start to introduce theoretical and industry perspectives where students are asked to compare and contrast their experiences. Guided meditative visualisation exercises are also used to guide students through developing deep and effective reflection. Although unfamiliar to traditional engineering education, guided meditation and visualisation provides an opportunity to think very specifically about previous experiences as facilitated by the narrator of the visualisation and provides an opportunity to think about how tasks may be undertaken differently in the future. Teamwork experiences are an excellent opportunity to develop reflective practice skills and students are asked to undertake reflective writing tasks as well as face to face evaluations of teamwork processes. The latter is a very powerful tool that needs to be well managed by the academic however this is well founded in practice with the methodology for conducting face to face performance review meetings based on the Public Works General Conditions Contract (GC21) which is commonly used to manage the construction of public assets in Australia.

Through experiences, understanding of theoretical perspectives and the reflective activities that compare the two, the student develops their own 'model of understanding' of a particular subject, topic or skill. This reflects their own developing understanding and is the framework from which they will undertake projects and interact with the engineering world. Models of understanding are founded in schema theory. A schema is a construct of how you develop what you know about a topic, concept or skill and how new information is integrated. The term 'models of understanding' is used to make the ideas more accessible to students.

When teaching this concept students are encouraged to visualise the process of forming a model of understanding using imagery, for example using the image of a brain dendrite network. The students are encouraged to think about the idea that new dendrites can be formed, modified, changed over time. New insights may see the need to remove whole sections of the model and replace with new knowledge and understanding. Other techniques are also presented and applied by the students to help develop their ability to explore their own understanding. These include brainstorming and mind mapping providing the student with a way to organize thinking in a non-linear fashion.

Models of understanding are complex and have as much to do with an individual's own psychological development, culture and social experiences as with the development of technical aspects. The application of their model of understanding in practice will demonstrate their level of competency at any point of time which may include demonstrations and/or writing about it. Experience has shown that the visualization process really assists the student to understand the process and enables them to link it in a real way to the idea of developing competency.

Part of the evolution of competency is deciding to do things differently based on reflection of our experiences and the development of our models of understanding around a particular competency. Importantly, students need to learn how to receive and integrate feedback from the coach/lecturer and their peers in order to self-reflect and self-regulate their learning approach. This is essential to the cyclic nature of competency development and is essential to the evolution of professional engineering competency. Different feedback forms through the program include self-evaluation, group evaluations, lecture feedback and feeding forward which encompasses the provision of feedback to current students from previous students' experiences and tasks.

The products and outputs of the model can be collected, collated, synthesised and articulated into expressions of competency and are representative of a student's competency level at any given point in time. These expressions can come in written forms such as competency statements, resumes and selection criteria. They can also be used to prepare for oral forms of competency expression such as preparation for presentations, interviews and other situations, where a practitioner needs to express their competency. The primary mechanism for collecting the outputs is through the use of a whole of course ePortfolio.

The cyclic nature of developing competency is explicit in this model and an assessment for learning approach is needed to force students to make the necessary cycles to firstly develop competency and secondly to understand and be able to articulate the nature of their developing competency. While competency development is incremental in nature development may not strictly happen in the cyclic nature presented in the model. Often connections and gains can be made by jumping all around the circle. However, the cyclic nature of the presented model represents the scaffolded and assessment for learning approach used within the Civil Engineering degree.

Implications and Concluding Remarks

The Civil Engineering degree at Southern Cross University has been designed from a whole of course perspective focusing on the key elements of: scaffolding; participation in authentic projects; self-assessment, reflective practice and critical thinking; competency development using ePortfolios; and is underpinned by an assessment for learning strategy. A theoretical competency development model was presented along with key implementation strategies that have the potential to not only enhance the quality of the student experience but can also assist students to understand and assess their readiness for professional life.

Critical factors for the high-quality design of authentic curriculum relevant to producing graduates that are work ready and can think like engineers are:

- Embracing a balanced experience profile of industry, academic and teaching and learning staff with high quality collegial conversations to collaboratively design curriculum that is relevant to industry
- Focusing on a whole of course approach supported by point 1 with a strong scaffold to support embedded and progressive skill development
- Supporting students to engage with the idea of competency development and provide a suitable framework to help to organise their understanding of their emerging competency over time
- Creating an environment for students where they can explore their meta-learning capacity and awareness of their understanding of their own learning processes and develop strategic control over their study and personal development
- Developing authentic assessment tasks that closely resemble the sorts of projects that graduate engineers would experience early in their careers
- Developing students' ability to think critically, reflect and self assess.
- Focusing on assessment for current and future learning.

The implications of a program that is designed and executed on these principles are that graduates should be well prepared for their early career from a technical perspective and should also have developed many of the professional and personal skills necessary to think and act like an engineer. Graduates should also be well prepared to engage in lifelong learning, which is so necessary for a successful career in engineering.

While the approach described above is designed to achieve the benefits outlined, it is important to understand that systems, frameworks and models on their own do not ensure quality and professionally relevant education. It is the people that control quality, in particular, the lecturing staff and their ability to engage students with engineering education. The concepts presented in this chapter do however provide an excellent foundation from which quality education can be framed.

Appendix: Engineers Australia (EA) Stage 1 Competency Standard Categories

Knowledge and skill base

- 1.1. Comprehensive, theory based understanding of the underpinning natural and physical sciences and the engineering fundamentals applicable to the engineering discipline.
- 1.2. Conceptual understanding of the mathematics, numerical analysis, statistics, and computer and information sciences which underpin the engineering discipline.
- 1.3. In-depth understanding of specialist bodies of knowledge within the engineering discipline.
- 1.4. Discernment of knowledge development and research directions within the engineering discipline.
- 1.5. Knowledge of engineering design practice and contextual factors impacting the engineering discipline.
- 1.6. Understanding of the scope, principles, norms, accountabilities and bounds of sustainable engineering practice in the specific discipline.

Application skills

- 2.1. Application of established engineering methods to complex engineering problem solving.
- 2.2. Fluent application of engineering techniques, tools and resources.
- 2.3. Application of systematic engineering synthesis and design processes.
- 2.4. Application of systematic approaches to the conduct and management of engineering projects.

Personal and professional skills

* 3.1. Ethical conduct and professional accountability.
* 3.2. Effective oral and written communication in professional and lay domains.
* 3.3. Creative, innovative and pro-active demeanor.
* 3.4. Professional use and management of information.
* 3.5. Orderly management of self and professional conduct.
* 3.6. Effective team membership and team leadership.

References

Adam, R. S., Turns, J., & Atman, C. J. (2003). Educating effective engineering designers: The role of reflective practice. *Design Studies, 24*(3), 275–294.

Argyris, C., & Schon, D. A. (1974). *Theory in practice: Increasing professional effectiveness*. San Francisco: Jossey-Bass.

Australian Qualifications Framework Council. (2013). *Australia Qualifications Framework* (2nd ed.). Retrieved from http://www.aqf.edu.au/wp-content/uploads/2013/05/AQF-2nd-Edition-January-2013.pdf

Beder, S. (1999). Beyond technicalities: Expanding engineering thinking. *Journal of Professional Issues in Engineering Education and Practice, 125*(1), 11–18.

Biggs, J. (2014). Constructive alignment in university teaching. *HERDSA Review of Higher Education, 1*, 5–22.

Biggs, J., & Tang, C. (2007). *Teaching for quality learning at university* (3rd ed.). Maidenhead, UK: Society for Research into Higher Education & Open University Press.

Biggs, J. B. (1985). The role of metalearning in study processes. *British Journal of Educational Psychology, 55*, 185–212.

Boud, D. (2000). Sustainable assessment: Rethinking assessment for the learning society. *Studies in Continuing Education, 22*(2), 151–167.

Boud, D., & Associates. (2010). *Seven propositions for assessment reform in higher education*. Sydney: Australian Learning and Teaching Council.

Boud, D., & Falchikov, N. (2006). Aligning assessment with long-term learning. *Assessment & Evaluation in Higher Education, 31*(4), 339–413. https://doi.org/10.1081/02602930600679050

Claxton, G. (2009). 3.4 Cultivating positive learning dispositions. In H. Daniel, H. Lauder, & J. Porter (Eds.), *Educational theories, cultures and learning: A critical perspective* (p. 177). Abingdon: Routledge.

Costa, A., & Kallick, B. (2002). *Discovering and exploring habits of mind*. Alexandria, VA: Association for Supervision and Curriculum Development.

Cousin, G. (2006). An introduction to threshold concepts. *Planet, 17*, 4–5. Retrieved April 18, 2012, from http://www.gees.ac.uk/planet/p17/gc.pdf

Engineers Australia. (n.d.). *Stage 1 competency standard for professional engineer*. Retrieved September 11, 2014, from https://www.engineersaustralia.org.au/sites/default/files/shado/Education/Program%20Accreditation/110318%20Stage%201%20Professional%20Engineer.pdf

Forneris, S. G., & Peden-McAlpine, C. J. (2006). Contextual learning: A reflective learning intervention for nursing education. *International Journal of Nursing Education Scholarship, 33*(1), Article 17.

Hammer, S. J., & Green, W. (2011). Critical thinking in a first year management unit: The relationship between disciplinary learning, academic literacy and learning progression. *Higher Education Research & Development, 30*(3), 303–315. https://doi.org/10.1080/07294360.2010.501075

Kift, S. M. (2009). *Articulating a transition pedagogy to scaffold and to enhance the first year student learning experience in Australian higher education*. Final report for ALTC Senior Fellowship Program. ALTC Resources. Retrieved from http://fyhe.com.au/wp-content/uploads/2012/10/Kift-Sally-ALTC-Senior-Fellowship-Report-Sep-09.pdf

Kilgore, D., Sattler, B., & Turns, J. (2012). From fragmentation to continuity: Engineering students make sense of experience through the development of a professional portfolio. *Studies in Higher Education, 38*(6), 807–826. https://doi.org/10.1080/03075079.2011.610501

Kinsella, E. A. (2007). Embodied reflection and the epistemology of reflective practice. *Journal of Philosophy of Education, 41*(3), 395–409.

Lucas, B., & Hanson, J. (2014). Thinking like an engineer: Using engineering habits of mind to redesign engineering education for global competitiveness. In *SEFI, 42nd Annual Conference*, Birmingham, UK.

Lucas, B., Hanson, J., & Claxton, G. (2014). *Thinking like an engineer: Implications for the education system*. A report for the Royal Academy of Engineering Standing Committee for Education and Training. Royal Academy of Engineering, UK.

Male, S. A., Bush, M. B., & Chapman, E. S. (2011). An Australian study of generic competencies required by engineers. *European Journal of Engineering Education, 36*(2), 151–163.

Meyer, J., Knight, D., Baldock, T., Kizil, M., O'Moore, L., & Callaghan, D. (2012). Scoping metalearning opportunity in the first three years of engineering. In *Profession of engineering education: Advancing teaching, research and careers: 23rd Annual Conference of the Australasian Association for Engineering Education*.

Osterman, K. F., & Kottkamp, R. B. (2004). *Reflective practice for educators: Improving schooling through professional development*. Newbury Park, CA: Corwin Press, Inc.

Resnick, L. (1999). Making America smarter. *Education Week Century Series, 18*(40), 38–40.

Schon, D. A. (1987). *Educating the reflective practitioner: Towards a new design for teaching and learning in the professions*. San Francisco: Jossey-Bass.

Sonntag, M. (2006). Reflexive pedagogy in the apprenticeship in design. *European Journal of Engineering Education, 31*(1), 109–117.

Spinks, N., Silburn, N., & Birchall, D. (2006). *Educating engineers for the 21st century: The industry view*. Henley-on-Thames, UK: Henley Management College.

Taffs, K. H., & Holt, J. I. (2013). Investigating student use and value of e-learning resources to develop academic writing within the discipline of environmental science. *Journal of Geography in Higher Education, 37*(4), 500–514.

Tan, K. (2013). A framework for assessment for learning: Implications for feedback practices within and beyond the gap. *Hindawi Publishing Corporation: ISRN Education*. Vol. 2013, Article ID 640609, 1–6. https://doi.org/10.1155/2013/640609

Tertiary Education Quality and Standards Agency. (2015). *TEQSA and quality assurance*. Retrieved from http://www.teqsa.gov.au/regulatory-approach/teqsa-and-quality-assurance

9

Incorporating Sustainable Engineering (SEng) Within a Course Featuring Social, Political and Economic Contexts

Ian Craig, David Thorpe, and Tara Newman

Introduction and Review

The first world environmental conference was held 10 years after Rachael Carson's book Silent Spring (Carson, 1962) which addressed pesticides and birdlife decline. From the Stockholm Conference in 1972 evolved the United Nations Environmental Program (UNEP). In 1987, the term 'sustainability' was formally defined under a UN commissioned report (UN-WCED, 1987) as 'development that meets the needs of the present without compromising the ability of future generations to meet their own needs'. For the sake of brevity, this is often shortened to 'preserving our lifestyle and environment for future generations'. But notice here, that 'lifestyle' comes before 'environment'. Did the Bruntland definition tend to imply that it was acceptable to keep exploiting the environment,

---

I. Craig (✉) • D. Thorpe
University of Southern Queensland, Toowoomba, QLD, Australia
e-mail: Ian.Craig@usq.edu.au

T. Newman
Texas State University, San Marcos, TX, USA

if it is for the purpose of preserving human lifestyle and well-being? In the Millennium Development Report (UN, 2015) this sentiment appears to be further endorsed, as the issue of environmental sustainability is listed as seventh, within a list of eight goals. The other Millennium Development Goals or MDGs, important though these are, address food security, economic and human welfare issues rather than the environment directly.

The year 1987 is when world population exceeded 5 billion people, regarded by many resource scientists as the world's 'sustainable carrying capacity'. Did the Bruntland definition fully appreciate the problem of enormous population growth of insatiable humans, expected to be 10 billion in a plus 5 °C world by 2050?. It is *strongly* suggested in this paper, that SEng engineers need to regard the three overlapping circles of economic, social and environment (Fig. 9.1) to be *absolutely* equal in size. It is also suggested, that a suitable definition for 'Sustainable Engineering (SEng)' might be 'any area of engineering or technological endeavour which holds minimisation of environmental impacts as its primary goal, whilst preserving social welfare and the economy'. There are over 50 definitions of sustainability out there, so one more will surely do no harm!

The first significant call for global action on the environment was made at the Rio de Janeiro Earth Summit (UNCED, 1992). Ten years later at the United Nations Environmental Program (UNEP, 2002) conference in Johannesburg, it was pointed out that very little progress had been made under the 800-page Rio Agenda 21 during the previous decade. A further UN conference (UNCSD, 2012) concluded that with world population now seven billion, the world had in fact become significantly less sustainable with each decade since 1992. This conference, known as Rio+20, was not attended by the most powerful world leaders, who were more concerned with the global financial crisis at that time.

Over the past 20 years, the area of SEng has been regarded more and more importantly, as key to the role of the professional engineer. Recognition of SEng issues by the Royal Academy of Engineering and the Institution of Civil Engineers, London is discussed by Duffell (1998). In 1999 the American Society for Engineering Education (ASEE) stated that engineering students 'should learn about sustainable development and sustainability in the general education component of the curriculum

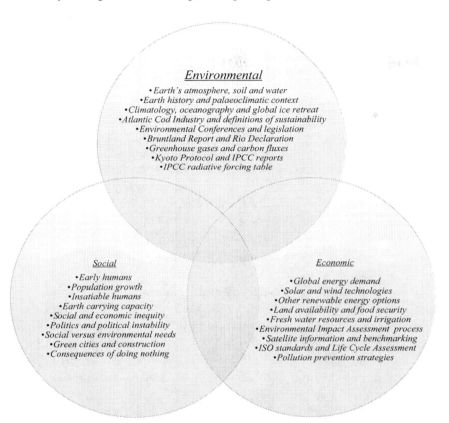

Fig. 9.1 Three overlapping circles illustrating sustainability, as it relates to engineering studies. The circles suggest 27 Sustainable Engineering (SEng) topics, for purposes of discussion across university engineering departments

use interdisciplinary teams to teach pollution prevention techniques and other sustainable engineering concepts.' In a pivotal paper in 2003, Mihelcic et al. described sustainability science and engineering as the 'emergence of a new meta-discipline'. But in 2005, Nath pointed out that despite the Bruntland definition, over 200 definitions still existed for sustainable development. The authors mention 'sustainable development' is generally equated with 'sustainable non-inflationary economic growth' by the economists and the business community, without any reference to environmental sustainability. The authors note that although some engineering courses are now starting to incorporate environmental sustainability, MBA and Law programmes rarely include any environmental modules, indicating the very low priority with which this subject is held. And it is of course MBA and Law graduates who mainly go on to be our politicians, decision makers and leaders.

Despite these problems, SEng was officially endorsed by the US Accreditation Board for Engineering and Technology (ABET) criteria set in 2007. Gaughran, Burke, and Quinn (2007) quote "There is hardly any industry sector in which the management of environmental sustainability is not of significant relevance. It is unfortunate that engineering and cognate areas of education have, for the most part, ignored these vital issues". These authors also mention European Union (EU) funded research project entitled 'Towards a sustainable future—Design, Quality and Environment' in which collaboration to develop specific course materials on SEng was sought across the universities of a number of countries including Ireland, Greece, Germany and Finland. Huntzinger, Hutchins, Gierke, and Sutherland (2007) provide a survey across selected universities about whether SEng is 'bolted on', built in' or 'courses completely redesigned'. Chau (2007) stated that 'the need arises to equip engineering students with a wider horizon of concepts in terms of environmental, economic and social attributes, to aid decision making in relation to sustainability issues', adding 'the emergence of sustainability as a concern within engineering has drastically changed the problem-solving model conventionally employed by the profession'. In the US Murphy et al. (2009) report a survey carried out across 270 universities, which pointed to the fact that only about half were addressing evaluation tools such as Life Cycle Assessment (LCA), only a quarter were integrating sustainability concepts into traditional engineering courses in order to broaden the student's skill set and awareness, and only 15% were delivering cross disciplinary courses taught in conjunction with other departments covering social economic and political aspects of sustainable engineering. Quinn, Gaughran, and Burke (2009) discuss incorporation of ISO14000, an Environmental Management System (EMS) which is now subscribed to by quarter of a million companies in 160 countries. The authors state that it would be 'difficult to find an industry sector in which the management of environmental sustainability is not of significant relevance'. Green construction (e.g. LEED) is discussed by Kevern (2011).

Since 2010, significantly more engineering courses are now incorporating sustainability concepts into existing courses or have significantly redesigned their curricula for better alignment with sustainability (Apul and Philpott 2011; UNESCO 2006). A useful review is provided of the rapidly growing body of SEng education literature, which shows that SEng is transforming not only the content, but also the format of engineering education delivery. Bauer, McFarland, Staehle, and Jahan (2012) suggest delivery of SEng via specific problems including solar panel design, wind turbines and derivation of biodiesel fuel from microalgae. The authors also mention group-based study involving discussion and team presentation of ethical issues in engineering. Providing stimulus to the teams, exposure of students to six documentary films is suggested. To this list, the present authors suggest the addition of the BBC documentaries "How Many People Can Live on Planet Earth" and "Hot Planet", presented by Sir David Attenborough and Professor Iain Stewart, respectively.

The main promise upon which SEng hopes to base itself into the future, so long as it is not reversed by a future right wing led US government, would be the recent '2015 Paris Agreement'. Conducted under the auspices of the United Nations Framework Convention on Climate Change (UNFCCC), this pivotal piece of legislation now strengthens the sentiments of the Kyoto 1997 Agreement. It for the first time firmly quotes target of +2 °C, as the maximum permitted global warming above pre-industrial levels. Presented by the 21st Conference of the Parties (COP21) in Paris on 12 December 2015, the 'language of the agreement' was endorsed by 195 countries and was actually ratified by 15. Unfortunately, the 2 °C target has some way to go until it comes into legal force across the globe.

Method

At the University of Southern Queensland (USQ) approximately ten years ago, new material on Sustainable Engineering (SEng) was introduced into an existing course entitled 'Technology and Society'. Three years ago, it was decided to rename the course to 'ENG2002 Technology, Sustainability and Society' and restructure the course as follows:-

- Module 1—Introduction
- Module 2—History of technology
- Module 3—Sustainability
- Module 4—Environmental impact assessment
- Module 5—Politics and power
- Module 6—The economy
- Module 7—Models of society
- Module 8—Cultural impacts
- Module 9—The legal framework
- Module 10—Management concepts in SEng

Thus, SEng is placed within economic and social contexts, with the course objectives are described as follows:

1. Converse proficiently upon general knowledge and current affairs of the day
2. Appreciate the history of technology, assess the basis of common criticisms of modern technology, and associated benefits to human society
3. Understand the basic concepts behind environmental sustainability and justify the need to move towards more sustainable practices
4. Understand the concepts behind and be able to apply the principles of effective environmental impact assessment
5. Understand the role of politics, politicians, power and government and illustrate the political dimension of engineering and surveying activities
6. Acquire a basic knowledge of economics and profitability forecasting, be able to perform a simple Net Present Value (NPV) exercise using Excel spreadsheet, and assess the likely effects of economic policies on technological enterprises
7. Appreciate the relevance of social structures and cultural values and deduce the causal factors behind technological developments during different periods of human history
8. Propose strategies for working effectively in multi-cultural environments, determine the relevance of social structure and cultural values to the engineering and surveying professions and demonstrate an

awareness of the key factors that may influence the practice of engineering in an overseas country
9. Acquire a basic knowledge of the International and Australian the legal system and identify ethical and legal constraints that are most likely to concern professional engineers or surveyors
10. Examine the basic philosophies behind modern technological management identify and discuss conflicts between client and societal expectations and recognise the impacts of globalisation in engineering industries

Selection of 27 topics relevant to SEng was carried out using consultation with professional colleagues over several years, and also tutorial based brainstorming sessions with students, in addition to substantial personal research into the relevant areas. Utilising a heuristic approach, 27 specific topics evolved as three groups of nine, are suggested here as a minimum for delivery of SEng across universities. Learning materials were then developed under these 27 topic headings, with specific information drawn from international peer reviewed publications and world recognised scientific bodies including UN/UNESCO, IPCC, and IEA. The subject matter is drawn from environmental engineering, and is distinct from environmental science, ecology and conservation biology taught under science degree programs.

Results

Presented below is an 'overlapping circles' diagram containing 27 topics thought appropriate to consider in the development of course unit devoted to SEng. These were split into nine groups, each relevant to the broad areas of (1) Environment, (2) Social and (3) Economic. Discussion and debate surrounding this of figure is positively encouraged across university departments. Although 'Introduction to ecosystems' is included, certain topics are not included e.g. biodiversity or rainforest ecology, as these topics are thought to be more suited to delivery by science, rather than an engineering department. Complex topics such as Gaussian Dispersion theory for air pollution and Streeter-Phelps for dissolved oxygen are avoided, as these are better delivered in a pure environmental engineering context (Davis & Cornwell, 2013). Student engineers just need to know that the various technologies exist, and this would enable them to consult with environmental specialists within that particular area.

Figure 9.1 is intentionally aimed at stimulating challenge and debate. Typical comments from readers of this paper might include 'I disagree with using the Atlantic Cod collapse as an example to best illustrate the concept of sustainability, and I think a much better example would be Southern Blue Fin Tuna'. If comments like this are stimulated, the authors most certainly welcome this, and feel that the central aim of this paper has been achieved. Not to leave this particular question unresolved, the defence for ocean fishery case studies in particular is the fascinating story of human behaviour (a true 'tragedy of the commons') which can easily be derived from brain storming students and getting them to interpret the shape of the yearly tonnage graph and interpreting the effects of advances in fishing technology (introduction of large trawlers, sonic fish finders etc). The graph of collapse of Newfoundland Cod (originally sourced from the Millenium Ecosystems Assessment Report, 2005) is freely available at the Wikipedia page on sustainability.

Or someone may comment 'I disagree with the requirement to teach engineers anything at all about palaeoclimate'. This stems from an actual comment from a civil engineering staff member 'climate has varied significantly in the distant past, so this variation now is surely nothing to worry about'. This emphasises that a great deal of confusion probably exists with some students and staff on this particular topic. The argument here, for some very basic training in palaeoclimate at least, is that if engineers in their future careers are going to actually put into practice low carbon engineering solutions, they need to wholeheartedly believe in the carbon threat to climate. For this they need to appreciate that we are actually in an ice age now, that it is called the Quaternary Ice Age (QIA), that it began about two million years ago, and that it actually assisted early humans. Students need to understand that in ice ages there are Milankovich (planetary) driven glacial/interglacial (cold/warm) cycles which feature advances and recessions of ice as natural phenomena. But they also need to appreciate that if we continue on our current path, represented by Option (1) of Fig. 9.2, that a climate tipping point may be reached and world sustainability and the very existence of the QIA (and all polar and mountain ice) is threatened.

It is strongly argued here that at least basic coverage of current climatology and palaeoclimatology information (perhaps in this case not PBL based) would certainly assist students with this understanding, and future commitment in their careers to SEng. The point should definitely be made, that as a fundamental concept in SEng, any continuance on with Option (1) of Fig. 9.2 is totally unacceptable, as it

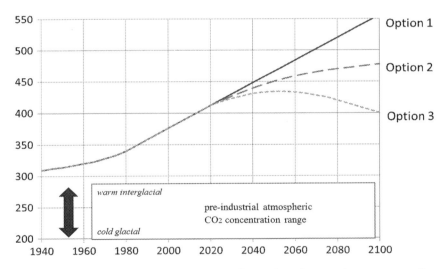

Fig. 9.2 Useful summary of climate information for engineers, regarding scenarios for future atmospheric carbon dioxide concentration (ppm), depicting three possible strategies: (1) 'Resilience' i.e. minimal incorporation of renewables into the energy mix, business as usual, strengthen emergency services, sharpen disaster response procedures, could be expensive and cost more than ~20% of global GDP in the longer term, according to Stern (2006), (2) 'Adaptation' i.e. gradual incorporation of renewable energy, deployment of major drought, fire and flood mitigation civil engineering projects, profitable, achievable, would provide employment, aim to stabilize CO_2 concentration at somewhere below 500 ppm, might cost 1–2% global GDP initially, and (3) 'Mitigation' i.e. rapid move to 100% renewable energy, appropriate engineering technology deployed with the aim to actually start decreasing atmospheric CO_2 concentration after 2050—would require an investment of ~5% global GDP initially

constitutes 'unsustainable engineering'. Engineers should now be more confident in stating this more clearly in their delivery of SEng education. Interesting here is emergence of a concept becoming known as resilience. Resilience appears to mean carrying on with a 'business as usual 3% economic growth rate within a closed system', and having the confidence to deal with any consequences via clever engineering technology, as they arise. There are many authors who warn against the dangers of this approach, notably Huesemann and Huesemann (2011). Their book 'Techno-Fix' is endorsed by many of our most famous resource scientists including William Rees, Richard Heinberg, David Suzuki and David Pimentel.

Conclusion

Very good signs that the Engineering community in Australia is responding positively to the SEng education challenge are visible in the in the formation of the Sustainable Engineering Society (SENG) and the fact that Engineers Australia (EA) now include full reference to sustainability in their Code of Ethics and Graduate Attribute documentation. After a slow start, educators are also now responding positively. Some preliminary studies concerning SEng education did appear during the 1990s, but serious discussion did not eventuate until the United Nations Decade of Education for Sustainable Development 2005–14 (UNESCO, 2006). Since about 2010, we have seen a sudden increase in SEng papers presented at engineering education conferences (Haselbach, 2015), and the Paris 2015 Agreement is certainly sign of good public awareness. Despite being a full 25 years since Bruntland, major improvements in SEng education are poised to happen in the near future. Teaching methods suitable for SEng delivery are intended as the subject of a future paper, but it is briefly suggested here that certain areas of SEng may be particularly suited to PBL, for example renewable energy and associated economics.

Until recently, it was thought that conceptually difficult areas (e.g. climate science) were best delivered with a dedicated traditional lecture, from a staff member preferably qualified, or else with good knowledge of earth science issues. However, just in the last three years or so, there has suddenly become available, several highly informed, high quality video documentaries covering this particular topic (see Appendix). With the outcomes of the recent Paris 2015 (COP21) meeting in mind, it is suggested that students as part of their studies are encouraged watch these videos (freely available from YouTube). The very positive impact of YouTube on how people learn, particularly STEM subjects, is undoubtedly here to stay (Khan, 2013). Students can then use them as debating stimuli, within facilitator led online discussion forums. If healthy criticism is encouraged in addition to personal opinion and comments, we believe that this would help develop strong critical thinking skills within students.

This paper has described SEng being incorporated into a dedicated engineering course which also features socio-political and economic contexts. Regarding content that should be incorporated into such a course, 27 essential concepts are suggested in this paper. In addition, an internet based database/discussion platform (www.sustainability.edu.au) has been formed—(Hargroves & Smith, 2005; Smith, Hargroves, Desha, & Palousis, 2007; Desha & Hargroves, 2014). This will undoubtedly help stimulate the area and facilitate uniformity of delivery of SEng across Australian universities and globally. Data of Hokanson, Mihelcic, and Phillips (2007) suggests that 'young women and men are not choosing careers in engineering because the profession is perceived to lack a connection to helping improve the world around them'. Invigoration of engineering courses with the important new area of SEng may refresh this connection. The notion that it takes governments and academia 25 years to respond to anything is clearly wrong, because it has taken at least half century since the birth of the environmental movement (Carson, 1962) for the importance SEng education to be fully realised. But now it appears that we are well underway with this task, our greatest challenge as engineers for the twenty-first century. Educators should not shy away from promoting SEng as a very important area in future engineering education.

Appendix: Notes on Some Recent One Hour Long Video Documentaries on Climate Science

PBS Global Warming the Signs and the Science, 2012

Alaska has warmed ~2 °C in just 50 years. Seasons are disrupted. Mountain glaciers are disappearing. Tropical type weather now more common at sub-tropical latitudes. Car ownership in China has increased by 500% since 1990. So far, we have emitted about 300 billion tonnes of carbon. In 50 years, we are on track to emit another 300 billion tonnes of carbon. And we could have 10 billion people on the planet. Number of days above 38 °C (100 °F) is increasing, across the globe. Cities 3–5% warmer than surrounding areas. Unhealthy air days increasing by up to 60%, in major US cities. Increase in new diseases and mosquito borne virus. El Nino. Peru 1983 25 years of rain (2.5 m) in 3 months. Sea-level rise. Katrina. US drought. Tree pest/disease. Colorado, low snow-pack, NCAR (Trenberth). Due to the effect of evaporation on water availability, we would need a 10% increase in rainfall, to make up for 1 °C of warming 1, IPCC (Parry). Rice (30% of world's food supply)—yield is reduced by 10%, with each 1 °C of warming. Nitrogen augmentation of soil bacteria CO_2 release. Forest outgassing of CO_2. Ocean freshening. Kyoto, 1997. Schneider, Stanford. Gelbspan. Landfill methane. 'The power company sends us a bill for $7 each month, and that's the cost of mailing us a bill!' Green construction. Solar energy hitting earth represents 9450 times our Primary Energy Demand (PED). Coal gasification reduces NOx and SOx, but CO_2 is still the same. Land clearance. Cassman (Nebraska). Calcium hydroxide, Lackner (Columbia). https://www.youtube.com/watch?v=xVQnPytgwQ0

Earth's Frozen Regions and Global Warming: PBS Documentary—Extreme Ice, 2014

A good update on glaciology to be had here. A billion people in Asia depend upon ice melt for their water, and this could be gone in 50 years. Columbia Glacier in Alaska has retreated 15 km in past 30 years, with ice velocities now 8x faster than 30 years ago. James Balog, Mark Serreze (NSIDC, Colorado). Tad Pfeffer, James White (Uni. Colorado at Boulder), Richard Alley (Penn State). Larsson B. ice shelf collapse 2002—this event meant some dramatic new thinking on what is happening in the Antarctic. In Greenland 125,000 years ago, a 3 °C warming occurred naturally, which produced a 3 m sea-level rise. But this took several thousand years to happen. The present warming in Greenland has been 3 °C in only 50 years. Jason Box, Ian Howat (Ohio State)—Jakobshavn Glacier, moving at 40 m per day, has now reached a threshold, whereby no-matter how much snow accumulates; there is net ice loss every year. Das and Youghin (Uni. Washington). https://en.wikipedia.org/wiki/Jakobshavn_Glacier, https://www.youtube.com/watch?v=__UgsLUxmos

Six Degrees Could Change the World, 2013

Good coverage here, of the consequences of climate change. Increased drought, fire and flood. Sydney/Victoria bushfires. Paris 2003 heatwave. Forest CO_2 outgassing. UK Hadley Centre climate modelling. Catastrophic Feedback Loops (CFL). Amazon drought/fire event, 2005. El Nino explained. New Orleans and the Katrina Hurricane, 2005. Water scarcity/famine. The Himalayas will lose what has been described as the 'largest frozen water tank in the world', the one which feeds the Ganges Delta, and approximately one billion people. Quote:-'I don't think that it's possible to dyke the whole planet' (Pachauri, IPCC) https://www.youtube.com/watch?v=R_pb1G2wIoA

Earth Under Water Global Warming Future Discovery Documentary, 2015

What is meant by resilience engineering? Does it reflect a willingness in humans to accept what is coming? The concept is gaining popularity amongst economists and politicians, because it essentially implies that we can carry on with our high emissions, and 'business-as-usual'. Huge coastal city sea-defences are now being planned for New York, Miami, New Orleans, San Francisco, London, Paris, Bangladesh? Some of the concepts described in this video can certainly be described as 'out-there'. Superdams (e.g. Golden Gate Project, Gibraltar Dam). What is your opinion on floating cities? And how about floating agriculture? https://www.youtube.com/watch?v=Jrp9cFjuYnM

Global Warming, What You Need to Know, with Tom Brokaw, 2012

Stefan Harrison (Uni Exeter) explains that glaciers in Patagonia are now less than 40 in number (down from the 150 they used to be, only 100 years ago). Stephen Pacala (Princeton Environmental Inst.) explains the effect of Milankovich Cycles (planetary motion) on climate. These natural cycles are enough to trigger ice advance and retreat, every 100,000 years or so. https://en.wikipedia.org/wiki/Quaternary_glaciation. We have had around twenty of these during the present Quaternary Ice Age, that we have been enjoying as humans, the past 2 million years. https://en.wikipedia.org/wiki/Timeline_of_glaciation. The stunning fact is these that the last eight of these (causing advances of ice as far south as New York and the European Alps) were based average global temperature differences of only a few degrees (±5–7 °C), between the cold (glacial), and the warmer (interglacial) phases. In Australia, 14 out the hottest 15 years on record have all happened since the year 2000. Globally, the 18 hottest years have happened since 1980. In January 2006, temperatures exceeded 44 °C in Sydney and South Australia and were the warmest on record. Micheal Oppenheimer (Prof. Geosciences, Princeton Uni.)—the role of the Amazon in CO_2 regulation. CO_2 outgassing may be due to the trees starting to die. Bob Spicer, Geologist (The Open University) explains the process of coal formation. Arhrenius, 1896. Charles Keeling. Churchill Polar Bears. James Hansen (NASA)—the rate of outflow of icebergs from Greenland has doubled, and then doubled again, during the past 15 years. Once we hit 4 °C rise, (highly likely, we've done 1 °C already), Greenland will contribute a 7 m sea-level rise (SLR). Western Antarctic will contribute another 6 m. John Hunter, (Uni. Tasmania). Might global warming send the Pacific in to a permanent El Nino state? 2005 hurricane season. 28 storms. Katrina, Aug 29.

80% New Orleans flooded, 1000 killed. Greg Holland (NCAR, Boulder CO)—warming is causing an increase in the number of cat 4 & 5 hurricanes. Holland believes that a cat 6 may be possible in the future. Drought in northern China. Desertification. Peter Cox (Hadley Centre). Three decades of warming has meant that climate zones have shifted, about 160 km. This is far quicker than many species can adapt to. Ove Hoegh-Guldberg (UQ)—coral bleaching events more frequent. West Nile Virus, Malaria, Yellow Fever. China is adding one coal fired power station per week. US has 5% of the world's population yet is responsible for 25% of emissions. CO_2 underground sequestration, Norway. Brazil now 100% ethanol from sugar. New York taxis now hybrids. Green construction. The air inside sky scrapers can now bed chilled and humidified using three storey high waterfalls, placed at the base of the building. The waterfall uses water collected on a solar powered roof. A return to wood, for all office furniture. Green construction is going to create a lot of high paid jobs (James Hansen). With simple changes using modern technology (e.g. LED lighting, hybrid vehicle, etc) the average American/Australian could reduce his/her annual emissions from 50 to 20 tonne per year. And the main point to be made here, is that these changes will not significantly impact upon the lifestyle that they presently enjoy. China's fearsome air pollution problem cannot be ignored (that's why we need to maintain emphasis on air pollution in this course!). What is more important, the GFC, or the GGE (Grand Global Experiment). The role of professional engineers is to wherever possible, 'air' on the side of caution, as we look to the stewardship of our planet. https://www.youtube.com/watch?v=xcVwLrAavyA

The History of Ice Age Era's, 2015

A useful crash course in palaeoclimate here. Peter Swart (Uni. Miami). Jim White (Uni. Colorado) explains the relationship between ice and sea level, as evidenced by ancient reefs located off the Miami coastline, and Foraminifera (ancient marine microfossils) located in ocean sediment off America's east coast. The data suggests that 2 million years ago that local temperature was 13 °C, but then it suddenly dropped to −3 °C, over about 100 years. Localised cooling, in close proximity to an advancing ice sheet one mile thick, is about 10 °C over 100 years (i.e. 0.1 °C/yr). During ice advance, global average temperature typically drops approximately 5 °C over 5000 years (i.e. 0.001 °C/yr). But humans have achieved a rate of global warming of 10 times the natural Milankovich rate i.e. 1 °C in 100 years (i.e. 0.01 °C/yr). https://www.youtube.com/watch?v=fTRZWQg_-os

References

Apul, D., & Philpott, S. (2011). Use of outdoor living spaces and Fink's taxonomy of significant learning in sustainability engineering education. *Journal of Professional Issues in Engineering Education and Practice*. Special issue: Sustainability in Civil and Environmental Engineering Education, *137*(2), 69–77.

Arrhenius, S. (1896, April). On the influence of carbonic acid in the air upon the temperature of the ground. *London, Edinburgh, and Dublin Philosophical Magazine and Journal of Science (fifth series), 41*, 237–275.

Bauer, S. K., McFarland, A. R., Staehle, M. M., & Jahan, K. (2012). Weaving sustainability into undergraduate engineering education through innovative pedagogical methods: A student's perspective. In *119th ASEE Annual Conference and Exposition, Conference Proceedings, 2012*.

Carson, R. (1962). Silent spring. *New Yorker Magazine* and Houghton Mifflin.

Chau, K. (2007). Incorporation of sustainability concepts into a civil engineering curriculum. *Journal of Professional Issues in Engineering Education and Practice, 133*(3), 188–191.

Davis, M. L., & Cornwell, D. A. (2013). *Introduction to environmental engineering* (5th ed.). New York: McGraw-Hill. 1040 pp. ISBN 978-0-07-340114-0.

Desha, C., & Hargroves, K. (2014). *Higher education and sustainable development: A model for curriculum renewal*. The Natural Edge Project (TNEP). London: Earthscan Press, Routledge. Retrieved from http://www.naturaledgeproject.net/HEandSD.aspx

Duffell, R. (1998). Toward the environment and sustainability ethic in engineering education and practice. *Journal of Professional Issues in Engineering Education and Practice, 124*(3), 78–90.

Gaughran, W., Burke, S., & Quinn, S. (2007). Environmental sustainability in undergraduate engineering education. In *ASEE Annual Conference and Exposition, Conference Proceedings, 2007*.

Hargroves, K., & Smith, M. (2005). *The natural advantage of nations: Business opportunities, innovation and governance in the 21st century.* London: Earthscan. Retrieved from http://www.naturaledgeproject.net/NAON.aspx

Haselbach, L. (2015). Special issue on sustainability engineering education—Keeping up with the world. *ACSC Journal of Professional Issues in Engineering Education and Practice, 141*(2), C2014001.

Hokanson, D. R., Mihelcic, J. R., & Phillips, L. D. (2007). Educating engineers in the sustainable futures model with a global perspective: Education, research & diversity initiatives. *International Journal of Engineering Education, 23*(2), 254–265.

Huesemann, Michael H., and Huesemann, Joyce A. (2011). Technofix: Why technology won't save us or the environment, Chapter 13, "The design of environmentally sustainable and appropriate technologies", New Society Publishers, Gabriola Island, BC, Canada, ISBN 0865717044, 464 pp. Retrieved from http://www.newtechnologyandsociety.org/

Huntzinger, D. N., Hutchins, M. J., Gierke, J. S., & Sutherland, J. W. (2007). Enabling sustainable thinking in undergraduate engineering education. *International Journal of Engineering Education, 23*(2), 218–230.

Kevern, J. (2011). Green building and sustainable infrastructure: Sustainability education for civil engineers. *Journal of Professional Issues in Engineering Education and Practice.* Special Issue: Sustainability in Civil and Environmental Engineering Education,, *137,* 107–112.

Khan, S. (2013). Let's use video to reinvent education. Retrieved from https://www.youtube.com/watch?v=nTFEUsudhfs

Mihelcic, J. R., Crittenden, J. C., Small, M. J., Shonnard, D. R., Hokanson, D. R., Zhang, Q., ... Schnoor, J. L. (2003). Sustainability science and engineering: The emergence of a new metadiscipline. *Environmental Science & Technology, 37*(23), 5314–5324.

Murphy, C. F., Allen, D., Allenby, B. J., Crittenden, J. C., Davidson, I. C., & Hendrickson, C. (2009, December 1). Sustainability in engineering education and research at US universities. *Environmental Science & Technology, 43*(15), 5558–5564.

Quinn, S., Gaughran, W., & Burke, S. (2009, June). Environmental sustainability in engineering education—Quo Vadis? *International Journal of Sustainable Engineering, 2*(2), 143–151.

Smith, M., Hargroves, K., Desha, C., & Palousis, N. (2007). *Engineering sustainable solutions program: Critical Literacies Portfolio—Introduction to sustainable development for engineering and built environment professionals.* The Natural Edge Project (TNEP), Australia.

Stern, N. (2006). *The stern review: The economics of climate change.* Cambridge: Cambridge University Press.

UN. (2015). *Millennium Development Goals (MDG) Report.* Department of Economic and Social Affairs of the United Nations Secretariat. Retrieved from www.un.org/millenniumgoals/2015_MDG_Report/pdf

UNCED. (1992). *United Nations Conference on Environment and Development.* Agenda 21: Program of Action for Sustainable Development. United Nations, New York.

UNCSD. (2012). *United Nations Conference on Sustainable Development.* Rio+21.

UNEP. (2002). *Johannesburg Earth Summit.* Retrieved from www.unep.org/pdf/annualreport/UNEP.

UNESCO. (2006). *Framework for the United Nations Decade of Education for Sustainable Development 2005–14: International Implementation Scheme.* ED/DESD/2006/PI/1.

UN-WCED. (1987). *UN World Commission on Environment and Development: 'Our Common Future'.* Oxford University Press. ISBN 019282080X.

10

The Transformative Dimensions of Professional Curriculum Quality Enhancement

Sara Hammer

Introduction

Quality assurance of undergraduate and postgraduate education programs for the professions is strongly associated with the assurance of specific learning outcomes and professional competencies or standards. Achievement of quality standards in higher education in Australia and elsewhere requires a focus on student participation and attainment, the learning environment, teaching, research and research training, institutional Quality Assurance processes, governance, and information management (Australian Government, 2015; ENQA, 2009). Accounts of authors in this second volume traverse a number of areas within these domains, such as learning outcomes and assessment, unit design and teaching, blended and simulated learning approaches, student diversity and equity, as well as support for and barriers to program quality enhancement.

S. Hammer (✉)
University of Southern Queensland, Toowoomba, QLD, Australia
e-mail: Sara.Hammer@usq.edu.au

© The Author(s) 2019
K. Trimmer et al. (eds.), *Ensuring Quality in Professional Education Volume II*,
https://doi.org/10.1007/978-3-030-01084-3_10

Case studies explored here illustrate the tensions faced by educators tasked with the design and implementation of curricula to produce work-ready Engineering and Surveying graduates. Whilst other layers of complexity do exist, this concluding chapter will focus particularly on the transformational nature of curriculum design and development and the way this enriches and complicates, in equal measure, the role of professional educators in universities.

Educational quality in the professions and the necessity for transformation are intimately related. However, this relationship manifests in various and interesting ways. For example, whilst current industry needs can drive complex processes of teaching and curriculum transformation, the reverse can also be true: as custodians and gatekeepers of higher education practices and values, universities may themselves instigate change in response to socio-political expectations, or in anticipation of future industry needs.

Consequently, it is possible to view some cases in this second volume of the series as instances where curriculum change becomes a lever for personal and professional transformation within universities. Curriculum change as transformation will be used as a framework for exploring author accounts of quality practice for the professions and include: transforming teacher conceptions, transformation as social and interpersonal; universities as enablers of quality transformation, and wider barriers to professional curriculum transformation.

Curriculum Change as Transformation

Professional educators in higher education arguably face barriers to the educational transformation required by curriculum change. These barriers may stem, firstly, from habitual, historically situated ways in which teachers and discipline groups conceptualise and enact the curriculum; and, secondly, from colleagues' resistance to the personal and professional disruption caused by curriculum change. By contrast, professional educators can also be innovators and drivers of transformative thinking and practice. At times, however broader national and sector trends will distort or even trump positive transformation at the program and discipline level.

Transforming Teacher Conceptions

One determinant of quality practice that sits firmly within the remit of higher education is the way teachers conceptualise and enact their program and unit curricula. Industry body feedback and engagement in the curriculum design process can impact on academic practice (Michelsen, Vabø, Kvilhaugsvik, & Kvam, 2017). However, professional educators are the principal drivers of the design and implementation process that determines whether students are provided with opportunities to achieve quality outcomes. Consequently, a focus on transforming teacher conceptions (Barrie, 2006; Trigwell & Prosser, 1996) and, therefore, teaching approaches is one way to assure quality practice.

Consequently, a key enabler of curriculum change is the transformation of individual teacher conception. This is particularly salient for academics in the professions who are coalface practitioners. As Padrò et al. argue in their chapter, the quality of professional education is a "many sided" phenomenon that is highly dependent on who is evaluating its purpose and desired outcomes. Thus, the concept of quality as 'fitness for purpose' may be refracted through the particular lenses of academics, as well as other major stakeholder groups of professional curricula. Consider the impact of professional teacher beliefs (Trigwell & Prosser, 1996) that privilege the idea of curriculum as "content" on initiatives to integrate sustainability education into university programs, particularly if one considers the United Nation definition of education for sustainable development (ESD) "as 'encouraging changes in behaviour that will create a more sustainable future'…(Cited in Desha & Hargroves, 2010, p. 652)". In this instance the focus on extending curriculum content in preference to the development of attributes or competencies may work counter to the assurance of expected quality educational outcomes.

In his chapter, Kinchin examines an effective way to investigate and transform academic conceptions of teaching and learning, based on visualising knowledge structures in professional education. He explains the theory and application of concept mapping of professional and disciplinary knowledge structures. These, he argues, not only enable teachers of the professions to visualise what is already known or theorised but also enable new perspectives to emerge. Thus, it assists teachers of the professions to unpack tacit knowledge, prevent resistance to change and short circuit the "unreflective maintenance of conservative teaching strategies", which can lead to what Kinchin refers to as "pedagogic frailty". However, a focus on useful transformation of teacher conception in professional disciplines does not, on its own, account for the material impact of curriculum change on a range of habitual, professional practices required of academics.

Curriculum designers of professional degrees need to negotiate with colleagues about what they perceive to be unnecessarily disruptive, organisational, practical changes that are associated with curriculum quality enhancement. This coalface resistance may thwart the expectations of professional bodies and other university stakeholders that the professional curriculum reflect recent societal and professional trends and issues. As Thorpe's chapter on project management in Engineering reminds us, it is anticipated that university graduates in Engineering will "break new ground" in their professional practice (Engineers Australia, 2013).

The reality is that significant curriculum change may present academics with affective and epistemological challenges, as well as professional development requirements that they must address to bring about the associated transformation of thinking and practice. This is reflected, albeit briefly, in Rose, Ryan, and Desha's (2015) account of embedding sustainable practice into Engineering curricula in an Australian university. They observe that a range of barriers face curriculum designers tasked with embedding Environmentally Sustainable Development (ESD) into the curriculum. They cite "cultural inertia", which is one cause of substantial "time lags" in curriculum renewal that can take between 15–20 years (Rose et al., 2015, pp. 229–230). One of their key recommendations focuses on capacity building (Desha, Robinson, & Sproul, 2015). They argue that to enable the integration of energy efficiency in Australian Engineering degrees, degree stakeholders, including government, industry and academics, should work collaboratively to ensure effective curriculum renewal. In their particular case, high levels of institutional support and government funding were available to support the change process. However, this is seldom the case for business-as-usual curriculum renewal at the coalface. In such cases, program teams will find themselves implementing required changes in institutions where there is little awareness of or support to navigate the deeper, political or cultural implications of this type of change.

Transformation as Social and Interpersonal

Enablers and barriers to educational transformation are not only personal and conceptual but also interpersonal and social. This is because curriculum renewal unavoidably involves a social, interpersonal dimension that may result in conflicting conceptions, disagreements, and power plays. Any of these may create barriers to meaningful curriculum transformation. Higher education leaders and change champions would do well to remember that the reality of curriculum change as a collective endeavour is far from the dry scholarly or procedural accounts one habitually sees in higher education research. Those charged with curriculum quality enhancement may find navigating this dimension personally and professionally challenging.

A study by King highlights affective aspects of the interpersonal dimension of curriculum change. Academic interviewees expressed frustration and anger as a result of loosely structured, re-iterative curriculum development processes, difficulties with scheduling because of clashing timetables, the negotiation and consensus-building required for collaborative decision-making processes, and issues of increased workload or role definition (King, 2006). Both of these examples are from the social sciences and with so little research in this space, to date, the affective, interpersonal labour associated with curriculum change in the professions is likely to remain unacknowledged by university managers and poorly understood by professional disciplines in the short to medium-term.

Some intended curriculum changes driven by shifting societal expectation, and relevant changes required by accreditation bodies may meet with short or long-term resistance at the disciplinary and teaching coalface that mirrors broader patterns of adoption and resistance within society. In Craig, Thorpe and Newman's account of introducing environmental sustainability into an Australian, Engineering unit a central concern was to avoid a "bolt-on" approach (Bath, Smith, Stein, & Swann, 2004) to sustainable engineering within the program by providing a unit curriculum that enables students to critically examine wider, historical, biological, philosophical and socio-political sustainability issues and debates. The authors trace the origins of "sustainable engineering" back to the first world environment conference in 1972 and the work of subsequent UN commissions and conferences. They admit that commensurate changes to university Engineering curricula have been a long time coming (See also Desha et al., 2015). However, Craig et al. note the present desire of younger Australians for degrees with greater social and environmental relevance and the emergence of the Sustainable Engineering Society as signs of acceptance of the sustainability agenda.

An extension of the important work in this case might usefully assess the general acceptance of the sustainable education agenda by academics themselves, including a comparison of their approaches to sustainability in both their research, and their teaching practice. This is because teacher beliefs in combination with interpersonal dynamics and wider discipline values may have an unintended effect on curriculum quality in professions, including Engineering. One implication of avoiding the affective, attitudinal dimension of curriculum renewal is a failure to address resistance amongst academic staff to holistic, curriculum change initiatives. Kolmos, Hadgraft, and Holgaard (2016) and others argue that internationally there has been a piecemeal approach in Engineering education to curriculum reform with early adopters incorporating sustainability elements in single units. Similar results have also been found in Australia (Desha & Hargroves, 2010). They (Kolmos et al., 2016) argue that a more systematic change should target both individual and organisational transformation, and would result in "epistemic" change within the discipline, as well shifts in practitioner and organisational values and identity. However, they note that such an approach requires high-level institutional support and buy-in, as well as explicit discussion of academic values and intentions.

Lake and Holt's account in this second volume illustrates a successful, collaborative, whole-of-program approach to curriculum transformation.

They examine an initiative to embed and scaffold Engineering competency development of students, using a program-wide ePortfolio, enabling reflective practice that emphasises improvement over time. In this new curriculum model, students are repositioned as future professionals with strategic control over their academic learning and professional competency development. Meanwhile the curriculum focus has shifted from historical pre-occupations with knowledge or content to a focus on competency development through a combination of theoretical grounding, holistic, authentic, real-world assessment tasks, and student reflection and self-awareness. Lake and Holt agree that one critical factor in their successful curriculum transformation process included embracing multiple views, including industry to enable high quality collegial conversations and collaborative curriculum design. Such an approach affirms, if somewhat obliquely, the importance of attending to the interpersonal, social drivers of curriculum transformation.

Baird's chapter explores barriers to quality curriculum transformation arising from culturally hegemonic perspectives on professional practice. Her chapter on "serving ethically" in the professions critically examines a case concerned with professional education in Papua New Guinea. She argues that traditional ethics instruction provided at her institution was largely theoretical, and did not acknowledge the ethical norms and practices of the local context. Consequently, this ethics instruction did not empower university graduates to successfully navigate the range of normative and situational challenges they would experience in their professional practice.

Universities as Enablers of Quality Transformation

Universities are not always change laggards in curriculum transformation. Indeed, despite the recent emphasis on external drivers of curriculum transformation (For example, TEQSA, 2015) in the professions, there are also cases where universities may contribute or drive innovation. Recent research suggests that institutional change can influence the way professional curricula are designed and taught in universities. Innovations may include embedding of graduate attributes within Engineering curricula in countries where more traditional forms of assessment, such as examinations, are dominant (Carvalho & Kotrashetti, 2016). In other research, a significant structural re-alignment of university degrees resulted in curriculum renewal, which represented a shift in the usual practice of change being driven by professional institutions (Hurlimann, March, & Robins, 2013). University-led innovation can also include the use of new curriculum design and implementation processes, such as that promoted by the "conceive-design-implement-operate" (CDIO) movement. CDIO emerged from Massachusetts Institute for Technology and Chalmers University in Sweden, amongst other institutions. Other curricular and pedagogical innovations include the use of problem or project-based learning, and a focus on self-identity development by positioning students as emerging student-professionals, rather than rather than university students of the professions (Edström & Kolmos, 2014; Finkel, 2013).

The case study illustration provided by Thorpe, Anteliz and Danaher provides an example of university-led curriculum quality transformation designed to develop and enhance professional currency and mobility. Their dual-site, comparative case critically examiners the role of university Engineering programs in Australia and Venezuela with a particular focus on providing "extension learning" opportunities with a sustainability focus. In this instance, universities offer practicing engineering professionals the opportunity to enrol in short courses that enable them to maintain and extend their professional currency, and to seek better re-numeration levels and career mobility.

Whether the impetus for curriculum change is external or internal, tensions and challenges created by potentially profound individual, disciplinary or professional transformation forms a frequently unseen or unacknowledged backdrop to the case Illustrations in quality practice presented here. Affective, personnel, and interpersonal issues can be treated as less important when compared with more commonly acknowledged challenges associated with curriculum renewal, such as fulfilling stakeholder expectations, meeting public demands for increased accountability, or issues of resourcing.

Wider Barriers to Professional Curriculum Transformation

Unfortunately, the sheer weight of external influence may ultimately trump positive curriculum transformation in professional programs with government and institutional agendas being felt at the level of the individual, higher education practitioner (O'Meara & MacDonald, 2004). Clarke's chapter focuses on the tensions created by demands for greater educational curriculum quality and academic accountability in an era of significant economic austerity. Her sobering account of the impact of austerity measures on the Irish university sector following the Global Financial Crisis of 2008 highlights in succinct terms the detrimental impact of funding cuts to the quality of infrastructure and support, increased student-staff ratios and, ultimately, Irish university global rankings. This case suggests the tipping point at which economic and budgetary context trump greater expectations of institutional performance by university stakeholders.

Similarly, the impact of institutional and sector approaches to assessing teaching quality may create unwanted risks for academics in the professions, amongst others. Clarke's chapter focuses on the intersection of individual identity and teaching practice as she explores an unintended consequence of institution and government use in Australia, the UK, the US and elsewhere, of student satisfaction surveys to monitor unit and program quality. She argues that uncritical use and interpretation of survey results within institutions, and by educational stakeholders, may discriminate unnecessarily against particular groups of academic teachers. Sharpe cites US research, which found that certain groups of academic staff including women, Non-English Speaking Background (NESB), and those from black or ethnic minority backgrounds, who consistently receive lower survey rankings. If one considers research, which shows that lecturers who adopt innovative approaches to learning and teaching are also at greater risk of receiving lower rankings (Jordan, 2008), the likelihood is that these evaluation regimes may create a barrier to positive curriculum transformation is increased.

Indeed, there is some question whether student satisfaction, on its own, is a sufficient or useful proxy for educational quality. This is supported by recent empirical research by Rienties and Toetenel (2016) of the Open University, which found that student satisfaction was related neither to academic progression, nor student-centred learning and teaching activities. Their research would seem to support the assertion of higher education researchers such as Gibbs (2010) who argue that students who are entirely satisfied are unlikely to be learning. Consequently, Sharpe argues for universities to: firstly, support program teams and individual teachers to responsibly interpret and apply survey data for the purposes of quality enhancement; and, secondly, to train teachers in the use of complimentary methods of unit and program evaluation. Addressing these recommendations would remove some of the disincentives for individual teachers to take greater risks in their professional practice.

Conclusion

Successful achievement of quality professional outcomes for university students that satisfy stakeholders such as government and professional bodies requires universities and their stakeholders to better understand the impact of personal and organisational transformation. Dry, procedural researcher narratives about the development of quality curricula that touch only briefly on the national, institutional, professional or institutional factors, or the attributes of individual players, provide incomplete accounts of quality enhancement in the professions and ignore key enablers and barriers, as well as dimensions of transformation that are required for genuine change. Through the lens of curriculum quality enhancement as transformation, this chapter has explored the role of teacher conceptions, beliefs and behaviours in curriculum renewal, as well the possible impact of social and interpersonal factors on the process of curriculum quality enhancement. It has also examined the role of academics and the university as sites of resistance to quality enhancement in the professions, or as important enablers of initiatives to improve the quality of professional education. Finally, it has examined national, sector and institutional barriers to the quality transformation of professional education. These dimensions have been offered as a framework to respectfully contextualise the case study illustrations in this second volume, and their challenges, failures and successes should be seen within this context.

References

Australian Government Department of Education & Training. (2015). *Higher Education Standards Framework (Threshold Standards)*. Retrieved from https://www.legislation.gov.au/Details/F2015L0163

Barrie, S. C. (2006). Understanding what we mean by the generic attributes of graduates. *Higher Education, 51*(2), 215–241. https://doi.org/10.1007/s10734-004-6384-7

Bath, D., Smith, C., Stein, S., & Swann, R. (2004). Beyond mapping and embedding graduate attributes: Bringing together quality assurance and action learning to create a validated and living curriculum. *Higher Education Research & Development, 23*(3), 313–328.

Carvalho, F., & Kotrashetti, A. (2016). Planning of a microwave engineering course guided by graduate attributes. In *2016 IEEE Eighth International Conference on Technology for Education (T4E 2016)* (pp. 260–261). Mumbai, India, Institute of the Electrical and Electronics Engineers, Inc, 2–4 December.

Desha, C., & Hargroves, K. (2010). Surveying the state of higher education in energy efficiency, in Australian engineering curriculum. *Journal of Cleaner Production, 18*(7), 652–658. https://doi.org/10.1016/j.jclepro.2009.07.004

Desha, C., Robinson, D., & Sproul, A. (2015). Working in partnership to develop engineering capability in energy efficiency. *Journal of Cleaner Production, 106*(C), 283–291. https://doi.org/10.1016/j.jclepro.2014.03.099

Edström, K., & Kolmos, A. (2014). PBL and CDIO: Complementary models for engineering education development. *European Journal of Engineering Education, 39*(5), 539–555. https://doi.org/10.1080/03043797.2014.895703

Engineers Australia. (2013). *Guide to assessment of eligibility for membership (stage 1 competency)*. Retrieved from http://www.engineersaustralia.org.au/sites/default/files/shado/Membership/Stage%201%20Assessment/ea_stage_1_guide-rev02_2013.pdf

ENQA. (2009). *ENQA report on standards and guidelines for quality assurance in the European higher education area*. Helsinki, Finland: European Association for Quality Assurance in Higher Education.

Finkel, A. (2013). *Innovative approaches to engineering education: The Australian experience*. Paper presented at the CAETS/HAE Symposium 2013, Budapest. Retrieved from http://www.caets.org/cms/7124/8123.aspx

Gibbs, G. (2010). *Dimensions of quality*. Retrieved from Heslington, York, UK: https://www.heacademy.ac.uk/system/files/dimensions_of_quality.pdf

Hurlimann, A., March, A., & Robins, J. (2013). University curriculum development—Stuck in a process and how to break free. *Journal of Higher Education Policy & Management, 35*(6), 639–651. https://doi.org/10.1080/1360080X.2013.844665

Jordan, J. T. (2008). Student ratings in a consumerist academy: Leveraging pedagogical control and authority. *Sociological Perspectives, 51*(2), 397–422. https://doi.org/10.1525/sop.2008.51.2.397

King, S. (2006). *Emotional dimensions of major educational change: A study of higher education PBL curriculum reform*. Paper presented at the Australian Association for Research in Education (AARE) Conference: 'Engaging pedagogies', Adelaide, South Australia. Retrieved from http://www.aare.edu.au/data/publications/2006/kin06834.pdf#page=1&zoom=auto,-35,792

Kolmos, A., Hadgraft, R. G., & Holgaard, J. E. (2016). Response strategies for curriculum change in engineering. *International Journal of Technology and Design Education, 26*(3), 391–411. https://doi.org/10.1007/s10798-015-9319-y

Michelsen, S., Vabø, A., Kvilhaugsvik, H., & Kvam, E. (2017). Higher education learning outcomes and their ambiguous relationship to disciplines and professions. *European Journal of Education, 52*(1), 56–67. https://doi.org/10.1111/ejed.12199

O'Meara, J., & MacDonald, D. (2004). Power, prestige and pedagogic identity: A tale of two programs recontextualizing teacher standards. *Asia-Pacific Journal of Teacher Education, 32*(2), 111–127. https://doi.org/10.1080/1359866042000234214

Rienties, B., & Toetenel, L. (2016). The impact of learning design on student behaviour, satisfaction and performance: A cross-institutional comparison across 151 modules. *Computers in Human Behavior, 60*, 333–341. https://doi.org/10.1016/j.chb.2016.02.074

Rose, G., Ryan, K., & Desha, C. (2015). Implementing a holistic process for embedding sustainability: A case study in first year engineering, Monash University, Australia. *Journal of Cleaner Production, 106*, 229–238. https://doi.org/10.1016/j.jclepro.2015.02.066

TEQSA. (2015). TEQSA and quality-assurance. Retrieved from http://www.teqsa.gov.au/regulatory-approach/teqsa-and-quality-assurance

Trigwell, K., & Prosser, M. (1996). Congruence between intention and strategy in university science teachers' approaches to teaching. *Higher Education, 32*(1), 77–87. https://doi.org/10.1007/Bf00139219

References

Aase, I., Bjørshol, C., Dieckmann, P., Aase, K., & Hansen, B. S. (2016). Interprofessional communication in a simulation-based team training session in healthcare: A student perspective. *Journal of Nursing Education and Practice, 6*(7), 91–100. https://doi.org/10.5430/jnep.v6n7p91

Aase, I., Hansen, B. S., & Aase, K. (2014). Norwegian nursing and medical students' perception of interprofessional teamwork: A qualitative study. *BMC Medical Education, 14*, 170–179.

Aase, I., Hansen, B. S., Aase, K., & Reeves, S. (2015). Interprofessional training for nursing and medical students in Norway: Exploring different professional perspectives. *Journal of Interprofessional Care*. https://doi.org/10.3109/13561820.2015.1054478

Abrami, P. C., Bernard, R. M., Bures, E. M., Borokhovski, E., & Tamim, R. M. (2012). Interaction in distance education and online learning: Using evidence and theory to improve practice. In L. Moller & J. B. Huett (Eds.), *The next generation of distance education: Unconstrained learning* (pp. 49–69). New York: Springer.

Adam, R. S., Turns, J., & Atman, C. J. (2003). Educating effective engineering designers: The role of reflective practice. *Design Studies, 24*(3), 275–294.

Alba, J. W., & Hutchinson, J. W. (1987). Dimensions of consumer expertise. *The Journal of Consumer Research, 13*(4), 411–454.

Al-Ghareeb, A. Z., & Cooper, S. J. (2016). Barriers and enablers to the use of high-fidelity patient simulation manikins in nurse education: An integrative review. *Nurse Education Today, 36*, 281–286.

Ali, I. M., Pascoe, C., & Warne, L. (2002, April). Interactions of organizational culture and collaboration in working and learning. *Journal of Educational Technology & Society, 5*(2), 60–68.

Alsharif, N. Z. (2012). Cultural humility and interprofessional education and practice: A winning combination. *American Journal of Pharmaceutical Education, 76*(7), 120. https://doi.org/10.5688/ajpe767120

Ambrosini, V., Bowman, C., & Collier, N. (2010). Using teaching case studies for management research. *Strategic Organization, 8*(3), 206–229.

Anderson, C., Bates, I., Brock, T., Brown, A., Bruno, A., Futter, B., & Rouse, M. (2012). Needs-based education in the context of globalization. *American Journal of Pharmaceutical Education, 76*(4), 1–56.

Anderson, J., & McCormick, R. (2005). *Ten principles for successful E-learning* [Online]. Retrieved August 23, 2014, from http://www.xplora.org/ww/en/pub/insight/thematic_dossiers/a

Andrade, H., & Valtcheva, A. (2009). Promoting learning and achievement through self-assessment. *Theory into Practice, 48*(1), 12–19. https://doi.org/10.1080/00405840802577544

Angelo, T. (2012). Designing subjects for learning: Practical research-based principles and guidelines. In L. Hunt & D. Chalmers (Eds.), *University teaching in focus: A learning-centred approach*. Melbourne, VIC: ACER Press.

Angelo, T. A., & Cross, K. P. (1993). *Classroom assessment techniques: A handbook for college teachers* (2nd ed.). San Francisco, CA: Jossey-Bass.

ANMAC. (2012). *ANMAC Registered Nurse Accreditation Standards*, Version 2, 15 August 2012. Canberra, Australia.

Apul, D., & Philpott, S. (2011). Use of outdoor living spaces and Fink's taxonomy of significant learning in sustainability engineering education. *Journal of Professional Issues in Engineering Education and Practice, 137*(2, Special Issue: Sustainability in Civil and Environmental Engineering Education), 69–77.

Arah, O., Hoekstra, J., Bos, A., & Lombarts, K. (2011). New tools for systematic evaluation of teaching qualities of medical faculty: Results of an ongoing multi-center survey. *PLoS ONE, 6*(10). https://doi.org/10.1371/journal.pone.0025983

Argyris, C., & Schon, D. A. (1974). *Theory in practice: Increasing professional effectiveness*. San Francisco, CA: Jossey-Bass.

Arieli, D., Mashiach, M., Hirschfeld, M. J., & Friedman, V. (2012). Cultural safety and nursing education in divided societies. *Nursing Education Perspectives, 33*(6), 364–368.

Armstrong, G. (2015). *Global Construction Survey 2015: Climbing the curve*. Zug, Switzerland: KPMG International Cooperative.

Arrhenius, S. (1896, April). On the influence of carbonic acid in the air upon the temperature of the ground. *London, Edinburgh, and Dublin Philosophical Magazine and Journal of Science (fifth series), 41*, 237–275.

Arnstein, S. R. (1969). A ladder of citizen participation. *Journal of the American Institute of Planners, 35*(4), 216–224.

Arora, B. (2015). A Gramscian analysis of the employability agenda. *British Journal of Sociology of Education, 36*(4), 635–648.

Arreola, R. A., Theall, M., & Aleamoni, L. M. (2003). *Beyond scholarship: Recognizing the multiple roles of the professoriate*. Paper presented at the 2003 AERA Convention, April 21–25, 2003, Chicago, IL.

Artess, J., Hooley, T., & Mellors-Bourne, R. (2016). *Employability: A review of the literature 2012–16. A report for the Higher Education Academy*. Higher Education Academy.

Arthur, M. B. (1994). The boundaryless career: A new perspective for organizational inquiry. *Journal of Organizational Behavior, 15*, 295–306. https://doi.org/10.1002/job.4030150402

Asian Development Bank. (2014). Country partnership strategy: Papua New Guinea, 2016–2020. Gender analysis strategy. Retrieved from https://www.adb.org/sites/default/files/linked-documents/cps-png-2016-2020-ga.pdf

Askenazy, P., & Galbis, E. M. (2007). The impact of technological and organizational changes on labor flows. Evidence on French establishments. *Labour, 21*(2), 265–301.

Astin, A. W. (1985). *Achieving educational excellence*. San Francisco, CA: Jossey-Bass.

Astin, A. W. (1993). *What matters in college: Four critical years revisited*. San Francisco, CA: Jossey-Bass.

Attwell, G. (2006). *A guide to the evaluation of E-learning* (Vol. 2). s.l.: Evaluate Europe Handbook.

Audi, R. (1988). *Epistemology: A contemporary introduction to the theory of knowledge*. New York: Routledge.

Austin, A. E. (2009). Cognitive apprenticeship theory and its implications for doctoral education: A case example from a doctoral program in higher and adult education. *International Journal for Academic Development, 14*(3), 173–183.

Austin, Z., & Gregory, P. (2007). Evaluating the accuracy of pharmacy students' self-assessment skills. *American Journal of Pharmaceutical Education, 71*(5), 1–89.

Australian Bureau of Statistics (ABS). (2008). *The health and welfare of Australia's Aboriginal and Torres Strait Islander peoples, 2008* (No. 4704.0). Health services—Provision, access and use. Retrieved from http://www.abs.gov.au/ausstats/abs@.nsf/0/84C63E845FED3BD2CA2574390014C9EB?opendocument

Australian Collaborative Education Network Limited. (2015). *National strategy on work integrated learning in university education* [Report No. CDN1]. Retrieved from http://acen.edu.au/

Australian Commission on Safety and Quality in Health Care. (2011). *Patient-centred care: Improving quality and safety through partnerships with patients and consumers.* Sydney: ACSQHC.

Australian Council for Educational Research (ACER). (2011). *Literature review relating to the current context and discourse of Indigenous tertiary education in Australia.* Canberra: Department of Education, Employment and Workplace Relations.

Australian Government Department of Education and Training. (2015). Higher Education Standards Framework (Threshold Standards) Retrieved from https://www.legislation.gov.au/Details/F2015L0163

Australian Government Department of Industry, Innovation, Science, Research and Tertiary Education. (2011). Higher Education Standards Framework (Threshold Standards) 2011. Retrieved from http://www.teqsa.gov.au/regulatory-approach/higher-education-standards-framework

Australian Health Promotion Association. (2009). Core competencies for health promotion practitioners. Australian Health Promotion Association. Retrieved from http://www.healthpromotion.org.au/images/stories/pdf/core%20competencies%20for%20hp%20practitioners.pdf

Australian Hospitals and Healthcare Association. (2014). Background research and consultation to inform the review of pharmacy competency standards. Retrieved April 7, 2015, from http://ahha.asn.au/sites/default/files/docs/page/consultation_paper_for_publication_revised_19.12.14_0.pdf

Australian Hospitals and Healthcare Association. (2015). Pharmacy standards review project—Final report. Deakin, ACT.

Australian Indigenous Health*InfoNet*. (2014). *Summary of Australian Indigenous health, 2013*. Retrieved from http://www.healthinfonet.ecu.edu.au/health-facts/summary

Australian Institute of Health and Welfare (AIHW). (2012). *Nursing and midwifery workforce 2011*. National Health Workforce Series No. 2. Cat. no. HWL 48. Canberra: AIHW. Retrieved from http://www.aihw.gov.au/WorkArea/DownloadAsset.aspx?id=10737422164

Australian Medical Association (AMA). (2014). *2010-11 AMA Indigenous Health Report Card—"Best Practice in Primary Health Care for Aboriginal Peoples and Torres Strait Islanders"*. Retrieved from https://ama.com.au/node/6629#anchorseven

Australian Nursing and Midwifery Accreditation Council (ANMAC). (2012). *ANMAC Registered Nurse Accreditation Standards*, Version 2, 15 August 2012. Canberra, Australia.

Australian Nursing and Midwifery Accreditation Council (ANMAC). (2014). *Midwife Accreditation Standards*. Retrieved from http://www.anmac.org.au/sites/default/files/documents/ANMAC_Midwife_Accreditation_Standards_2014.pdf

Australian Pharmacy Council. (2012). Accreditation Standards for Pharmacy Programs in Australia and New Zealand. Retrieved February 26, 2015, from http://pharmacycouncil.org.au/content/index.php?id=17

Australian Psychological Society. (2015). *Study pathways*. Retrieved from http://www.psychology.org.au/studentHQ/studying/study-pathways/

Australian Psychology Accreditation Council. (2012). *Student information*. Retrieved from https://www.psychologycouncil.org.au/student-information/

Australian Qualifications Framework Council. (2013a). *Australia Qualifications Framework* (2nd ed.). Retrieved from http://www.aqf.edu.au/wp-content/uploads/2013/05/AQF-2nd-Edition-January-2013.pdf

Australian Qualifications Framework Council. (2013b). *Australian Qualifications Framework Second Edition*. Retrieved from http://www.aqf.edu.au/aqf/in-detail/aqf-levels/

Avci, E. (2017). Learning from experiences to determine quality in ethics education. *International Journal of Ethics Education, 2*, 3–16. https://doi.org/10.1007/s40889-016-0027-6

Ayius, A., & May, R. J. (Eds.). (2007). *Corruption in Papua New Guinea: Towards an understanding of issues*. NRI Special Publication No. 47. Port Moresby, PNG: The National Research Institute.

Backof, J. F., & Martin, C. L., Jr. (1991). Historical perspectives: Development of the codes of ethics. *Journal of Business Ethics, 10*(2), 99.

Bailey, G. (2014). Accountability and the rise of 'play safe' pedagogical practices. *Education + Training, 56*(7), 663–674.

Baker, C., Pulling, C., McGraw, R., Dagnone, J. D., Hopkins-Rosseel, D., & Medves, J. (2008). Simulation in interprofessional education for patient—Centered collaborative care. *Journal of Advanced Nursing, 64*(4), 372–379.

Banks, S. (2010). Integrity in professional life: Issues of conduct, commitment and capacity. *British Journal of Social Work, 40*, 2168–2184.

Barnett, R. (1994). *The limits of competence*. Berkshire: Open University Press.

Barr, H., Koppel, I., Reeves, S., Hammick, M., & Freeth, D. (2005). *Effective interprofessional education: Argument, assumption and evidence*. London: Blackwell Publishing.

Barrie, S. C. (2007). A conceptual framework for the teaching and learning of generic graduate attributes. *Studies in Higher Education, 32*(4), 439–458. https://doi.org/10.1080/03075070701476100

Barrie, S., Hughes, C., & Smith, C. (2009). *The national graduate attributes report: Integration and assessment of graduate attributes in curriculum (Research Report)*. Retrieved from http://espace.library.uq.edu.au/view/UQ:201570

Barry, M. (2010). CompHP: Developing competencies and professional standards for health promotion capacity building in Europe, 1–17. Retrieved from http://www.iuhpe.org/?page=614&lang=en

Basart, J. M., & Serra, M. (2013, March). Engineering ethics beyond engineers' ethics. *Science and Engineering Ethics, 19*(1), 179–187. https://doi.org/10.1007/s11948-011-9293-z

Bass, L., Garn, G., & Monroe, L. (2010). Using JCEL case studies to meet ELCC standards. *Journal of Cases in Educational Leadership, 14*(1), 1–12.

Bate, P., & Robert, G. (2007). *Bringing user experience to healthcare improvement: The concepts, methods and practices of experience-based design*. Abingdon, UK: Radcliffe Publishing.

Bath, D., Smith, C., Stein, S., & Swann, R. (2004). Beyond mapping and embedding graduate attributes: Bringing together quality assurance and action learning to create a validated and living curriculum. *Higher Education Research & Development, 23*(3), 313–328.

Battiste, M. (2000). Introduction: Unfolding the lesson of colonization. In M. Battiste (Ed.), *Reclaiming Indigenous voice and vision*. Vancouver, BC: University of British Columbia Press.

Bauer, S. K., McFarland, A. R., Staehle, M. M., & Jahan, K. (2012). Weaving sustainability into undergraduate engineering education through innovative pedagogical methods: A student's perspective. In *119th ASEE Annual Conference and Exposition, Conference Proceedings, 2012*.

Baum, F. (2008). *The new public health* (3rd ed.). South Melbourne, VIC: Oxford University Press.

Baxter-Magolda, M. B. (2014). Self-authorship. In C. Hanson (Ed.), *In search of self: Exploring student identity development: New Directions for Higher Education, Number 166* (pp. 25–34). San Francisco, CA: Jossey-Bass.

Beder, S. (1999). Beyond technicalities: Expanding engineering thinking. *Journal of Professional Issues in Engineering Education and Practice, 125*(1), 11–18.

Bedggood, R. E., & Donovan, J. D. (2012). University performance evaluations: What are we really measuring? *Studies in Higher Education, 37*(7), 825–842.

Beetham, H. (2005). *e-Portfolios in post-16 learning in the UK: Developments, issues and opportunities*. A report prepared for the JISC e-Learning and Pedagogy Strand of the JISC e-Learning Programme. Retrieved from http://www.webarchive.org.uk/wayback/archive/20140615085615/http://www.jisc.ac.uk/media/documents/themes/elearning/eportfolioped.pdf

Behrendt, L., Larkin, S., Griew, R., & Kelly, P. (2012). *Review of higher education access and outcomes for Aboriginal and Torres Strait Islander people.* Canberra: Department of Education & Training.

Beine, M., Docquier, F., & Rapoport, H. (2008). Brain drain and human capital formation in developing countries: Winners and losers. *The Economic Journal, 118*, 631–652. https://doi.org/10.1111/j.1468-0297.2008.02135.x

Bekkers, V., & Edwards, A. (2007). Legitimacy and democracy: A conceptual framework for assessing governance practices. In V. Bekkers, G. Dijkstra, A. Edwards, & M. Fenger (Eds.), *Governance and the democratic deficit: Assessing the democratic legitimacy of governance practices* (p. 3560). Aldershot, Hampshire: Ashgate.

Bernstein, B. (1975). *Class, codes and control. Vol 3, Towards a theory of educational transmissions.* London: Routledge and Kegan Paul.

Bernstein, B. (1999). Vertical and horizontal discourse: An essay. *British Journal of Sociology of Education, 20*(2), 157–173.

Bernstein, B. (2000). *Pedagogy, symbolic control and identity.* Oxford: Rowman & Littlefield.

von Bertalanffy, L. (1968). *Organismic psychology and general systems theory.* Barre, MA: Barre Publishers.

von Bertalanffy, L. (1969). *General system theory: Foundations, development, application* (Rev. ed.). New York: George Braziller.

Bhabha, H. K. (1994). *The location of culture.* London: Routledge.

Biggs, J. (1996). Enhancing teaching through constructive alignment. *Higher Education, 32*(3), 347–364.

Biggs, J. (1999). What the student does: Teaching for enhanced learning. *Higher Education Research and Development, 18*(1), 57–75.

Biggs, J. (2001). The reflective institution: Assuring and enhancing the quality of teaching and learning. *Higher Education, 41*(3), 221–238.

Biggs, J. (2012). What the student does: Teaching for enhanced learning. *Higher Education Research and Development, 31*(1), 39–55. https://doi.org/10.1080/07294360.2012.642839

Biggs, J. (2014). Constructive alignment in university teaching. *HERDSA Review of Higher Education, 1*, 5–22.

Biggs, J., & Collis, K. (1982). *A system for evaluating learning outcomes: The SOLO taxonomy*. New York: Academic Press.

Biggs, J., & Tang, C. (2007a). Aligning assessment tasks with intended learning outcomes. In J. Biggs & C. Tang (Eds.), *Teaching for quality learning at university: What the student does* (pp. 37–68). Berkshire: Open University Press.

Biggs, J., & Tang, C. (2007b). *Teaching for quality at university: What the student does* (3rd ed.). Berkshire, UK: Open University Press & McGraw-Hill Education.

Biggs, J. B. (1985). The role of metalearning in study processes. *British Journal of Educational Psychology, 55*, 185–212.

Biggs, J. B., Kember, D., & Leung, D. Y. P. (2001). The revised two factor study process questionnaire: R-SPQ2F. *British Journal of Educational Psychology, 71*, 133–149.

Billett, S. (2010). Emerging perspectives of work: Implications for university learning and teaching. In J. Higgs, I. Goulter, S. Loftus, J. Reid, & F. Trede (Eds.), *Education for future practice* (pp. 97–112). Rotterdam, Netherlands: Sense Publishers.

Bird, B. (1988). Implementing entrepreneurial ideas: The case for intention. *The Academy of Management Review, 13*(3), 442–453.

BIS. (2016, September). Teaching Excellence Framework: Year 2 specification. Department for Business Innovation and Skills. Retrieved from https://www.gov.uk/government/publications/teaching-excellence-framework-year-2-specification

Black, P., & William, D. (2012). The reliability of assessments. In J. Gardner (Ed.), *Assessment and learning*. London: Sage Publications.

Blackie, M. (2017). Semantic waves and pedagogic frailty. In I. M. Kinchin & N. E. Winstone (Eds.), *Pedagogic frailty and resilience in the university* (pp. 49–61). Rotterdam, Netherlands: Sense Publishers.

Blackie, M. A. L. (2014). Creating semantic waves: Using legitimation code theory as a tool to aid the teaching of chemistry. *Chemistry Education Research and Practice, 15*(4), 462–469.

Bleakley, A. (2012). The curriculum is dead! Long live the curriculum! Designing an undergraduate medicine and surgery curriculum for the future. *Medical Teacher, 34*(7), 543–547. https://doi.org/10.3109/0142159X.2012.678424

Bloomfield, R. D. (1994). Cultural sensitivity and health care. *Journal of the National Medical Association, 86*(11), 819–820.

Bluestacks. (2017). [Online]. Retrieved December 8, 2017, from http://www.bluestacks.com/

Boblin, S. L., Ireland, S., Kirkpatrick, H., & Robertson, K. (2013). Using Stake's qualitative case study approach to explore implementation of evidence-based practice. *Qualitative Health Research, 23*(9), 1267–1275. https://doi.org/10.1177/1049732313502128

Bohle Carbonell, K., Stalmeijer, R. E., Könings, K. D., Segers, M., & van Merriënboer, J. J. G. (2014). How experts deal with novel situations: A review of adaptive expertise. *Educational Research Review, 12*, 14–29.

Bohr, N. (1963). *Essays 1958–1962 on atomic physics and human knowledge.* Bungay, Suffolk: Richard Clay and Company, Ltd.

Boland, T. (2015). Speech at Royal Irish Academy. A dialogue on higher education funding. Royal Irish Academy, 23 September 2015. Retrieved from http://www.hea.ie/sites/default/files/ ria_tb_funding_speech_v2_002.pdf

Boni, A., & Gasper, D. (2012). Rethinking the quality of universities: How can human development thinking contribute. *Journal of Human Development and Capabilities: A Multi-disciplinary Journal for People-Centred Development, 13*(3), 451–470. https://doi.org/10.1080/19452829.2012.679647

Boocock, S. S. (1973). The school as a social environment for learning: Social organization and micro-social process in education. *Sociology of Education, 46*(1), 15–50, JSTOR. Retrieved from www.jstor.org/stable/2112204

Bordieu, P., & Passeron, J.-C. (2000). *Reproduction in education, society and culture* (2nd ed.). London: Sage Publications.

Bot, L., Gossiaux, P.-B., Rauch, C.-P., & Tabiou, S. (2005). "Learning by doing": A teaching method for active learning in scientific graduate education. *European Journal of Engineering Education, 30*(1), 105–119. https://doi.org/10.1080/03043790512331313868

Botterill, M., Allan, G., & Brooks, S. (2008). Building community: Introducing ePortfolios in university education. In *Proceedings of the Ascilite Conference, Melbourne, Australia.* Retrieved from http://www.ascilite.org.au/conferences/melbourne08/procs/botterill-poster.pdf

Boud, D. (1998). *Assessment and learning—Unlearning bad habits of assessment.* Presentation to the Conference Effective Assessment at University, University of Queensland, 4–5 November 1998.

Boud, D. (1999). Avoiding the traps: Seeking good practice in the use of self assessment and reflection in professional courses. *Social Work Education, 18*(2), 121–132. https://doi.org/10.1080/02615479911220131

Boud, D. (2000). Sustainable assessment: Rethinking assessment for the learning society. *Studies in Continuing Education, 22*(2), 151–167.

Boud, D. (2010). Assessment for developing practice. In J. Higgs, I. Fish, S. Goulter, J.-A. Loftus, & F. Trede (Eds.), *Education for future practice* (pp. 251–262). Rotterdam, Netherlands: Sense Publishers.

Boud, D., & Associates. (2010). *Seven propositions for assessment reform in higher education.* Sydney: Australian Learning and Teaching Council.

Boud, D., & Falchikov, N. (2005). Redesigning assessment for learning beyond higher education. *Research and Development in Higher Education, 28*, 34–41.

Boud, D., & Falchikov, N. (2006). Aligning assessment with long-term learning. *Assessment & Evaluation in Higher Education, 31*(4), 339–413. https://doi.org/10.1081/02602930600679050

Boud, D., & Soler, R. (2015). Sustainable assessment revisited. *Assessment & Evaluation in Higher Education*, 1–14. https://doi.org/10.1080/02602938.2015.1018133

Bound, D. (2010). Sustainable assessment: Rethinking assessment for the learning society. *Studies in Continuing Education, 22*(2), 151–167.

Bourdieu, P. (1991). *Language and symbolic power* (G. Raymond & M. Adamson, Trans.). Oxford: Polity Press.

Bourke, R. (2014). Self-assessment in professional programmes within tertiary institutions. *Teaching in Higher Education, 19*(8), 908–918. https://doi.org/10.1080/13562517.2014.934353

Bovill, C., & Bulley, C. J. (2011). A model of active student participation in curriculum design: Exploring desirability and possibility. In C. Rust (Ed.), *Improving Student Learning (ISL) 18: Global theories and local practices: Institutional, disciplinary and cultural variations.* Oxford Brookes University: Oxford Centre for Staff and Learning Development.

Bradley, J. H., Paul, R., & Seeman, E. (2006). Analyzing the structure of expert knowledge. *Information Management, 43*, 77–91.

Bradley, P. (2006). The history of simulation on medical education and possible future directions. *Medical Education, 40*(3), 254–262. https://doi.org/10.1111/j.1365-2929.2006.02394.x

Brady, J. M. (2010). Cultural nursing implications in an integrated world. *Journal of PeriAnesthesia Nursing, 25*(6), 409–412. https://doi.org/10.1016/j.jopan.2010.10.005

Brady, N. (2012). From "moral loss" to "moral reconstruction"? A critique of ethical perspectives on challenging the neoliberal hegemony in UK universities in the 21st century. *Oxford Review of Education, 38*(3), 343–355. https://doi.org/10.1080/03054985.2012.698987

Bråten, I., & Strømsø, H. I. (2008). Job values in professional education: The role of achievement goals. *Scandinavian Journal of Educational Research, 52*(3), 259–277.

Braun, V., & Clarke, V. (2014). What can "thematic analysis" offer health and wellbeing researchers? *International Journal of Qualitative Studies in Health and Well-being, 9*(1). https://doi.org/10.3402/qhw.v9.26152

Brewer, M. L., & Stewart-Wynne, E. G. (2013). An Australian hospital-based student training ward delivering safe, client-centered care while developing students' interprofessional practice capabilities. *Journal of Interprofessional Care, 27*(6), 482–488.

Bridgstock, R. (2009). The graduate attributes we've overlooked: Enhancing graduate employability through career management skills. *Higher Education, Research, and Development, 28*(1), 31–44. https://doi.org/10.1080/07294360802444347

Bridgstock, R., & Cunningham, S. (2016). Creative labour and graduate outcomes: Implications for higher education and cultural policy. *International Journal of Cultural Policy, 22*(1), 10–26.

Bronfenbrenner, U., & Ceci, S. J. (1994). Nature-nurture reconceptualized in developmental perspective: A bioecological model. *Psychological Review, 101*(4), 568–586.

Bronfenbrenner, U., & Morris, P. A. (2006). The bioecological model of human development. In W. Damon & R. M. Lerner (Eds.), *Handbook of child psychology* (6th ed., pp. 793–828). Hoboken, NJ: Wiley.

Brookfield, S. (1998). Critically reflective practice. *The Journal of Continuing Education in the Health Professions, 18*, 197–205.

Broom, A., Good, P., Kirby, E., & Lwin, Z. (2013). Negotiating palliative care in the context of culturally and linguistically diverse patients. *Internal Medicine Journal, 43*(9), 1043–1046. https://doi.org/10.1111/imj.12244

Brooman, S., Darwent, S., & Pimor, A. (2015). The student voice in higher education curriculum design: Is there value in listening? *Innovations in Education and Teaching International, 52*(6). https://doi.org/10.1080/14703297.2014.910128

Brown, A., Gilbert, B., Bruno, A., & Cooper, G. (2012). Validated competency framework for delivery of pharmacy services in Pacific-Island countries. *Journal of Pharmacy Practice and Research, 42*(4), 268–272.

Brown, E. F., Day, P. A., Limb, G. E., Pellebon, D. A., Proctor, E. C., & Weaver, H. N. (2009). *Task Force on Native Americans in Social Work Education—Final report: Status of Native Americans in Social Work Higher Education.* Alexandria, VA: Council on Social Work Education Retrieved from http://www.cswe.org/File.aspx?id=55342

Brown, G. (2002). Commentary on: 'Accountability of accounting educators and the rhythm of the university: Resistance strategies for postmodern blues'. *Accounting Education, 11*(2), 173–174. https://doi.org/10.1080/0963928021000031718

Brown, R., Ashley, R., & Farrelly, M. (2011, December). Political and professional agency entrapment: An agenda for urban water research. *Water Resources Management, 25*(15), 4037–4050. https://doi.org/10.1007/s11269-011-9886-y

Brown, S. L., & Eisenhardt, K. M. (1997). The art of continuous change: Linking complexity theory and time-paced evolution in relentlessly shifting organizations. *Administrative Science Quarterly, 42*(1), 1–34.

Browne, A. J., Smye, V. L., & Varcoe, C. (2005). The relevance of postcolonial theoretical perspectives to research in Aboriginal health. *Canadian Journal of Nursing Research, 37*(4), 16–37.

Brownie, S., Bahnisch, M., & Thomas, J. (2011). *Competency-based education and competency-based career frameworks: Informing Australia health workforce development.* Adelaide: National Health Workforce Planning & Research Collaboration.

Brualdi, A. (1996). *Multiple intelligences: Gardener's theory* [Online]. Retrieved April 23, 2014, from http://www.springhurst.org/articles/MItheory.htm

Bruner, J. (1996). Frames for thinking: Ways of making meaning. In D. R. Olson & N. Torrance (Eds.), *Modes of thought: Explorations in culture and cognition* (pp. 93–105). Cambridge, UK: Cambridge University Press.

Bucher, R., & Strauss, A. (1961). Professions in process. *The American Journal on Sociology, 66*(4), 325–334.

Buckley, A. (2012). *"Making it count": Reflecting on the National Student Survey (NSS) in the process of enhancement.* York: Higher Education Academy Retrieved from https://www.heacademy.ac.uk/making-it-count-reflections-national-student-survey-nss-process-enhancement

Buckley, A. (2013). *Engagement for enhancement: Report of a UK survey pilot.* York: Higher Education Academy.

Buckley, A. (2014). *The UK Engagement Survey 2014: The second pilot year.* York: Higher Education Academy.

Buckley, S., Coleman, J., Davison, I., Khan, K., Zamora, J., Malick, S., … Sayers, J. (2009). The educational effects of portfolios on undergraduate student learning: A Best Evidence Medical Education (BEME) systematic review. BEME Guide No. 11. *Medical Teacher, 31*(4), 282–298.

Bunce, L., Baird, A., & Jones, S. E. (2016). The student-as-consumer approach in higher education and its effects on academic performance. *Studies in Higher Education.* https://doi.org/10.1080/03075079.2015.1127908

Busoni, F. B. (1911). *A new esthetic of music* (T. Baker, Trans.). New York: G. Schirmer.

Butcher, N., & Wilson-Strydom, M. (2012). *A guide to quality in online learning.* s.l.: Academic Partnerships.

Büthe, T. (2002). Taking temporality seriously: Modeling history and the use of narratives as evidence. *The American Political Science Review, 96*(3), 481–493.

Butler, P. (2006). E-Portfolios, pedagogy and implementation in higher education: Considerations from the literature. In N. Buzzetto-More (Ed.), *The e-Portfolio paradigm: Informing, educating, assessing and managing with e-portfolios* (pp. 109–139). Santa Rosa, CA: Informing Science Press.

Button, D., Harrington, A., & Belan, I. (2014). E-learning & information communication technology (ICT) in nursing education: A review of the literature. *Nurse Education Today, 34*(10), 1311–1323. https://doi.org/10.1016/j.nedt.2013.05.002

Calhoun, C. (2006). The university and the public good. *Thesis Eleven, 84*, 7–43. https://doi.org/10.1177/0725513606060516

Cameron, J., Banko, K. M., & Pierce, W. D. (2001). Pervasive negative effects of rewards on intrinsic motivation: The myth continues. *The Behavior Analyst, 24*, 1–44.

Cañas, A. J., Novak, J. D., & Reiska, P. (2015). How good is my concept map? Am I a good Cmapper? *Knowledge Management & E-Learning, An International Journal, 7*(1), 6–19.

Cant, R. P., & Cooper, S. J. (2017). Use of simulation-based learning in undergraduate nurse education: An umbrella systematic review. *Nurse Education Today, 49*, 63–71.

Cantle, T. (n.d.). *Interculturalism—Community cohesion.* Institute of Community Cohesion (iCoCo). Retrieved from http://tedcantle.co.uk/publications/about-interculturalism/

Cantle, T. (2012). Interculturalism: For the era of globalisation, cohesion diversity. *Political Insight, 3*(3), 38–41. https://doi.org/10.1111/j.2041-9066.2012.00124.x

Carey, H. M. (2011). Bushmen and bush parsons: The shaping of a rural myth: The 2010 Russel Ward annual lecture, University of New England, 15 April 2010. *Journal of Australian Colonial History, 13*, 1–26.

Carey, P. (2013). Student as co-producer in a marketised higher education system: A case study of students' experience of participation in curriculum design. *Innovations in Education and Teaching International, 50*(3), 250–260. https://doi.org/10.1080/14703297.2013.796714

Carvalho, F., & Kotrashetti, A. (2016). Planning of a microwave engineering course guided by graduate attributes. In 2016 IEEE Eighth International Conference on Technology For Education (T4E 2016) (pp.260–261). Mumbai India 2–4 December, Institute of the Electrical and Electronics Engineers, Inc.

Carper, B. (1978). Fundamental patterns of knowing in nursing. *Advances in Nursing Science, 1*(1), 13–23.

Carson, R. (1962). *Silent Spring*. New Yorker magazine and Houghton Mifflin.

Cash, R. (2005). Ethical issues in health workforce development. *Bulletin of the World Health Organization, 83*(4), 280–284.

Cave, M., Hanney, S., Henkel, M., & Kogan, M. (1997). *The use of performance indicators in higher education: The challenge of the quality movement* (3rd ed.). London: Jessica Kingsley.

Cecilia, M. R., & De Gasperis, G. (2016). A study on teaching and learning the von Neumann Machine in a 3D learning environment. In M. Caporuscio, F. De la Prieta, T. Di Mascio, R. Gennari, J. Gutiérrez Rodríguez, & P. Vittorini (Eds.), *Methodologies and intelligent systems for technology enhanced learning*. Advances in Intelligent Systems and Computing, Vol. 478. Cambridge: Springer.

Cerdeira, L., Machado-Taylor, M., Cabrito, B., Patrocínio, T., Brites, R., Gomes, R., ... Ganga, R. (2016). Brain drain and the disenchantment of being a higher education student in Portugal. *Journal of Higher Education Policy and Management, 38*(1), 68–77.

Cerra, V. (2017). How can a strong currency or drop in oil prices raise inflation and the black-market premium? *Economic Modelling*. https://doi.org/10.1016/j.econmod.2017.05.015

Chalmers, D., & Fuller, R. (1996). *Teaching for learning at university*. London: Kogan Page.

Chamberlain, J. M. (2012). *The sociology of medical regulation: An introduction*. Dordrecht, The Netherlands: Springer Netherlands.

Changfu, C., Mei, Z., & Chen, Z. J. (2012). Cultures matter: An alternative model of teaching evaluations. *China Media Research, 8*(2), 86–93.

Chau, K. (2007). Incorporation of sustainability concepts into a civil engineering curriculum. *Journal of Professional Issues in Engineering Education and Practice, 133*(3), 188–191.

Chaudhuri, D., Mukhopadhyay, A. R., & Ghosn, S. K. (2011). Assessment of engineering colleges through application of the Six Sigma metrics in a State of India. *International Journal of Quality & Reliability Management, 28*(9), 969–1001.

Chen, C.-S. 2013. *Advanced Engineering Project Management.* Syllabus. Florida International University. Retrieved from http://web.eng.fiu.edu/chen/Spring%202015/ESI%206455%20MSIT/ESI%206455%20Spring%202015%20Regular.html

Cheng, M. (2016). *Quality in education: Developing a virtue of professional practice.* Rotterdam, Netherlands: Sense Publishers.

Chinn, P. L., & Kramer, M. K. (2004). *Integrated knowledge development in nursing.* St. Louis: Mosby.

Clark, B. R. (1989). The academic life: Small worlds, different worlds. *Educational Researcher, 18*(5), 4–8.

Clark, B. R. (1997). The modern integration of research activities with teaching and learning. *The Journal of Higher Education, 68*(3), 241–255.

Clarke, F. (2011). Injecting expertise: Developing an expertise-based pedagogy for teaching local anaesthesia in dentistry. *Higher Education Network Journal, 2*, 29–43.

Clarke, J. (1991). Nursing: An intellectual activity. *British Medical Journal, 303*, 377–378.

Clarke, M., Drennan, J., Harmon, D., Hyde, A., & Politis, Y. (2015). *The academic profession in Ireland.* Dublin: University College Dublin.

Clarke, V., & Braun, V. (2014). Thematic analysis. In T. Teo (Ed.), *Encyclopedia of critical psychology* (pp. 1947–1952). New York: Springer.

Clarke, V., & Braun, V. (2017). Thematic analysis. *The Journal of Positive Psychology, 12*(3), 297–298. https://doi.org/10.1080/17439760.2016.1262613

Claxton, G. (2009). 3.4 Cultivating positive learning dispositions. In H. Daniel, H. Lauder, & J. Porter (Eds.), *Educational theories, cultures and learning: A critical perspective* (p. 177). Abingdon: Routledge.

Closing the Gap Clearinghouse (AIHW & AIFS). (2013). *Strategies and practices for promoting the social and emotional wellbeing of Aboriginal and Torres Strait Islander people.* Resource sheet no. 19. Produced for the Closing the Gap Clearinghouse. Canberra: Australian Institute of Health and Welfare & Melbourne: Australian Institute of Family Studies. Retrieved from www.aihw.gov.au/uploadedFiles/ClosingTheGap/Content/Publications/2013/ctgc-rs19.pdf

Coates, H., & McCormick, A. (Eds.). (2014). *Engaging university students: International insights from system-wide studies*. London: Springer.

Coffee, J. C. (2006). *Gatekeepers: The professions and corporate governance*. Oxford: Oxford University Press.

Coleman, H., Rogers, G., & King, J. (2002). Using portfolios to stimulate critical thinking in social work education. *Social Work in Education, 21*, 583–595.

Coles, M. (2015). *National Qualifications Frameworks: Reflections and trajectories. Qualifications policies insights*. Quality and Qualifications Ireland.

Colley, S. (2003). Nursing theory: Its importance to practice. *Nursing Standard, 17*(46), 33–37.

Collins, H. (2014, October). Rejecting knowledge claims inside and outside science. *Social Studies of Science, 44*(5), 722–735. https://doi.org/10.1177/0306312714536011

Commonwealth Department of Education, Science and Training. (2002). *Striving for quality: Learning, teaching and scholarship*. Canberra: Department of Education, Science and Training.

Connaughton, J., & Edgar, S. (2012). *What is the relevance of reflective practice in undergraduate e-portfolios to professional work practices?* Presentation at Australian Collaborative Education Network (ACEN) Conference, 29 October–2 November, Geelong. Retrieved from http://acen.edu.au/2012conference/wp-content/uploads/2012/11/61_What-is-the-relevance-of-reflective-practice-in-undergraduate-e.pdf

Connell, R. W. (1985). How to supervise a PhD. *Vestes, 2*, 38–41.

Cook, D. A., & Helms, J. E. (1988). Visible racial/ethnic group supervisees' satisfaction with cross-cultural supervision as predicted by relationship characteristics. *Journal of Counseling Psychology, 35*(3), 268–274.

Coombes, I., Bates, I., Duggan, C., & Galbraith, K. (2011). Developing and recognising advanced practitioners in Australia: An opportunity for a maturing profession? *Journal of Pharmacy Practice and Research, 41*(1), 17.

Cooper, L., Orrell, J., & Bowden, M. (2010). *Work integrated learning: A guide to effective practice*. London: Routledge.

Corey, G., Schneider Corey, M., Corey, C., & Callinan, P. (2014). *Issues and ethics in the helping professions* (9th ed.). Stamford, CT: Cengage Learning.

Cortés, P., & Pan, J. (2014). Foreign nurse importation and the supply of native nurses. *Journal of Health Economics, 37*, 164–180. https://doi.org/10.1016/j.jhealeco.2014.06.008

Costa, A., & Kallick, B. (2002). *Discovering and exploring habits of mind*. Alexandria, VA: Association for Supervision and Curriculum Development.

Coulter, A. (2011). *Engaging patients in healthcare*. New York: Open University Press.

Council of Australian Governments (COAG). (2012). *Closing the gap in Indigenous disadvantage*. Retrieved from https://www.coag.gov.au/closing_the_gap_in_indigenous_disadvantage

Cousin, G. (2006). An introduction to threshold concepts. *Planet, 17*, 4–5. Retrieved April 18, 2012, from http://www.gees.ac.uk/planet/p17/gc.pdf

Cozzens, R. (2017). *The effectiveness of hybrid and online delivery methods to rural high schools in the context of engineering and technology curriculum*. Unpublished PhD thesis, Leeds Beckett University, Leeds, UK

Cranmer, S. (2006). Enhancing graduate employability: Best intentions and mixed outcomes. *Studies in Higher Education, 31*(2), 169–184.

Cranney, J., Morris, S., Martin, F., Provost, S., Zinkiewicz, L., Reece, J., … McCarthy, S. (2011). Psychological literacy and applied psychology in undergraduate education. In J. Cranney & D. S. Dunn (Eds.), *The psychologically literate citizen: Foundations and global perspectives* (pp. 146–164). New York: Oxford University Press.

Creed, P. A., Fallon, T., & Hood, M. (2009). The relationship between career adaptability, person and situation variables, and career concerns in young adults. *Journal of Vocational Behavior, 74*(2), 219–229. https://doi.org/10.1016/j.jvb.2008.12.004

Creswell, J. (2013). *Research design qualitative, quantitative and mixed methods approaches* (2nd ed.). Thousand Oaks, CA: Sage Publications.

Crigger, N., & Godfrey, N. (2014). From the inside out: A new approach to teaching professional identity formation and professional ethics. *Journal of Professional Nursing, 30*(5), 376–382. https://doi.org/10.1016/j.profnurs.2014.03.004

Cristóvão, A., Koutsouris, A., & Kügler, M. (2012). Extension systems and change facilitation for agricultural and rural development. In L. Darnhofer, D. Gibbon, & B. Dedieu (Eds.), *Farming systems research into the 21st century: The new dynamic* (pp. 201–227). Dordrecht, The Netherlands: Springer.

Croskerry, P. (2003). Cognitive forcing strategies in clinical decision making. *Annals of Emergency Medicine, 41*(1), 110–120. https://doi.org/10.1067/mem.2003.22

Cross, S. L., Brown, E. F., Day, P. A., Limb, G. E., Pellebon, D. A., Proctor, E. C., & Weaver, H. N. (2009). *Task Force on Native Americans in social work education final report: Status of Native Americans in social work higher education*. Council on Social Work Education. Retrieved from http://www.cswe.org/File.aspx?id=55342

Crowden, A. (1994). On the moral nature of nursing practice. *Journal of Advanced Nursing, 20*(6), 1104–1110, 7p. https://doi.org/10.1046/j.1365-2648.1994.20061104.x

Crowe, J. (2007). Dworkin on the value of integrity. *Deakin Law Review, 12*(1), 167–180.
Croxford, L. (2001). Global university education: Some cultural considerations. *Higher Education in Europe, 26*(1), 53–60.
Cuellar, N. G., Walsh Brennan, A. M., Vito, K., & de Leon Siantz, M. L. (2008). Special section: Cultural competency: Cultural competence in the undergraduate nursing curriculum. *Journal of Professional Nursing, 24*(3), 143–149. https://doi.org/10.1016/j.profnurs.2008.01.004
Currant, N. (2015). Strategies of belonging: Counterstories of black students at a predominately white university. *Brookes eJournal of Learning and Teaching, 7*(2). Retrieved from bejlt.brookes.ac.uk
Dahl, R. A. (1957). The concept of power. *Behavioral Science, 2*(3), 201–215.
Dall'Alba, G. (2009). Learning professional ways of being: Ambiguities of becoming. *Educational Philosophy and Theory, 41*(1), 34–45.
Daly, Y. M., & Higgins, N. (2011). The place and efficacy of simulations in legal education: A preliminary examination. *AISHE-J, 3*(2), 1–20.
Damsa, C., de Lange, T., Elken, M., Esterhazy, R., Fossland, T., Frølich, N., …, Aamodt, P. O. (2015). *Quality in Norwegian higher education: A review of research on aspects affecting student learning*. NIFU Report 2015: 24. Oslo: Nordic Institute for Studies in Innovation, Research and Education.
Darbyshire, C., & Fleming, V. E. M. (2008). Governmentality, student autonomy and nurse education. *Journal of Advanced Nursing, 62*(2), 172–179.
Darbyshire, P., & McKenna, L. (2013). Nursing's crisis of care: What part does nursing education own? *Nurse Education Today, 33*(4), 305–307.
Davies, H., & O'Callaghan, C. (2014). All in this together? Feminisms, academia, austerity. *Journal of Gender Studies, 23*(3), 227–232.
Davis, K. E. (2008, Fall). Extension in sub-Saharan Africa: Overview and assessment of past and current models, and future prospects. *Journal of International Agricultural and Extension Education, 15*(3), 15–28. Retrieved from https://www.aiaee.org/attachments/article/111/Davis-Vol-15.3-2.pdf
Davis, M. (2015). Engineering as profession: Some methodological problems in its study. In S. H. Christensen, C. Didier, A. Jamison, M. Meganck, C. Mitcham, & B. Newberry (Eds.), *Engineering identities, epistemologies and values: Engineering education and practice in context (Philosophy of Engineering and Technology Vol. 21)* (Vol. 2, pp. 65–79). Zug, Switzerland: Springer International Publishing.
Davis, M. L., & Cornwell, D. A. (2013). *Introduction to environmental engineering* (5th ed., 1040pp.). New York: McGraw-Hill. 978-0-07-340114-0

de Carvalho, M., Patah, L., & de Souza Bido, D. (2015). Project management and its effects on project success: Cross-country and cross-industry comparisons. *International Journal of Project Management, 33*, 1509–1522.

De Corte, J. (2017, November 21). *Locked in a stalemate: The Organization of American States and the Venezuelan democratic crisis.* Retrieved from https://papers.ssrn.com/sol3/papers.cfm?abstract_id=3073692

De, D., & Richardson, J. (2008). Cultural safety: An introduction. *Paediatric Nursing, 20*(2), 39–43.

Dearnley, C., Haigh, J., & Fairhall, J. (2008). Using mobile technologies for assessment and learning in practice settings: A case study. *Nurse Education in Practice, 8*(3), 197–204.

DeBourgh, G. A. (2012). Synergy for patient safety and quality: Academic and service partnerships to promote effective nurse education and clinical practice. *Journal of Professional Nursing, 28*(1), 48–61.

Deci, E. L., & Ryan, R. M. (2000). The "what" and "why" of goal pursuits: Human needs and the self-determination of behavior. *Psychological Inquiry, 11*(4), 227–268.

Deleuze, G., & Guattari, F. (1987). *A thousand plateaus: Capitalism and schizophrenia* (B. Massumi, Trans.). Minneapolis, MN: University of Minnesota Press.

Deming, W. E. (1994). *The new economics for industry, government, education* (2nd ed.). Cambridge, MA: MIT Press.

Department of Education and Skills. (2017). *Proposed Exchequer—Employer investment mechanism for higher education and future education and training.* Consultation Paper. Retrieved from https://www.education.ie/en/Publications/Education-Reports/pub_ed_proposed_exchequer_employer_investment_higher_further_training_2017.pdf

Department of Education and Training. (2013). *Australian Qualifications Framework* (2nd ed.). Canberra: Australian Government.

Department of Education and Training. (2016). *Selected higher education statistics—Time series data and publications.* Australian Government. Retrieved from https://education.gov.au/selected-highereducation-statistics-2015-student-data

Department of Education, Science and Training. (2002). *Employability skills for the future.* Retrieved from http://www.detya.gov.au/ty/publications/employability_skills/final_report.pdf

Department of Foreign Affairs and Trade, Australia. (2015, September 30). *Aid Investment Plan Papua New Guinea: 2015–16 to 2017–18.* Retrieved from http://dfat.gov.au/about-us/publications/Pages/aid-investment-plan-aip-papua-new-guinea-2015-16-to-2017-18.aspx

Department of Personnel Management, PNG. (2014). *Public sector ethics and values based executive leadership and management capability framework.* Port Moresby, PNG: DPM.

Derven, M. (2014). *Leveraging diversity & inclusion for a global economy* (E. Gundling & P. Leri, Eds.). Washington, DC: Info-line. Retrieved from http://ezproxy.usq.edu.au/login?url=http://library.books24x7.com/library.asp?^B&bookid=66702

Desha, C., & Hargroves, K. (2014). *Higher education and sustainable development: A model for curriculum renewal.* London: The Natural Edge Project (TNEP), Earthscan Press and Routledge Retrieved from http://www.naturaledgeproject.net/HEandSD.aspx

Devlin, M. (2006). Challenging accepted wisdom about the place of conceptions of teaching in university teaching improvement. *International Journal of Teaching and Learning in Higher Education, 18*(2), 112–119.

Dewey, J. (1887). *Psychology.* New York: Harper & Brothers.

Deyo, Z., Huynh, D., Rochester, C., Sturpe, D., & Kiser, K. (2011). Readiness for self-directed learning and academic performance in an abilities laboratory course. *American Journal of Pharmaceutical Education, 75*(2), 1–25. https://doi.org/10.1177/0001848191041002003

Dickinson, I., Green, M., Smith, M., Bown, A., & Gorse, C. A. (2008, Summer). Virtual site as an aid to first-year learning. *Assessment, Learning & Teaching Journal, 4*, 45–48.

Dieckmann, P. (2009). *Using simulations for educations, training and research.* Lengerich: Pabst Science Publishers. ISBN:978-3-89967-539-9.

Dieckmann, P., et al. (2017). Variation and adaptation: Learning from success in patient safety-oriented simulation training. *Advances in Simulation, 2*, 21. https://doi.org/10.1186/s41077-017-0054-1

Dieckmann, P., Gaba, D., & Rall, M. (2007). Deepening the theoretical foundations of patient simulation as a social practice. *Simulation in Healthcare: Journal of the Society for Simulation in Healthcare, 2*(3), 183–193.

Dieckmann, P., Molin Friis, S., Lippert, A., & Østergaard, D. (2012). Goals, success factors, and barriers for simulation-based learning. A qualitative interview study in health care. *Simulation Gaming, 43*(5), 627–697.

Dietsch, E., Martin, T., Shackleton, P., Davies, C., McLeod, M., & Alston, M. (2011). Australian aboriginal kinship: A means to enhance maternal well-being. *Women and Birth, 24*(2), 58–64. https://doi.org/10.1016/j.wombi.2010.06.003

Dill, D. D. (2007). Are public research universities effective communities of learning?: The collective action dilemma of assuring academic standards. In R. L. Geiger, C. L. Colbeck, R. L. Williams, & C. K. Anderson (Eds.), *Future of the American Public Research University* (pp. 187–203). Rotterdam, Netherlands: Sense Publishers.

Dill, D. D., & Beerkens, M. (2013). Designing the framework conditions for assuring academic standards: Lessons learned about professional, market, and government regulation of academic quality. *Higher Education, 65*(3), 341–357.

Dill, D. D., & Soo, M. (2005). Academic quality, league tables, and public policy: A cross-national analysis of university ranking systems. *Higher Education, 49*(4), 495–533.

Direk, Z. (2014). Law, justice, and politics: Derrida on deconstruction and democracy to come. *CR: The New Centennial Review, 14*(2), 111–126.

Donate-Bartfield, E., & Lausten, L. (2002). Why practice culturally sensitive care? Integrating ethics and behaviour sensitive science. *Journal of Dental Education, 66*(9), 1006–1011.

Donley, R. (1985). A social mandate for nursing: Prescription for the future. *The Journal of Contemporary Health Law and Policy, 1*(1), 39.

Doppelt, G. (2008). The value ladenness of scientific knowledge. In H. Kincaid, J. Dupré, & A. Wylie (Eds.), *Value-free science? Ideals and illusions*. Oxford University Press. ISBN:9780195308969.

Doris, J. M., & Plakias, A. (2008). How to argue about disagreement: Evaluative diversity and moral realism. In W. Sinnott-Armstrong (Ed.), *Moral psychology, Vol 2: The cognitive science of morality: Intuition and diversity*. Cambridge, MA: MIT Press.

Doubleday, A., & Lee, L. (2016). Dissecting the voice: Health professions students' perceptions of instructor age and gender in an online environment and the impact on evaluations for faculty. *Anatomical Sciences Education, 9*(6), 537–544.

Dreijmanis, J. (Ed.). (2008). *Max Weber's complete writings on academic and political vocations* (G. C. Wells, Trans.). New York: Algora Publishers.

Ducasse, A. (2009). *Toeing the line: Mapping graduate attributes on to assessment in the Humanities and Social Sciences*. Paper presented at the HERDSA Conference, Darwin.

Duderstadt, J. J. (2010). Engineering for a changing world: A roadmap to the future of American engineering practice, research, and education. In D. Grasso & M. B. Burkins (Eds.), *Holistic engineering education* (pp. 17–35). New York: Springer.

Duffell, R. (1998). Toward the environment and sustainability ethic in engineering education and practice. *Journal of Professional Issues in Engineering Education and Practice, 124*(3), 78–90.

Duffy, M. E. (2001). A critique of cultural education in nursing. *Journal of Advanced Nursing, 36*(4), 487–495. https://doi.org/10.1046/j.1365-2648.2001.02000.x

Duncan-Pitt, L., & Sutherland, S. (2006). An introduction to the use of eportfolios in professional practice. *Journal of Radiotherapy in Practice, 5,* 69–75.

Durey, A., Hill, P., Arkles, R., Gilles, M., Peterson, K., Wearne, S., & Pulver, L. J. (2008). Overseas-trained doctors in Indigenous rural health services: Negotiating professional relationships across cultural domains. *Australian & New Zealand Journal of Public Health, 32*(6), 512–518. https://doi.org/10.1111/j.1753-6405.2008.00301.x

Dworkin, R. (1986). *Law's empire.* Cambridge, MA: Belknap Press.

DWU. (2016a). Vision statement. Retrieved March 10, 2017, from http://www.dwu.ac.pg/en/index.php/vision-mission-core-values

DWU. (2016b). MBBS program specification document (Internal working document).

Dyke, J., Gidman, W., Wilson, S., & Becket, G. (2009). Personal development planning: First-year Master of Pharmacy students' engagement with, and attitudes towards, reflective self-assessment. *The International Journal of Pharmacy Practice, 17*(1), 61–66.

Earl, L. (2013). *Assessment as learning: Using classroom assessment to maximise student learning* (2nd ed.). Thousand Oaks, CA: Corwin Press.

East, L., Stokes, R., & Walker, M. (2014). Universities, the public good and professional education in the UK. *Studies in Higher Education, 39*(9), 1617–1633.

Easterby, L. M., Siebert, B., Woodfield, C. J., Holloway, K., Gilbert, P., Zoucha, R., & Turk, M. W. (2012). A transcultural immersion experience: Implications for nursing education. *ABNF Journal, 23*(4), 81–84.

Eaton, J. S. (2012). The future of accreditation? *Planning for Higher Education, 40*(3), 8–15.

Edgar, A., & Pattison, S. (2011). Integrity and the moral complexity of professional practice. *Nursing Philosophy, 12,* 94–106.

Edwards, S. D. (2014). Moral realism in nursing. *Nursing Philosophy, 15*(2), 81–88. https://doi.org/10.1111/nup.12030

Elassy, N. (2015). The concepts of quality, quality assurance and quality enhancement. *Quality Assurance in Education, 23*(3), 250–261.

El-Khawas, E. (2000). The impetus for organisational change: An exploration. *Tertiary Education and Management, 6*(1), 37–46.

Ellis, R. C. T., Dickinson, I., Green, M., & Smith, M. (2006). The implementation and evaluation of an undergraduate virtual reality surveying application. In *BEECON 2006 Built Environment Education Conference*, Bonnington Hotel, Bloomsbury, London, 12–13 September 2006.

Elvira, Q., Imants, J., Dankbaar, B., & Segers, M. (2016). Designing education for professional expertise development. *Scandinavian Journal of Educational Research*. https://doi.org/10.1080/00313831.2015.1119729

Emerson, R. M. (1962). Power-dependence relations. *American Sociological Review, 27*(1), 31–41.

Engineers Australia. (2012). *Australian engineering competency standards stage 2—Experienced professional engineer*. Canberra, ACT: Author.

Engineers Australia. (2013). *Guide to assessment of eligibility for membership (stage 1 competency)* (pp. 1–24). Canberra, ACT: Author.

Engineers Australia. (n.d.). *Stage 1 competency standard for professional engineer*. Retrieved November 9, 2014, from https://www.engineersaustralia.org.au/sites/default/files/shado/Education/Program%20Accreditation/110318%20Stage%201%20Professional%20Engineer.pdf

Engineers Australia. (2017). Apply for membership. Retrieved from https://www.engineersaustralia.org.au/Membership

Engineers Ireland. (2017). Budget Submission 2017. Retrieved from https://www.engineersireland.ie/EngineersIreland/media/SiteMedia/communications/publications/Engineers-Ireland-2017-Budget-Submission-b.pdf

ENQA. (2003). *Quality procedures in European Higher Education*. ENQA Occasional Papers 5, Helsinki.

ENQA. (2009). *ENQA report on standards and guidelines for quality assurance in the European higher education area*. Helsinki, Finland: European Association for Quality Assurance in Higher Education.

Entwistle, N., & Ramsden, P. (1983). *Understanding student learning*. London: Croom Helm.

Epstein, R., Siegel, D., & Silberman, J. (2008). Self-monitoring in clinical practice: A challenge for medical educators. *Journal of Continuing Education in the Health Professions, 28*, 5–13.

Eraut, M. (1994). *Developing professional knowledge and competence*. London and Washington, DC: The Falmer Press.

Eraut, M. (2006). Professional knowledge and learning at work. *Knowledge, Work & Society—Savoir, Travail et Société, 3*(4), 45–62.

Eraut, M. (2008). Learning from other people in the workplace. In K. Hall, P. Murphy, & J. Soler (Eds.), *Pedagogy and practice: Culture and identities* (pp. 40–57). Los Angeles: Sage and The Open University.

Eraut, M., Alderton, A., Boylan, A., & Wraight, A. (1995). *Learning to use scientific knowledge in education and practice settings: An evaluation of the contribution of the biological behavioural and social sciences to pre-registration nursing and Midwifery programmes. Research Report 3*. London: ENB and University of Sussex, Institute of Continuing and Professional Education.

Ericsson, K. A. (2008). Deliberate practice and acquisition of expert performance: A general overview. *Academy Emergency Medicine, 15*, 988–994.

Eriksen, A. (2015). What is professional integrity? *Nordic Journal of Applied Ethics, 9*(2), 3–17.

Eteläpelto, A., Vähäsantanen, K., Hökkä, P., & Paloniemi, S. (2013, December). What is agency? Conceptualizing professional agency at work. *Educational Research Review, 10*, 45–65. https://doi.org/10.1016/j.edurev.2013.05.001

Etzioni, A. (1969). *The semi-professions and their organization: Teachers, nurses, social workers*. New York: Free Press.

European Ministers of Education. (1999). *The Bologna Declaration of 19 June 1999. Joint declaration of the European Ministers of Education*. Brussels: European Union.

Eva, K., & Regehr, G. (2008). "I'll never play professional football" and other fallacies of self-assessment. *Journal of Continuing Education in the Health Professions, 28*(1), 14–19.

Evans, L. (2008). Professionalism, professionality and the development of education professionals. *British Journal of Educational Studies, 56*(1), 20–38.

Evans, L. (2010). Professionalism, professionality and the development of education professionals. *British Journal of Educational Studies, 56*(1), 20–38.

Evetts, J. (2006). Introduction: Trust and professionalism: Challenges and occupational changes. *Current Sociology, 54*, 515–531.

Ewell, P. T. (1999). Linking performance measures to resource allocation: Exploring unmapped terrain. *Quality in Higher Education, 5*(3), 191–209.

Farmer, J., Kenny, A., McKinstry, C., & Huysmans, R. D. (2015). A scoping review of the association between rural medical education and rural practice location. *Human Resources of Health, 13*, 27. https://doi.org/10.1186/s12960-015-0017-3

Farrand, P., McMullan, M., Jowett, R., & Humphreys, A. (2006). Implementing competency recommendations into pre-registration nursing curricula: Effects upon levels of confidence in clinical skills. *Nurse Education Today, 26*(2), 97–103.

Fawns, T., & McKenzie, K. (2010). How to ensure eportfolios are a resource to students' learning. *Nursing Times*. Retrieved from http://www.nursingtimes.net/how-to-ensure-e-portfolios-are-a-valuable-resource-to-students-learning/5017919.article

Feigenbaum, A. V. (1983). *Total quality control* (3rd ed.). New York: McGraw-Hill.

Felder, R. M., & Brent, R. (2003, Fall). Learning by doing. *Chemical Engineering Education, 37*(4), 282–283.

Fenton, G. (2014). Involving a young person in the development of a digital resource in nurse education. *Nurse Education in Practice, 14*(1), 49–54. https://doi.org/10.1016/j.nepr.2013.04.014

Ferns, S., Russel, L., Smith, C., & Cretchley, P. (2014). *The impact of work integrated learning on student work-readiness* [Report No. SI11_2139]. Retrieved from www.olt.gov.au

Fewings, P. (2009). *Ethics for the built environment*. London: Taylor and Francis.

Flanagan, B. (2008). Debriefing: Theory and technique. In R. H. Riley (Ed.), *Manual of simulation in healthcare* (pp. 155–170). Oxford: Oxford University Press.

Flexner, A. (1930). *Universities: American, English, German*. New York: Oxford University Press.

Fontaine, S. I. (2002). Teaching with the beginner's mind: Notes from my karate journal. *College Composition and Communication, 54*(2), 208–221.

Forneris, S. G., & Peden-McAlpine, C. J. (2006). Contextual learning: A reflective learning intervention for nursing education. *International Journal of Nursing Education Scholarship, 33*(1)., Article 17.

Foucault, M. (1991). *Discipline and punish: The birth of a prison*. London: Penguin.

Foucault, M. (2007/1978). *Security, territory, population: Lectures at the Collège de France, 1977–1978* (G. Burchell, Trans.). New York: Palgrave Macmillan.

Franz, N., Garst, B. A., Baughman, S., Smith, C., & Peters, B. (2009, August). Catalyzing transformation: Conditions in extension educational environments that promote change. *Journal of Extension, 47*(4). Retrieved from https://www.joe.org/joe/2009august/rb1.php

Freeman, R. E., Harrison, J. S., Wicks, A. C., Parmar, B., & de Colle, S. (2010). *Stakeholder theory: The state of the art*. Cambridge, UK: Cambridge University Press.

Freeth, D., & Fry, H. (2005). Nursing students' and tutors' perceptions of learning and teaching in a clinical skills centre. *Nurse Education Today, 25*(4), 272–282. https://doi.org/10.1016/j.nedt.2005.01.007

Freeth, D., Hammick, M., Reeves, S., Koppel, I., & Barr, H. (2005). *Effective interprofessional education. Development, delivery & evaluation*. Blackwell Publishing Ltd. and UK. CAIPE.

Freidson, E. (2001). *Professionalism: The third logic—On the practice of knowledge*. Chicago: University of Chicago Press.

French, E., Summers, J., Kinash, S., Lawson, R., Taylor, T., Herbert, J., & Hall, C. (2014). The practice of quality in assuring learning in higher education. *Quality in Higher Education, 20*(1), 24–43. https://doi.org/10.1080/135383 22.2014.889432

French, J. R. P., Jr., & Raven, B. (1959). The bases of social power. In D. Cartwright (Ed.), *Studies in social power* (pp. 150–167). Ann Arbor, MI: Institute of Social Research, University of Michigan.

Fried Foster, N. (Ed.). (2013). *Studying students: A second look*. Chicago: Association of College and Research Libraries.

Friedman, A., Hogg, K., Nadarajah, K., & Pitts, R. (2017). *Professional body accreditation in higher education institutions in Ireland*. Quality and Qualifications, Ireland.

Friedman, L. (1995). C.S. Peirce's transcendental and immanent realism. *Transactions of the Charles S. Peirce Society, 31*(2), 374–392.

Friesen, M. R. (2011). Immigrants' integration and career development in the professional engineering workplace in the context of social and cultural capital. *Engineering Studies, 3*(2), 79–100. https://doi.org/10.1080/19378629.2 011.571260

Frost, H. D., & Regehr, G. (2013). "I am a doctor": Negotiating the discourses of standardization and diversity in professional identity construction. *Academic Medicine, 88*(10), 1570–1577. https://doi.org/10.1097/ACM.0b013e3182a34b05

Fry, J. D., & Ibrahim, E. (2013, September). Reassessing Venezuela's organic hydrocarbon law: A balance between sovereignty and efficiency? *Journal of World Energy Law & Business, 6*(3), 234–259. https://doi.org/10.1093/jwelb/jwt005

Fulton, A., Fulton, D., Tabart, T., Ball, P., Champion, S., Weatherley, J., & Heinjus, D. (2003, May). *Agricultural extension, learning and change: A report for the Rural Industries Research and Development Corporation*. Barton, ACT: Rural Industries Research and Development Corporation.

Fung, L., et al. (2015). Impact of crisis resource management simulation-based training for interporfessional and interdisciplinary teams: A systematic review. *Journal of Interprofessional Care, 29*(5), 433–444.

Gainer, J. (2012). Critical thinking: Foundational for digital literacies and democracy. *Journal of Adolescent & Adult Literacy, 56*(1), 14–17. https://doi.org/10.1002/JAAL.00096

Garel, G. (2013). A history of project management models: From pre-models to the standard models. *International Journal of Project Management, 31*, 663–669.

Garrett, B., MacPhee, M., & Jackson, C. (2013). Evaluation of an eportfolio for the assessment of clinical competence in a baccalaureate nursing program. *Nurse Education Today, 33*(10), 1207–1213.

Gartner. (2017). Worldwide smartphone sales to end users by operating system in 2016 [Online]. Retrieved March, 30, 2017, from http://www.gartner.com/newsroom/id/3415117

Gaughran, W., Burke, S., & Quinn, S. (2007). Environmental sustainability in undergraduate engineering education. In *ASEE Annual Conference and Exposition, Conference Proceedings, 2007*.

Geraldi, J., Turner, J., Maylor, H., Söderholm, A., Hobday, M., & Brady, T. (2008). Innovation in project management: Voices of researchers. *International Journal of Project Management, 26*(5), 586–589.

Gerbic, P., Lewis, L., & Northover, M. (2009). *Student perspectives of eportfolios: A longitudinal study of growth and development*. Paper presented at the Ascilite 2009, Auckland, New Zealand. Retrieved from http://www.ascilite.org/conferences/auckland09/procs/gerbic.pdf

Gerholm, T. (1990). On tacit knowledge in academia. *European Journal of Education, 25*(3), 263–271.

Gherardi, S. (2008). Situated knowledge and situated action: What do practice-based studies promise? In D. Barry & H. Hansen (Eds.), *The Sage handbook of new approaches to management and organization* (pp. 516–525). London: Sage Publications.

Gibbons, S. (2013). Techniques to understand the changing needs of library users. *IFLA Journal, 39*(2), 162–167.

Gibbs, G. (1988a). *Learning by doing: A guide to teaching and learning methods*. Oxford: Further Education Unit, Oxford Brookes University.

Gibbs, G. (1988b). *Learning by doing, a guide to teaching and learning methods* (p. 134). London: Further Education Unit.

Gibbs, G. (2010). *Dimensions of quality*. Heslington, York: Higher Education Academy.

Gibbs, G. (2013). Reflections on the changing nature of educational development. *International Journal for Academic Development, 18*(1), 4–14.

Gibbs, G., & Simpson, C. (2004). Conditions under which assessment supports student learning. *Learning and Teaching in Higher Education, 1*, 3–31.

Giddens, A. (1968). 'Power' in the recent writings of Talcott Parsons. *Sociology, 2*(3), 257–272.

Gill, T. M. (2017). Unpacking the world cultural toolkit in socialist Venezuela: National sovereignty, human rights and anti-NGO legislation. *Third World Quarterly, 38*(3), 621–635. https://doi.org/10.1080/01436597.2016.119925

Gjeraa, K., Møller, T. P., & Østergaard, D. (2014). Efficacy of simulation-based trauma team training of non-technical skills. A systematic review. *Acta Anaesthesiologica Scandinavica, 58*, 775–787.

Gobet, F., Lane, P. C. R., Croker, S., Cheng, P. C.-H., Jones, G., Oliver, I., & Pine, J. M. (2001). Chunking mechanisms in human learning. *Cognitive Sciences, 5*(6), 236–243.

Goggins, J. (2012). Engineering in communities: Learning by doing. *Campus-Wide Information Systems, 29*(4), 238–250. https://doi.org/10.1108/10650741211253831

Golde, C. M. (2000). Should I stay or should I go? Student descriptions of the doctoral attrition process. *The Review of Higher Education, 23*(2), 199–227.

Golde, C. M. (2005). The role of the department and discipline in doctoral student attrition: Lessons from four departments. *The Journal of Higher Education, 76*(6), 669–700.

GoPNG [Government of Papua New Guinea]. (2010). Vision 2050. Retrieved from www.treasury.gov.pg/html/publications/files/pub_files/.../2011.png.vision.2050.pdf

Gordon, J., & Campbell, C. (2013). The role of ePortfolios in supporting continuing professional development in practice. *Medical Teacher, 35*(4), 287–294.

Gore, J., Ladwig, J., Elsworth, W., & Ellis, H. (2009). Quality assessment: Linking assessment tasks and teaching outcomes in the social sciences. Retrieved from http://www.olt.gov.au/resource-library

Gorman, D., & Toombs, M. (2009). Matching research methodology with Australian Indigenous culture. *Aboriginal and Islander Health Worker Journal, 33*(3), 1–7.

Gorman, E. H., & Sandelfur, R. L. (2011, August). "Golden age", quiescence, and revival: How the sociology of professions became the study of knowledge-based work. *Work and Occupations, 38*(3), 275–302. https://doi.org/10.1177/0730888411417565

Gosling, D. (2009). Educational development in the UK: A complex and contradictory reality. *International Journal for Academic Development, 14*(1), 5–18.

Government of Western Australia, Department of Health—Aboriginal Health. (2012). *WA Health Aboriginal Cultural Learning Framework*. Retrieved from http://ww2.health.wa.gov.au/Improving-WA-Health/About-Aboriginal-Health/Aboriginal-Cultural-Learning-Framework-2012-2016

Grace, P. J. (2014). Philosophical foundations of applied and professional ethics. In P. J. Grace (Ed.), *Nursing ethics and professional responsibility in advanced practice* (2nd ed., pp. 1–43). Burlington, MA: Jones & Bartlett Learning.

Grant, B., & McKinley, E. (2011). Colouring the pedagogy of doctoral supervision: Considering supervisor, student and knowledge through the lens of indigeneity. *Innovations in Education and Teaching International, 48*(4), 377–386.

Grant, B. M. (2010). The limits of 'teaching and learning': Indigenous students and doctoral supervision. *Teaching in Higher Education, 15*(5), 505–517.

Gray, L. (2008). *Effective practice with e-Portfolios*. Bristol: JISC Retrieved from http://www.webarchive.org.uk/wayback/archive/20140615090512/http://www.jisc.ac.uk/media/documents/publications/effectivepracticeeportfolios.pdf

Green, B. (2012). Addressing the curriculum problem in doctoral education. *Australian Universities Review, 52*(1), 10–18.

Green, D. A. (2009). New academics' perceptions of the language of teaching and learning: Identifying and overcoming linguistic barriers. *International Journal for Academic Development, 14*(1), 33–45.

Green, W., Hammer, S., & Star, C. (2009). Facing up to the challenge: Why is it so hard to develop graduate attributes? *Higher Education Research & Development, 28*(1), 17–29. https://doi.org/10.1080/07294360802444339

Gresalfi, M., & Barab, S. (2011). Learning for a reason: Supporting forms of engagement by designing tasks and orchestrating environments. *Theory into Practice, 50*(4), 300–310.

Guest, G. (2006). Lifelong learning for engineers: A global perspective. *European Journal of Engineering Education, 31*(3), 273–281. https://doi.org/10.1080/03043790600644396

Gulikers, J. T. M., Bastiaens, T. J., & Kirschner, P. A. (2004a). A five-dimensional framework for authentic assessment. *Educational Technology Research and Development, 52*(3), 67–86.

Gulikers, J. T. M., Bastiaens, T. J., & Kirschner, P. A. (2004b). Perceptions of authentic assessment: Five dimensions of authenticity. In *Proceedings, Second Biannual Northumbria/EARLI SIG Assessment Conference*, Bergen.

Guo, S., Cockburn-Wootten, C., & Munshi, D. (2014). Negotiating diversity: Fostering collaborative interpretations of case studies. *Business Communication Quarterly, 77*(2), 169–182. https://doi.org/10.1177/2329490614530464

Hafferty, F. W. (1998). Beyond curriculum reform: Confronting medicines hidden curriculum. *Academic Medicine, 73*(4), 403–407.

Hagström, L., & Scheja, M. (2014). Using meta-reflection to improve learning and throughput: Redesigning assessment procedures in a political science course on power. *Assessment & Evaluation in Higher Education, 39*(2), 242–252.

Haig, K., Sutton, S., & Whittington, J. (2006). SBAR: A shared mental model for improving communication between clinicians. *Joint Commission Journal on Quality and Patient Safety, 32*(3), 167–175.

Hall, S. (1996). Who needs identity. In S. Hall & P. du Gay (Eds.), *Questions of cultural identity* (pp. 1–17). London: SAGE.

Hallam, G., Harper, W., McCowan, C., Hauville, K., McAllister, L. & Creagh, T. (2008). *ePortfolio use by university students in Australia: Informing excellence in policy and practice*. Final project report August 2008. Brisbane: Queensland University of Technology.

Halloran, L. (2009). Teaching transcultural nursing through literature. *Journal of Nursing Education, 48*(9), 523–528. https://doi.org/10.3928/01484834-20090610-07

Hamilton, G., Byatt, G., & Hodgkinson, J. (2011). *The color coded project portfolio—Where is the balance?* Retrieved May 24, 2016, from http://www.pmhut.com/the-color-coded-project-portfolio-where-is-the-balance

Hammer, S. J., Chardon, T., Collins, P., & Hart, C. (2012). Legal educators' perceptions of lifelong learning: Conceptualisation and practice. *International Journal of Lifelong Education, 31*(2), 187–201. https://doi.org/10.1080/02601370.2012.663803

Hammer, S. J., & Green, W. (2011). Critical thinking in a first year management unit: The relationship between disciplinary learning, academic literacy and learning progression. *Higher Education Research & Development, 30*(3), 303–315. https://doi.org/10.1080/07294360.2010.501075

Happell, B., Byrne, L., McAllister, M., Lampshire, D., Roper, C., Gaskin, C. J., … Hamer, H. (2014). Consumer involvement in the tertiary-level education of mental health professionals: A systematic review. *International Journal of Mental Health Nursing, 23*(1), 3–16. https://doi.org/10.1111/inm.12021

Harding, T. (2013). Cultural safety: A vital element for nursing ethics. *Nursing Praxis in New Zealand, 29*(1), 4–11.

Hargroves, K., & Smith, M. (2005). *The natural advantage of nations: Business opportunities, innovation and governance in the 21st century.* London: Earthscan Retrieved from http://www.naturaledgeproject.net/NAON.aspx

Harris, C. E., Pritchard, M. S., Rabins, M. J., James, R., & Englehardt, E. (2014). *Engineering ethics: Concepts and cases* (5th ed.). Boston, MA: Wadsworth/Cengage Learning.

Hartman, N. (2004). The development of expertise in the use of constraint-based CAD tools: Examining practicing professionals. *Engineering Design Graphics Journal, 68*(2), 14–26.

Hartung, P. J., Porfeli, E. J., & Vondracek, F. W. (2008). Career adaptability in childhood. *Career Development Quarterly, 57*, 63–74. https://doi.org/10.1002/j.2161-0045.2008.tb00166.x

Harvey, L., Locke, W., & Morey, A. (2002). *Enhancing employability, recognising diversity. Making links between higher education and the world of work.* London: Universities UK.

Harwood, J. (2010). Understanding academic drift: On the institutional dynamics of higher technical and professional education. *Minerva, 48*(4), 413–427. https://doi.org/10.1007/s11024-010-9156-9

Haselbach, L. (2015). Special issue on sustainability engineering education—Keeping up with the world. *ACSC Journal of Professional Issues in Engineering Education and Practice, 141*(2), C2014001.

Hassel, A. (2015). Public policy. In J. Wright (Ed.), *International encyclopedia of the social and behavioral science* (2nd ed.). Elsevier.

Hattie, J. (2008). *Visible learning: A synthesis of over 800 meta-analyses relating to achievement.* Retrieved from http://UTAS.eblib.com.au/patron/FullRecord.aspx?p=367685

Hay, D. B., Williams, D., Stahl, D., & Wingate, R. (2013). Using drawings of the brain cell to exhibit expertise in neuroscience: Exploring the boundaries of experimental culture. *Science Education, 97*(3), 468–491.

Hays. (2010). *Accountancy practices Ireland Employment Report 2010.* Hays Recruiting Experts in Accountancy and Finance.

Health Personnel Act. (1999). Lov om helsepersonell m.v. (Helsepersonelloven). Retrieved from https://lovdata.no/dokument/NL/lov/1999-07-02-64 (in Norwegian).

Heat Loss Calculator app Google Play Store listing. (n.d.). [Online]. Retrieved December 8, 2017, from https://play.google.com/store/apps/details?id=leedsbeckett.ac.uk.heatloss&hl=en_GB

References

Hedlund, J., Forsythe, G. B., Horvath, J. A., Williams, W. M., Snook, S., & Sternberg, R. J. (2006). Identifying and assessing tacit knowledge: Understanding the practical intelligence of military leaders. *The Leadership Quarterly, 14*, 117–140.

Heery, E., & Salmon, J. (Eds.). (2000). *The insecure workforce*. London: RoutledgeFalmer.

HEFCE. (2014). UK review of the provision of information about higher education. National Student Survey results and trends analysis 2005–2013. Retrieved from http://www.hefce.ac.uk/pubs/year/2014/201413/

Heidegger, M. (2008/1927). *Being and time* (J. Macquarrie & E. Robinson, Trans.). New York: HarperPerennial.

Heitmann, G. (2005). Challenges of engineering education and curriculum development in the context of the Bologna Process. *European Journal of Engineering Education, 30*(4), 447–458. https://doi.org/10.1080/03043790500213136

Hennessy, B. (2016, October 7). Decolonising the university: Lessons from Oceania. *Demos*. Retrieved from http://www.demosproject.net/decolonising-the-university-lessons-from-oceania/

Henry, J. (2007). Supervising Aboriginal doctoral candidates. In C. Denholm & T. Evans (Eds.), *Supervising doctorates downunder: Keys to effective supervision in Australia and New Zealand* (pp. 155–163). Camberwell, VIC: ACER Press.

Herbert, J. (2005). Owning the discourse: Seizing the power! *Australian Association for Research in Education*. University of Western Sydney. Retrieved from http://www.aare.edu.au/05pap/her05217.pdf

Hernes, G. (2013). Super resilient organization. In J. E. Karlsen & R. M. O. Pritchard (Eds.), *Resilient universities: Confronting changes in a challenging world* (pp. 381–402). Oxford: Peter Lang.

Herreid, C. F. (2012). Introduction. In C. F. Herreid, N. A. Schiller, & K. F. Herreid (Eds.), *Science stories using case studies to teach critical thinking* (pp. vii–xiii). Arlington, VA: National Science Teachers Association.

Hershey, J. L. (2007). *The lived experience of becoming a professional nurse for associate degree nursing graduates: A phenomenological study*. Doctoral dissertation, The Pennsylvania State University.

HESA. (2016). Synthesis of consultation responses in support of HESA's fundamental review of destinations and outcomes data for graduates from higher education. Higher Education Statistics Agency, October 2016.

Heywood, J. (2005). *Engineering education: Research and development in curriculum and instruction*. Hoboken, NJ: Wiley-IEEE Press.

Higgs, J., & Titchen, A. (2001). Rethinking the practice-knowledge interface in an uncertain world: A model for practice development. *British Journal of Occupational Therapy, 64*(11), 526–533.

Higher Education Authority. (2016). *Higher education system performance 2014–2016.* Dublin.

Higher Education Authority. (2017). *Review of the allocation model for funding of higher education institutions: Working Paper 1. The higher education sector in Ireland.* Dublin.

Hilton, P., & Pollard, C. (2004). Supporting clinical skills developments. *Nursing Standard, 18*(35), 31–36. https://doi.org/10.7748/ns2004.05.18.35.31.c3608

Hindle, K., Klyver, K., & Jennings, D. F. (2009). An 'informed' intent model: Incorporating human capital, social capital, and gender variables into the theoretical model of entrepreneurial intentions. In A. L. Carsrud & M. Brännback (Eds.), *Understanding the entrepreneurial mind: Opening the black box* (pp. 35–50). Dordrecht, The Netherlands: Springer Science+Business Media.

Hinett, K., & Weeden, P. (2000). How am I doing?: Developing critical self-evaluation in trainee teachers. *Quality in Higher Education, 6*(3), 245–257. https://doi.org/10.1080/13538320020005981

Hinton, A., & Chirgwin, S. (2010). Nursing education: Reducing reality shock for graduate Indigenous nurses—It's all about time. *Australian Journal of Advanced Nursing, 28*(1), 60–66.

Ho, E. S.-C. (2009). Educational leadership for parental involvement in an Asian context: Insights from Bourdieu's theory of practice. *The School Community Journal, 19*(2), 101–122.

Hoare, L. (2013). Swimming in the deep end: Transnational teaching as culture learning? *Higher Education Research & Development, 32*(4), 561–574. https://doi.org/10.1080/07294360.2012.700918

Hodgson, C., & Pyle, K. (2010). A literature review of assessment for learning in science. Retrieved May 24, 2016, from http://nfernew.dudobi.com/nfer/publications/AAS01/AAS01.pdf

Hoffman, R. R., & Lintern, G. (2006). Eliciting and representing the knowledge of experts. In K. A. Ericsson, N. Charness, P. J. Feltovich, & R. R. Hoffman (Eds.), *The Cambridge handbook of expertise and expert performance* (pp. 203–222). Cambridge, UK: Cambridge University Press.

Hofstadter, R., & Metzger, W. P. (1955). *The development of academic freedom in the United States.* New York: Columbia University Press.

Hokanson, D. R., Mihelcic, J. R., & Phillips, L. D. (2007). Educating engineers in the sustainable futures model with a global perspective: Education, research & diversity initiatives. *International Journal of Engineering Education, 23*(2), 254–265.

Hökkä, P., Eteläpelto, A., & Rasku-Puttonen, H. (2012). The professional agency of teacher educators amid academic discourses. *Journal of Education for Teaching: International Research & Pedagogy, 38*(1), 83–102.

Hollanda, P. J., Allena, B. C., & Coopera, B. K. (2013). Reducing burnout in Australian nurses: The role of employee direct voice and managerial responsiveness. *The International Journal of Human Resource Management, 24*(16), 3146–3162. https://doi.org/10.1080/09585192.2013.775032

Hollander, E. P., & Willis, R. H. (1967). Some current issues in the psychology of conformity and nonconformity. *Psychological Bulletin, 68*(1), 62–76.

Holmes, D., & Gastaldo, D. (2002). Nursing as a means of governmentality. *Journal of Advanced Nursing, 38*(6), 557–565.

Holmes, D., & Gastaldo, D. (2004). Rhizomatic thought in nursing: An alternative path for the development of the discipline. *Nursing Philosophy, 5*, 258–267.

Hood, C. (2004). Conclusion: Making sense of controls over government. In C. Hood, O. James, B. G. Peters, & C. Scott (Eds.), *Controlling modern government: Variety, commonality, and change* (pp. 185–205). Cheltenham, UK: Edward Elgar.

Hopwood, N. (2017). Practice architectures of simulation pedagogy: From fidelity to transformation. In K. Mahon, S. Francisco, & S. Kemmis (Eds.), *Exploring education and professional practice* (pp. 63–81). Singapore: Springer.

Hossain, D., Gorman, D., Williams-Mozely, J., & Garvey, D. (2008). Bridging the gap: Identifying needs and aspirations of Indigenous students to facilitate their entry into university. *Australian Journal of Indigenous Education, 37*, 9–17.

Howard, S. A. (2015). Metaemotional intentionality. *Pacific Philosophical Quarterly, 98*, 406–428.

Howell, R. (2013). Grading rubrics: Hoopla or help? *Innovations in Education and Teaching International, 51*(4), 400–410. https://doi.org/10.1080/14703297.2013.785252

Howieson, B., Hancock, P., Segal, N., Kavanagh, M., Tempone, I., & Kent, J. (2014). Who should teach what? Australian perceptions of the roles of universities and practice in the education of professional accountants. *Journal of Accountancy Education, 32*, 259–275.

Hoyle, E. (1982). The professionalization of teachers: A paradox. *British Journal of Educational Studies, 30*(2), 161–171.

Hu, S., & Kuh, G. (2002). Being (dis)engaged in educationally purposeful activities: The influences of student and institutional characteristics. *Research in Higher Education, 43*(5), 555–575.

Huddle, T., & Heudebert, G. (2007). Viewpoint: Taking apart the art: The risk of anatomizing clinical competence. *Academic Medicine, 82*(6), 536–541.

Huesemann, M. H., & Huesemann, J. A. (2011). *Technofix: Why technology won't save us or the environment.* Chapter 13, "The design of environmentally sustainable and appropriate technologies". New Society Publishers, Gabriola Island, BC, Canada, ISBN 0865717044, 464p. Retrieved from http://www.newtechnologyandsociety.org/

Humphries, N., McAleese, S., Matthews, A., & Brugha, R. (2015). Emigration is a matter of self-preservation. The working conditions … are killing us slowly': Qualitative insights into health professional emigration from Ireland. *Human Resources Health* 13 (35). Retrieved October 15, 2017, from https://www.ncbi.nlm.nih.gov/pmc/articles/PMC4437248/

Hunt, L., & Chalmers, D. (Eds.). (2012). *University teaching in focus: A learning centred approach.* Camberwell, VIC: ACER Press.

Hunter, D. (2015, April). The new face of blended learning. *DeakinCo*. Retrieved December 20, 2017, from http://deakinprime.com/news-and-publications/news/the-new-face-of-blended-learning

Hunter, I. (2008). The desire for deconstruction: Derrida's metaphysics of law. *Communication, Politics & Culture, 41*(1), 6–29.

Huntzinger, D. N., Hutchins, M. J., Gierke, J. S., & Sutherland, J. W. (2007). Enabling sustainable thinking in undergraduate engineering education. *International Journal of Engineering Education, 23*(2), 218–230.

Hurlimann, A., March, A., & Robins, J. (2013). University curriculum development—Stuck in a process and how to break free. *Journal of Higher Education Policy & Management, 35*(6), 639–651. https://doi.org/10.1080/1360080X.2013.844665

Husserl, E. (1931). *Ideas: General introduction to pure phenomenology* (W. R. B. Gibson, Trans.). London: George Allen & Unwind LTD.

IFAC Education Committee. (2005). *Professional ethics for accountants: Approaches to the development and maintenance of professional values, ethics and attitudes in accounting education programs.* Retrieved from https://www.iaesb.org/system/files/meetings/files/1625.pdf

Ingersoll, R. M., & Perda, D. (2008). The status of teaching as a profession. In J. H. Ballantine & J. Z. Spade (Eds.), *Schools and society: A sociological approach to education* (3rd ed., pp. 106–118). Thousand Oaks, CA: Sage Publications.

Institute of National Affairs. (2016). *PNG at 40 Symposium: Learning from the past and engaging with the future.* Papers from Alotau Symposium, 1–3 March 2016. Port Moresby, PNG: Institute of National Affairs. Retrieved from www.inapng.com/pdf_files/PNG%20at%2040%20Symposium%20ReportPB.pdf

International Confederation of Midwives (ICM). (2008). *Position statement basic and ongoing education for midwives.* Retrieved from www.internationalmidwives.org

International Pharmaceutical Federation. (2009). FIP statement of policy quality assurance of pharmacy education. Retrieved February 3, 2014, from http://www.fip.org/pe_resources

International Pharmaceutical Federation Pharmacy Education Taskforce. (2012). A global competency framework for services provided by pharmacy workforce. Retrieved February 3, 2015, from http://www.fip.org/pe_resources

IOM (Institute of Medicine). (2003). *Health professions education: A bridge to quality* (A. Greiner & E. Knebel, Eds.). Washington, DC: The National Academies Press.

IOM (Institute of medicine). (2015). *Measuring the impact of interprofessional education on collaborative practice and patient outcomes.* Washington, DC: The National Academies Press Retrieved from http://iom.nationalacademies.org/reports/2015/impact-of-ipe.aspx

Irish Medical Organisation. (2017). IMO Pre-Budget Submission 2018. Retrieved from http://www.imo.ie/news-media/news-press-releases/2017/imo-budget-submission-201/index.xml

Irish Survey of Student Engagement [ISSE]. (2016). HEA, IUA, THEA and USI: Dublin. Retrieved October 16, 2017, from www.studentsurvey.ie

Iser, W. (1979). *The act of reading.* London: Routledge and Kegan Paul.

Ito, J. K., & Brotheridge, C. M. (2005). Does supporting employees' career adaptability lead to commitment, turnover, or both? *Human Resource Management, 44,* 5–19. https://doi.org/10.1002/hrm.20037

Jairam, D., & Kahl, D. H., Jr. (2012). Navigating the doctoral experience: The role of social support in successful degree completion. *International Journal of Doctoral Studies, 7,* 311–329.

James, W. (1890). *The principles of psychology. Volume I.* New York: Henry Holt and Company.

Janke, K., Traynor, A., & Sorensen, T. (2011). Refinement of strengths instruction in a pharmacy curriculum over eight years. *American Journal of Pharmaceutical Education, 75*(3), 1–45.

Jarvis, C., & Gouthro, P. (2013). The role of the arts in professional education; making the invisible, visible. In *Research in work and learning*, 18–21 June 2013, University of Stirling. Retrieved October 16, 2017, from http://eprints.hud.ac.uk/id/eprint/18339/

Jarvis, P. (1999). *The practitioner-researcher: Developing theory from practice*. San Francisco, CA: Jossey-Bass.

Jeffries, P. R. (2005). A framework for designing, implementing, and evaluating: Simulations used as teaching strategies in nursing. *Nursing Education Perspectives, 26*(2), 96–103.

Jeffries, P. R. (2007). *Simulation in nursing education. From conceptualization to evaluation*. New York: The National League for Nursing.

Jeffries, P. R., Rew, S., & Cramer, J. M. (2002). A comparison of student-centered versus traditional methods of teaching basic nursing skills in a learning laboratory. *Nursing Education Perspectives, 23*(1), 14.

Jeffs, L., Abramovich, I. A., Hayes, C., Smith, O., Tregunno, D., Chan, W. H., & Reeves, S. (2013). Implementing an interprofessional patient safety learning initiative: Insights from participants, project leads and steering committee members. *BMJ Quality & Saftey, 22*, 923–930. https://doi.org/10.1136/bmjqs-2012-001720

Jenkins, K. D. (1983). *Towards professionalization*. Paper presented at the Annual Conference of the Southern Regional Council on Education. ERIC Document, ED 248 576.

Jisc. (2008). *Effective practice with e-Portfolios*. Retrieved from http://www.jisc.ac.uk/eportfolio

Jisc. (2015). Enhancing the student digital experience: A strategic approach—Supporting institutions to develop digital environments which meet students' expectations and help them to progress to higher study and employment. Retrieved December, 20, 2017, from https://www.jisc.ac.uk/full-guide/enhancing-the-digital-student-experience

John, D. A., Kawachi, I., Lathan, C. S., & Ayanian, J. Z. (2014). Disparities in perceived unmet need for supportive services among patients with lung cancer in the cancer care outcomes research and surveillance consortium. *Cancer, 120*, 3178–3191. https://doi.org/10.1002/cncr.28801

Johns, C. (1995). Framing learning through reflection within Carper's fundamental ways of knowing in nursing. *Journal of Advanced Nursing, 22*(2), 226–234.

Jolly, H. (2016). *Understanding pedagogical content knowledge for engineering education: The effect of field and habitus*. Doctoral dissertation, University of Southern Queensland.

Jones, M. (2013). Issues in doctoral studies—Forty years of journal discussions: Where have we been and where are we going? *International Journal of Doctoral Studies, 8*, 83–104.

Jones, M. E., Bond, M. L., & Mancini, M. E. (1998). Developing a culturally competent work force: An opportunity for collaboration. *Journal of Professional Nursing, 14*(5), 280–287.

Jonnergård, K., & Erlingsdóttir, G. (2012, September). Variations in professions' adaption of quality reforms: The cases of doctors and auditors in Sweden. *Current Sociology, 60*(5), 672–689. https://doi.org/10.1177/0011392112440440

Jordan, J. T. (2008). Student ratings in a consumerist academy: Leveraging pedagogical control and authority. *Sociological Perspectives, 51*(2), 397–422. https://doi.org/10.1525/sop.2008.51.2.397

Jørgensen, S., Skyttermoen, T., & Syversen, T. L. (2011). 'I pose og sekk? Mot en prakademisk utdanning i organisasjons- og ledelsesfag—et studieutviklingsprosjekt som ble «kronet med gull»' [Report from the design of a 'pracademic' program in management education]. In I. G. Bjørke, O. Eikeland, & H. Jarning (Eds.), *Ny Praksis—ny kunnskap* (pp. 211–226). Oslo: ABM Media.

Jørgensen, U., & Valderrama, A. (2016). The politics of engineering professionalism and education. In U. Jørgensen & S. Brodersen (Eds.), *Engineering professionalism (Professional practice and education: A diversity of voices)* (pp. 283–309). Rotterdam, Netherlands: Sense Publishers.

Josephson, P. (2004). Lehrfreiheit, Lernfreiheit, Wertfreiheit: Max Weber and the University Teachers' Congress in Jena 1908. *Max Weber Studies, 4*(2), 201–219.

Juran, J. M., & Godfrey, A. B. (1999). The quality control process. In J. M. Juran, A. B. Godfrey, R. E. Hoogstoel, & E. G. Schilling (Eds.), *Juran's quality handbook* (5th ed., pp. 4.1–4.29). New York: McGraw-Hill.

Juran, J. M., & Gryna, F. M., Jr. (1970). *Quality planning and analysis: From product development through usage*. New York: McGraw-Hill.

Kahneman, D. (2012). *Thinking, fast and slow*. Melbourne, VIC: Penguin Books.

Kahneman, D., & Tversky, A. (1979). Prospect theory: An analysis of decision under risk. *Econometrica, 47*(2), 263–292.

Kandiko Howson, C., & Matos, F. (2014). *UK Engagement Survey 2014: Full report of cognitive testing*. York: Higher Education Academy Retrieved from https://www.heacademy.ac.uk/system/files/resources/ukes_2014_cognitive_testing_report.pdf

Karapanos, E., Zimmerman, J., Forlizzi, J., & Martens, J-B. (2009). User experience over time: An initial framework. In *Proceedings of the 27th International Conference on Human Factors in Computing Systems, CHI 2009* (pp. 729–738). Boston, MA, 4–9 April 2009.

Kastenhofer, K., Lansu, A., van Dam-Mieras, R., & Sotoudeh, M. (2010, March). The contribution of university curricula to engineering education for sustainable development. *GAIA—Ecological Perspectives for Science and Society, 19*(1), 44–51. https://doi.org/10.14512/gaia.19.1.10

Katz, D., & Kahn, R. L. (1978). *The social psychology of organizations* (2nd ed.). New York: Wiley.

Kaufman, H. G. (1972). Relations of ability and interest to currency of professional knowledge among engineers. *Journal of Applied Psychology, 56*(6), 495–499. https://doi.org/10.1037/h0033751

Kavanamur, D., & Okole, H. (2004). *Understanding reform in Papua New Guinea: An analytical evaluation.* Port Moresby, PNG: Institute of National Affairs.

Kawan, M. M. S., Kondalsamy-Chennakesavan, S., Ranmuthugala, G., Toombs, M. R., & Nicholson, G. C. (2017, July 7). The rural pipeline to longer-term rural practice: General practitioners and specialists. *PLOS One.* https://doi.org/10.1371/journal.pone.0180394

Kek, M. Y. C. A., & Huijser, H. (2017). *Problem-based learning into the future: Imagining an agile PBL ecology for learning.* Singapore: Springer.

Kek, M. Y. C. A., Padró, F. F., & Huijser, H. (under review). Exploring the contributions of co-curricular learning programs to student success in a holistic learning ecology for student development and support.

Kember, D. (2000). *Action learning and action research: Improving the quality of teaching and learning.* London: Kogan Page.

Kember, D., & Ginns, P. (2012). *Evaluating teaching and learning.* New York: Routledge.

Kemmis, S. (2005). Knowing practice: Searching for salience. *Pedagogy, Culture and Society, 13*(3), 391–426.

Keskitalo, T., & Ruokamo, H. (2016). Students' expectations and experiences of meaningful simulation-based medical education. *Seminar.net. International Journal of Media, Technology and Lifelong Learning, 12*(2), 110–123 Retrieved from http://seminar.net/104-frontpage/269-students-expectations-and-experiences-of-meaningful-simulation-based-medical-education

Kevern, J. (2011). Green building and sustainable infrastructure: Sustainability education for civil engineers. *Journal of Professional Issues in Engineering Education and Practice, 137*, Special Issue: Sustainability in Civil and Environmental Engineering Education, 107–112.

Keys, B., & Wolfe, J. (1990). The role of management game and simulation in education and research. *Journal of Management, 16*(2), 307–336.

Khan, S. (2013). Let's use video to reinvent education. Retrieved from https://www.youtube.com/watch?v=nTFEUsudhfs

Kift, S. M. (2009). *Articulating a transition pedagogy to scaffold and to enhance the first year student learning experience in Australian higher education*. Final report for ALTC Senior Fellowship Program. ALTC Resources. Retrieved from http://fyhe.com.au/wp-content/uploads/2012/10/Kift-Sally-ALTC-Senior-Fellowship-Report-Sep-09.pdf

Kilgore, D., Sattler, B., & Turns, J. (2012). From fragmentation to continuity: Engineering students make sense of experience through the development of a professional portfolio. *Studies in Higher Education, 38*(6), 807–826. https://doi.org/10.1080/03075079.2011.610501

Killen, R. (2007). *Effective teaching strategies: Lessons from research and practice* (4th ed.). South Melbourne, VIC: Thomson Social Science Press.

Kinchin, I. M. (1994). *The biology of tardigrades*. London: Portland Press.

Kinchin, I. M. (2014). Concept mapping as a learning tool in higher education: A critical analysis of recent reviews. *The Journal of Continuing Higher Education, 62*(1), 39–49.

Kinchin, I. M. (2016). *Visualising powerful knowledge: A knowledge structures perspective on teaching and learning at university*. Rotterdam, Netherlands: Sense Publishers.

Kinchin, I. M., & Cabot, L. B. (2010). Reconsidering the dimensions of expertise: From linear stages towards dual processing. *London Review of Education, 8*(2), 153–166.

Kinchin, I. M., & Winstone, N. E. (2017). *Pedagogic frailty and resilience in the university*. Rotterdam, Netherlands: Sense Publishers.

Kinchin, I. M., Alpay, E., Curtis, K., Franklin, J., Rivers, C., & Winstone, N. E. (2016). Charting the elements of pedagogic frailty. *Educational Research, 58*(1), 1–23.

Kinchin, I. M., Baysan, A., & Cabot, L. B. (2008). Towards a pedagogy for clinical education: Beyond individual learning differences. *Journal of Further and Higher Education, 32*(4), 373–387.

Kinchin, I. M., Cabot, L. B., & Hay, D. B. (2008a). Visualising expertise: Towards an authentic pedagogy for higher education. *Teaching in Higher Education, 13*(3), 315–326.

Kinchin, I. M., Cabot, L. B., & Hay, D. B. (2008b). Using concept mapping to locate the tacit dimension of clinical expertise: Towards a theoretical framework to support critical reflection on teaching. *Learning in Health and Social Care, 7*(2), 93–104.

Kinchin, I. M., Lygo-Baker, S., & Hay, D. B. (2008). Universities as centres of non-learning. *Studies in Higher Education, 33*(1), 89–103.

Kinchin, I. M., & Miller, N. L. (2012). 'Structural Transformation' as a threshold concept in university teaching. *Innovations in Education and Teaching International, 49*(2), 207–222.

King, K. P. (2004). Both sides now: Examining transformative learning and professional development of educators. *Innovative Higher Education, 29*(2), 155–174.

King, M., & Thornhill, C. (2003). *Niklas Luhmann's theory of politics and law.* Hampshire, UK: Palgrave Macmillan.

King, S. (2006). *Emotional dimensions of major educational change: A study of higher education PBL curriculum reform.* Paper presented at the Australian Association for Research in Education (AARE) Conference: 'Engaging Pedagogies', Adelaide, South Australia. Retrieved from http://www.aare.edu.au/data/publications/2006/kin06834.pdf#page=1&zoom=auto,-35,792

Kingsbury, D. V. (2016, October). Oil's colonial residues: Geopolitics, identity, and resistance in Venezuela. *Bulletin of Latin American Research, 35*(4), 423–436. https://doi.org/10.1111/blar.12477

Kinsella, E. A. (2007). Embodied reflection and the epistemology of reflective practice. *Journal of Philosophy of Education, 41*(3), 395–409.

Kipfer, S., Goonewardena, K., Schmid, C., & Milgrom, R. (2008). On the production of Henri Lefebvre. In K. Goonewardena, S. Kipfer, R. Milgrom, & C. Schmid (Eds.), *Space, difference, everyday life: Reading Henri Lefebvre* (pp. 1–24). New York: Routledge.

Kiraly, M., James, J., & Humphreys, C. (2014). 'It's a family responsibility': Family and cultural connection for aboriginal children in kinship care. *Children Australia, 40*(1), 23–32. https://doi.org/10.1017/cha.2014.36

Kirkpatrick, D. L., & Kirkpatrick, J. D. (2008). *Evaluating training programs. The four levels.* San Francisco, CA: Berrett-Koehler Publishers, Inc.

Kirschner, P. A. (2015). Do we need teachers as designers of technology enhanced learning? *Instructional Science, 43*(2), 309–322. https://doi.org/10.1007/s11251-015-9346-9

Kis, V. (2005). *Quality assurance in tertiary education: Current practices in OECD countries and literature review on potential effects.* Paper contribution to the OECD Thematic Review of Tertiary Education. Retrieved from www.oecd.org/edu/tertiary/review

Knowles, M. (1975). *Self directed learning: A guide for learners and teachers.* New York: Association Press.

Kolb, D. A. (1984). *Experiential learning: Experience as the source of learning and development*. Englewood Cliffs, NJ: Prentice-Hall/Harris.

Kolb, D. A., & Fry, R. (1975). Toward an applied theory of experiential learning. In C. Cooper (Ed.), *Theories of group process*. London: John Wiley.

Könings, K. D., Brand-Gruwel, S., & van Merriënboer, J. J. G. (2010). An approach to participatory instructional design in secondary education: An exploratory study. *Educational Research, 52*(1), 45–59. https://doi.org/10.1080/00131881003588204

Kools, S., Chimwaza, A., & Macha, S. (2015). Cultural humility and working with marginalized populations in developing countries. *Global Health Promotion, 22*(1), 52–59. https://doi.org/10.1177/1757975914528728

Kozulin, A., Gindis, B., Ageyev, V. S., & Miller, S. M. (2003). *Vygotsky's educational theory in cultural context*. Cambridge, UK: Cambridge University Press.

Kraiger, K. (2008). Transforming our models of learning and development: Web-based instruction as enabler of third-generation instruction. *Industrial and Organizational Psychology, 1*, 454–467.

Krathwohl, D. (2002). A revision of Bloom's taxonomy: An overview. *Theory into Practice, 41*(4), 212–218.

Krause, K.-L., Scott, G., Aubin, K., Alexander, H., Angelo, T., Campbell, S., & Pattison, P. (2014). *Assuring learning and teaching standards through inter-institutional peer review and moderation*. Final report of the project. Retrieved from University of Western Sydney website: http://www.uws.edu.au/__data/assets/pdf_file/0007/576916/External_Report_2014_Web_3.pdf

Kuh, G. D., Kinzie, J., Shuh, J. H., Whitt, E. J., & Associates. (2005). *Student success in college: Creating conditions that matter*. San Francisco, CA: Jossey-Bass.

Kula-Semos, M. A. (2009). *Seeking transformative partnerships: Schools, university and the practicum in Papua New Guinea*. PhD thesis, James Cook University.

Kula-Semos, M. A. (2014). An interpretation of the competing values framework in PNG's multicultural higher education landscape. *Contemporary PNG Studies, 21*, 29–43.

Kutob, R. M., Bormanis, J., Crago, M., Harris, J. M., Senf, J., & Shisslak, C. M. (2013). Cultural competence education for practicing physicians: Lessons in cultural humility, nonjudgmental behaviors, and health beliefs elicitation. *Journal of Continuing Education in the Health Professions, 33*(3), 164–173. https://doi.org/10.1002/chp.21181

Kuzich, S., Groves, R., Hara, S., & Pelliccione, L. (2010). *Building team capacity: Sustaining quality in assessment and moderation practices in a fully on-line unit*. Paper presented at the ATN Assessment Conference.

Kwak, Y. H. (2005). A brief history of project management. In G. Carayannis, Y. H. Kwak, & F. T. Anbari (Eds.), *The story of managing projects* Retrieved from http://home.gwu.edu/~kwak/PM_History.pdf

Laaksonen, R., Bates, I., & Duggan, C. (2007). Training, clinical medication review performance and self-assessed competence: Investigating influences. *Pharmacy Education, 7*(3), 257–265. https://doi.org/10.1080/15602210701610367

Labaree, D. F. (2006). Mutual subversion: A short history of the liberal and the professional in American higher education. *History of Education Quarterly, 46*(1), 1–15.

Lahenius, K. (2012). Communities of practice supporting doctoral studies. *The International Journal of Management Education, 10*, 29–38.

Lahenius, K., & Martinuso, M. (2011). Different types of doctoral study processes. *Scandinavian Journal of Educational Research, 55*(6), 609–623.

Larkin, J. H., & Simon, H. A. (1987). Why a diagram is (sometimes) worth ten thousand words. *Cognitive Science, 11*, 65–99.

Larmour, P. (2012). *Interpreting corruption: Culture and politics in the Pacific Islands*. Honolulu: University of Hawaii Press.

Larson, E. W., & Gray, C. F. (2011). *Project management—The managerial process* (5th ed.). International Edition, NY: McGraw-Hill Irwin.

Lave, J., & Wenger, E. (1991). *Situated learning: Legitimate peripheral participation*. Cambridge: Cambridge University Press.

Law Society of Ireland. (2014). *The Solicitors' profession: Contribution to the Irish economy*. Fitzpatrick Associates Economic Consultants.

Lawless, E. (2014, March 10). Technology in education: If students aren't worried why are teachers? Teacher Network. *The Guardian*. Retrieved from http://www.pewglobal.org/2016/02/22/internet-access-growing-worldwide-but-remains-higher-in-advanced-economies/

Laycock, A., Walker, D., Harrison, N., & Brands, J. (2009). *Supporting Indigenous researchers: A practical guide for supervisors*. Darwin: Cooperative Research Centre for Aboriginal Health Retrieved from https://www.lowitja.org.au/sites/default/files/docs/supervisors_guide1_0.pdf

Lee, A. (2009). How are doctoral students supervised? Concepts of doctoral research supervision. *Studies in Higher Education, 33*(3), 267–281.

Lee, A., & Green, B. (2009). Supervision as metaphor. *Studies in Higher Education, 34*(6), 615–630.

Lee, A., Steketee, C., Rogers, G., & Moran, M. (2013). Towards a theoretical framework for curriculum development in health professional education. *Focus on Health Professional Education, 14*(3), 64–77.

Lee, D. H., & Olshavsky, R. W. (1994). Toward a predictive model of the consumer inference process: The role of expertise. *Psychology & Marketing, 11*(2), 109–127.

Lefebvre, H. (1991/1974). *The production of space* (D. Nicholson-Smith, Trans.). Oxford: Blackwell.

Lent, R. W., Sheu, H.-B., Singley, D., Schmidt, J. A., Schmidt, L. C., & Gloster, C. S. (2008, October). Longitudinal relations of self-efficacy to outcome expectations, interests, and major choice goals in engineering students. *Journal of Vocational Behavior, 73*(2), 328–335. https://doi.org/10.1016/j.jvb.2008.07.005

Levi, H. E. (1972). The place of professional education in the life of the university. *Ohio State Law Journal, 32*, 229–239.

Leydesdorff, L. (2008). The communication of meaning in anticipatory systems: A simulation study of the dynamics of intentionality in social interactions. In D. M. Dubois (Ed.), *Proceedings of the 8th International Conference on Computing Anticipatory Systems CASYS'07, Liège, Belgium, 6–11 August 2007* (Vol. 1051, pp. 33–49). Melville, NY: American Institute of Physics Conference Proceedings.

Lieberherr, E. (2013). *The role of throughput in the input-output legitimacy debate: Insights from public and private governance modes in the Swiss and English water sectors.* Paper presented at ICPP 2013, Panel 39: The New Policies of Privatization, June 26–28, Grenoble, France. Retrieved from http://archives.ippapublicpolicy.org/IMG/pdf/panel_39_s2_lieberherr.pdf

Lim, P. H., Gan, S., & Ng, H. K. (2010). Student evaluation of engineering modules for improved teaching-learning effectiveness. *Engineering Education, 5,* 52–63.

Lin, Q. (2008). Preservice teachers' learning experiences of constructing e-portfolios online. *Internet and Higher Education, 11,* 194–200.

Lincoln, Y. S., & Guba, E. (1985). *Naturalistic inquiry.* Beverly Hills, CA: Sage Publications.

Lind, G. (2008). The meaning and measurement of moral judgment competence: A dual-aspect model. In D. Fasko Jr. & W. Willis (Eds.), *Contemporary philosophical and psychological perspectives on moral development and education* (pp. 185–220). Creskill: Hampton Press Retrieved from https://www.uni-konstanz.de/ag-moral/pdf/Lind-2008_Meaning_measurement.pdf

Lindberg, M. (2014). Implications of the Bologna Process for throughput in the higher education sector: An empirical illustration based on a Finnish-British comparison. *European Journal of Education, 49*(2), 259–271.

Litchfield, B. C., & Dempsey, J. V. (2015, Summer). Authentic assessment of knowledge, skills, and attitudes. *New Directions for Teaching & Learning, 2015*(142), 65–80. https://doi.org/10.1002/tl.20130

Liu, S. (2016). Higher education quality assessment and university change: A theoretical approach. In S. Liu (Ed.), *Quality assurance and institutional transformation, the Chinese experience* (pp. 15–46). Springer.

Lloyd, S., Byrne, M., & McCoy, T. (2012). Faculty-perceived barriers of online education. *MERLOT Journal of Online Learning and Teaching, 8*(1), 1–12.

Locke, J. (1689/1952). *An enquiry concerning human understanding*. Chicago: Encyclopedia Britannica.

Loftin, C., Newman, S. D., Dumas, B. P., Gilden, G., & Bond, M. L. (2012). Perceived barriers to success for minority nursing students: An integrative review. *International Scholarly Research Network*, 9. https://doi.org/10.5402/2012/806543

Lomas, L. (2004). Embedding quality: The challenges for higher education. *Quality Assurance in Education, 12*(4), 157–165.

London, M. (1993). Relationships between career motivation, empowerment, and support for career development. *Journal of Occupational and Organizational Psychology, 66*, 55–69. https://doi.org/10.1111/j.2044-8325.1993.tb00516.x

Long, T. B. (2012). Overview of teaching strategies for cultural competence in nursing students. *Journal of Cultural Diversity, 19*(3), 102–108.

Lopez-Fernandez, O., & Rodriguez-Illera, J. (2009). Investigating university students' adaptation to a digital learner course portfolio. *Computers & Education, 52*, 608–616.

Loue, S., Wilson-Delfosse, A., & Limbach, K. (2015). Identifying gaps in the cultural competence/sensitivity components of an undergraduate medical school curriculum: A needs assessment. *Journal of Immigrant and Minority Health, 17*(5), 1412–1419. https://doi.org/10.1007/s10903-014-0102-z

Lowi, T. J. (1972). Four systems of policy, politics and choice. *Public Administration Review, 32*(4), 314–325.

Lucas, B., & Hanson, J. (2014). Thinking like an engineer: Using engineering habits of mind to redesign engineering education for global competitiveness. In *SEFI, 42nd Annual Conference*, Birmingham, UK.

Lucas, B., Hanson, J., & Claxton, G. (2014). *Thinking like an engineer: Implications for the education system*. A report for the Royal Academy of Engineering Standing Committee for Education and Training. Royal Academy of Engineering, UK.

Luhmann, N. (1995). *Social systems* (J. Bednarz, Jr. & D. Baecker, Trans.). Stanford, CA: Stanford University Press.

Luhmann, N. (1997). The limits of steering. *Theory, Culture and Society, 14*(1), 41–57.

Lund, K. D., Berland, A., & Huda, N. (2013). Teaching nurses in Bangladesh. *American Journal of Nursing, 113*(8), 66–70.

Lunenburg, F. C. (2011). Theorizing about curriculum: Conceptions and definitions. *International Journal of Scholarly Intellectual Diversity, 13*(1), 1–6.

Lusted, D. (1986). Why pedagogy? *Screen, 27*(5), 2–14.

Lynch, S. (2017). *European policy on teaching and learning in higher education.* Presentation to EUA 1st European Learning and Teaching Forum, Pierre and Marie Curie University, Paris.

M.St. nr 13. (2011–2012). Utdanning for velferd. Samspill i praksis. Retrieved from https://www.regjeringen.no/contentassets/ac91ff2dedee43e1be825fb-097d9aa22/no/pdfs/stm201120120013000dddpdfs.pdf (in Norwegian)

M.St. nr. 10. (2012–2013). God kvalitet—Trygge tjenester. Retrieved from http://www.regjeringen.no/no/dokumrnt/meld-st-10-20122013/id7090251 (in Norwegian)

Macfarlane, B. (2012). Reframing student academic freedom: A capability perspective. *Higher Education, 63*, 719–732.

Macnaught, L., Maton, K., Martin, J. R., & Matruglio, E. (2013). Jointly constructing semantic waves: Implications for teacher training. *Linguistics and Education, 24*, 50–63.

Maier-Lorentz, M. (2008). Transcultural nursing: Its importance in nursing practice. *Journal of Cultural Diversity, 15*(1), 37–43.

Male, S. A., Bush, M. B., & Chapman, E. S. (2011). An Australian study of generic competencies required by engineers. *European Journal of Engineering Education, 36*(2), 151–163.

Malone, K., & Supri, S. (2012). A critical time for medical education: The perils of competence-based reform of the curriculum. *Advances in Health Sciences Education, 17*(2), 241–246.

Manathunga, C. (2015). Intercultural doctoral supervision: The centrality of place, time and other forms of knowledge. *Arts & Humanities in Higher Education, 0*(0), 1–12.

Mancuso-Murphy, J. (2007). Distance education in nursing: An integrated review of online nursing students' experiences with technology-delivered instruction. *Journal of Nursing Education, 46*(6), 252–260.

Mandernach, J. (2012). *Indicators of engagement in online classroom*. Madison, WI: Magna Publication.

Manser, T. (2009). Teamwork and patient safety in dynamic domains of healthcare: A review of the literature. *Acta Anaesthesiologica Scandinavica, 53*(2), 143–151. https://doi.org/10.1111/j.1399-6576.2008.01717

Manzo, K. (2002, May 9). E-defining education. *Education Week*, p. 38.

Markauskaite, L., & Goodyear, P. (2016). *Epistemic fluency and professional education*. Dordrecht, The Netherlands: Springer.

Marsh, H. W., & Cheng, J. H. S. (2008). Dimensionality, multi-level structure and differentiation at the level of the university and discipline: Preliminary results. Retrieved from https://www.heacademy.ac.uk/resource/national-student-survey-teaching-uk-universities-dimensionality-multilevel-structure-and

Marsh, H. W., Ginns, P., Morin, A. J. S., Nagengast, B., & Martin, A. J. (2011). Use of student ratings to benchmark universities: Multilevel modelling of responses to the Australian Course Experience Questionnaire (CEQ). *Journal of Educational Psychology, 103*, 733–748.

Marsh, H. W., & Roche, L. (1993). The use of students' evaluations and an individually structured intervention to enhance university teaching effectiveness. *American Education Research Journal, 30*, 217–251.

Marshall, C., & Rossman, G. B. (2016). *Designing qualitative research* (6th ed.). Thousand Oaks, CA: Sage Publications.

Marshall, S., & Flanagan, B. (2010). Simulation-based education for building clinical teams. *Journal of Emergencies, Trauma and Shock, 3*(4), 360–368.

Marsico, G. (2012). The double uncertainty: Trajectories and professional identity in changing contexts. *Culture & Psychology, 18*(1), 121–132.

Martin, D. E., & Kipling, A. (2006). Factors shaping Aboriginal nursing students' experiences. *Nurse Education Today, 26*(8), 688–696.

Martin, M., & Stella, A. (2007). *External quality assurance in higher education: Making choices*. Paris: UNESCO, International Institute for Educational Planning.

Martin, R. (Host). (2014, November 18). *First Contact* [Television broadcast]. Sydney, NSW: Special Broadcasting Service Corporation (SBS). Retrieved from http://www.sbs.com.au/programs/first-contact

Mathews, M. R. (2004). Accounting curricula: Does professional accreditation lead to uniformity within Australian bachelor's degree programmes? *Accounting Education, 13*(Suppl. 1), 71–89. https://doi.org/10.1080/0963928042000310805

Maton, K. (2009). Cumulative and segmented learning: Exploring the role of curriculum structures in knowledge building. *British Journal of Sociology of Education, 31*(1), 43–57.

Maton, K. (2014). *Knowledge and knowers: Towards a realist sociology of education*. London: Routledge.

Maturana, H., & Varela, F. J. (1980). *Autopoiesis and cognition: The realization of the living*. Dordrecht, The Netherlands: D. Reidel Publishing Company.

McCarthy, W. (2006). Ethics in education—Which ethics? *Contemporary PNG Studies, 5*, 96–108.

McConvell, P., Keen, I., & Hendery, R. (2013). *Kinship systems: Change and reconstruction*. Salt Lake City: The University of Utah Press.

McCormack, C. (2004). Tensions between student and institutional conceptions of postgraduate research. *Studies in Higher Education, 29*(3), 319–334.

McCurry, M. K., Revell, S. M. H., & Roy, S. C. (2010). Knowledge for the good of the individual and society: Linking philosophy, disciplinary goals, theory, and practice. *Nursing Philosophy, 11*(1), 42–52. https://doi.org/10.1111/j.1466-769X.2009.00423.x

McDonald, H. (2006). East Kimberley concepts of health and illness: A contribution to intercultural health programs in northern Australia. *Australian Aboriginal Studies, 2006*(2), 86–97.

McEwen, C., & Trede, F. (2016). Educating deliberate professionals: Beyond reflective and deliberative practitioners. In F. Trede & C. McEwen (Eds.), *Educating the deliberate professional: Preparing for future practices* (pp. 223–230). New York: Springer.

McGregor, R. (1996). An Aboriginal Caucasian: Some uses for racial kinship in early twentieth century Australia. *Australian Aboriginal Studies, 1*, 11–20.

McInnis, C. (2005). *The Australia qualifications framework. Public Policy for Academic Quality Research Program*. Chapel Hill: University of North Carolina Retrieved from http://www.unc.edu

McKenna, H. (1997). *Nursing theories and models*. London: Routledge.

McKeown, M., & Carey, L. (2015). Editorial: Democratic leadership: A charming solution for nursing's legitimacy crisis. *Journal of Clinical Nursing, 24*(3–4), 315–317.

McKinley, E., Grant, B., Middleton, S., Irwin, K., & Williams, L. R. T. (2011). Working at the interface: Indigenous students' experience of undertaking doctoral studies in Aotearoa New Zealand. *Equity & Excellence in Education, 44*(1), 115–132.

McLean, M., & Walker, M. (2016). A capabilities approach to educating the deliberate professional: Theory and practice. In F. Trede & C. McEwen (Eds.), *Educating the deliberate professional: Preparing for future practices* (pp. 141–155). New York: Springer.

McLeod, P. J., Meagher, T., Steinert, Y., Schuwirth, L., & McLeod, A. H. (2004). Clinical teachers' tacit knowledge of basic pedagogic principles. *Medical Teacher, 26*, 23–27.

McMahon, N., & Henman, M. (2007). *Introduction of competency based assessment to MSc in hospital pharmacy programme.* Paper presented at the Monash and King's Pharmacy Education Symposium 2007, Prato, Italy.

McMullan, M. (2005). Students' perceptions on the use of portfolios in pre-registration nursing education: A questionnaire survey. *International Journal of Nursing Studies, 43*(3), 333–343.

Mduma, E. R., et al. (2015). Frequent brief on-site simulation training and reduction in 24h neonatal mortality—An educational intervention study. *Resuscitation, 93*, 1–7.

Melville, C., Rees, M., Brookfield, D., & Anderson, J. (2004). Portfolios for assessment of paediatric specialist registrars. *Medical Education, 38*, 1117–1125.

Merriam, S. B. (2009). *Qualitative research: A guide to design and implementation.* San Francisco, CA: Jossey-Bass.

Merriam, S. B., & Bierema, L. L. (2013). *Adult learning: Linking theory and practice.* San Francisco: John Wiley & Sons.

Merrifield, N. (2016, August 31). Best and worst UK universities for nursing, as rated by students.

Merrow, E. W. (2011). *Industrial megaprojects—Concepts, strategies and practices for success.* Hoboken, NJ: Wiley.

Mészáros, K., Barnett, M., McDonald, K., Wehring, H., Evans, D., Sasaki-Hill, D., & Knapp, K. (2009). Progress examination for assessing students' readiness for advanced pharmacy practice experiences. *American Journal of Pharmaceutical Education, 73*(6), 1–109.

Meyer, J., Knight, D., Baldock, T., Kizil, M., O'Moore, L., & Callaghan, D. (2012). Scoping metalearning opportunity in the first three years of engineering. In *Profession of Engineering Education: Advancing Teaching, Research and Careers: 23rd Annual Conference of the Australasian Association for Engineering Education.*

Mezirow, J. (1997). Transformative learning: Theory to practice. In P. Cranton (Ed.), *Transformative learning in action: Insights from practice—New directions for adult and continuing education, No. 74.* (pp. 5–12). San Francisco, CA: Jossey-Bass.

Mezirow, J. (2000). Learning to think like an adult: Core concepts of Transformation Theory. In J. Mezirow (Ed.), *Learning as transformation: Critical perspectives on a theory in progress* (pp. 3–34). San Francisco, CA: Jossey-Bass.

Mihelcic, J. R., Crittenden, J. C., Small, M. J., Shonnard, D. R., Hokanson, D. R., Zhang, Q., ... Schnoor, J. L. (2003, December 1). Sustainability science and engineering: The emergence of a new metadiscipline. *Environmental Science & Technology, 37*(23), 5314–5324.

Miles, R. E., & Snow, C. C. (1978). *Organizational strategy, structure, and process.* New York: McGraw-Hill.

Miller, G. (1990). The assessment of clinical skills, competence, performance. *Academic Medicine, 65*(9), S63–S67.

Miller, G. A. (1956). The magical number seven, plus or minus two: Some limits on our capacity for processing information. *Psychological Review, 101*(2), 343–352.

Mitchell, R. K., Agle, B. R., & Wood, D. J. (1997). Toward a theory of stakeholder identification and salience: Defining the principle of who and what really counts. *Academy of Management Review, 22*(4), 853–886.

Mizikaci, F. (2006). A systems approach to program evaluation model for quality in higher education. *Quality Assurance in Education, 14*(1), 37–53.

Mockler, N. (2018). *Teaching quality is not teacher quality. How we talk about 'quality' matters, here's why.* EduResearch Matters (blog). Retrieved from Australian Education Research Association website http://www.aare.edu.au/blog/?p=2845&utm_campaign=website

Moll, L. C., & González, N. (1994). Lessons from the research with language— Minority children. *Journal of Reading Behavior, 26*(4), 439–456.

Moore, M. G. (1989). Editorial: Three types of interaction. *The American Journal of Distance Education, 3*(2), 1–7.

Morley, L. (2001). Producing new workers: Quality, equality and employability in higher education. *Quality in Higher Education, 7*(2), 131–138.

Motola, I., et al. (2013). Simulation in healthcare education: A best evidence practical guide. AMEE Guide No. 82. *Medical Teacher, 35,* 1511–1530.

Motycka, C., Rose, R., Ried, D., & Brazeau, G. (2010). Self-assessment in pharmacy and health science education and professional practice. *American Journal of Pharmaceutical Education, 74*(5), 1–7.

Mumm, K., Karm, M., & Remmik, M. (2015). Assessment for learning: Why assessment does not always support student teachers' learning. *Journal of Further and Higher Education*, 1–24. https://doi.org/10.1080/03098 77x.2015.1062847

Murphy, C. F., Allen, D., Allenby, B. J., Crittenden, J. C., Davidson, I. C., & Hendrickson, C. (2009). Sustainability in engineering education and research at US universities. *Environmental Science & Technology, 43*(15), 5558–5564.

Murphy, P. (2008). Defining pedagogy. In K. Hall, P. Murphy, & J. Soler (Eds.), *Pedagogy and practice: Culture and identities*. London: SAGE.

Murray, C., & Lawry, J. (2011, August). Maintenance of professional currency: Perceptions of occupational therapists. *Australian Occupational Therapy Journal, 58*(4), 261–269. https://doi.org/10.1111/j.1440-1630.2011.00927.x

Namaliu, R., & Garnaut, R. (2010). *PNG universities review: Report to Prime Ministers Somare and Rudd*. Retrieved from dfat.gov.au/about-us/publications/documents/png-universities-review.doc

Nash, R., Chalmers, L., Brown, N., Jackson, S., & Peterson, G. (2015). An international review of program wide use of competency standards in pharmacy education. *Pharmacy Education Journal, 15*(1), 131–141.

Nasser, R. N., & Romanowski, M. H. (2016). Social justice and the engineering profession: Challenging engineering education to move beyond the technical. In M. Abdulwahed, M. O. Hasna, & J. E. Froyd (Eds.), *Advances in engineering education in the Middle East and North Africa: Current status, and future insights* (pp. 409–428). Zug, Switzerland: Springer International Publishing.

National Competency Standards Framework for Pharmacists in Australia. (2010) Retrieved January 30, 2015, from http://www.psa.org.au/supporting-practice/national-competency-standards

National Employer Survey. (2015). *Employers' views on Irish Further and Higher Education and Training Outcomes*. Dublin: Higher Education Authority, SOLAS, QQI, Department of Education and Skills.

National Health and Medical Research Council [NHMRC]. (2003). *Values and ethics: Guidelines for ethical conduct in Aboriginal and Torres Strait Islander health research*. Canberra: Commonwealth of Australia.

NCHE (The Norwegian Association of Higher Education Institutions). (2016). *Kvalitet i praksisstudiene i helse- og sosialfaglig høyere utdanning: Praksisprosjektet [Quality in the practice studies in health and social provision higher education. The Practice Project]*. Oslo: Universitets- og høgskolerådet.

Nelson, S., Tassone, M., & Hodge, B. D. (2014). *Creating the healthcare team of the future. The Toronto model for interprofessional education and practice*. Ithaca, NY: Cornell University Press.

Nerad, M. (2012). Conceptual approaches to doctoral education: A community of practice. *Alternation, 19*(2), 57–72.

Nerland, M., & Prøitz, T. S. (Eds.). (2018, January). *Quality in higher education: Case studies of educational practices in eight courses*. NIFU Report 2018:1. Oslo: Nordic Institute for Studies in Innovation, Research and Education.

Newman, D. (2017, July 18). Top 6 Digital Transformation trends in education. *CMO Network, Forbes*. Retrieved from https://www.forbes.com/sites/danielnewman/2017/07/18/top-6-digital-transformation-trends-in-education/#404e72342a9a

Newman, S. (2001). Derrida's deconstruction of authority. *Philosophy & Social Criticism, 27*(3), 1–20.

Nguyen, T., & Walker, M. (2014). Sustainable assessment for lifelong learning. *Assessment & Evaluation in Higher Education*, 1–15. https://doi.org/10.1080/02602938.2014.985632

Nicholson, N. (2002). Policy choices and the uses of state power: The work of Theodore J. Lowi. *Policy Sciences, 35*(2), 163–177.

Nicol, D. J., & Macfarlane-Dick, D. (2006). Formative assessment and self-regulated learning: A model and seven principles of good feedback practice. *Studies in Higher Education, 31*(2), 199–218. https://doi.org/10.1080/03075070600572090

Noordegraaf, M. (2011a). Remaking professionals? How associations and professional education connect professionalism and organizations. *Current Sociology, 59*(4), 465–488.

Noordegraaf, M. (2011b, October). Risky business: How professionals and professional fields (must) deal with organizational issues. *Organization Studies, 32*(10), 1349–1371. https://doi.org/10.1177/0170840611416748

Norwegian Ministry of Education and Research. (2008). *Rammeplan for sykepleierutdanning (National curriculum Regulations for Nursing programs)*. Oslo: Norwegian Ministry of Education and Research.

NOU. (2015: 3). *Advokaten i samfunnet—Lov om advokater og andre som yter rettslig bistand. [The Lawyer in Society—The Law concerning lawyers and others who provide legal advice]*. Oslo: Ministry of Justice and Public Security.

Novak, J. D. (2010). *Learning, creating, and using knowledge: Concept maps as facilitative tools in schools and corporations* (2nd ed.). Oxford: Routledge.

Novak, J. D., & Cañas, A. J. (2006). The origins of concept maps and the continuing evolution of the tool. *Information Visualization Journal, 5*(3), 175–184.

Novak, J. D., & Cañas, A. J. (2007). Theoretical origins of concept maps, how to construct them, and uses in education. *Reflecting Education, 3*(1), 29–42.

Novak, J. D., & Symington, D. J. (1982). Concept mapping for curriculum development. *Victoria Institute for Educational Research Bulletin, 48*, 3–11.

Nursing and Midwifery Board of Australia (NMBA). 2016. *Continuing Professional Development Registration Standard*. Retrieved from http://www.nursingmidwiferyboard.gov.au/Codes-Guidelines-Statements/FAQ/CPD-FAQ-for-nurses-and-midwives.aspx

Nursing and Midwifery Council. (2010). *Standards for pre-registration nursing education*. London: NMC.

O'Donovan, B., Price, M., & Rust, C. (2004). Know what I mean? Enhancing student understanding of assessment standards and criteria. *Teaching in Higher Education, 9*(3), 325–335. https://doi.org/10.1080/1356251042000216642

OECD. (2004). *Review of National Policies for Education: Review of Higher Education in Ireland Examiners' Report*. OECD Retrieved from http://www.hea.ie/sites/default/files/oecd_review_of_higher_education_2004.pdf

Oliver, B. (2016). *Assuring graduate capabilities*. Retrieved from http://www.assuringgraduatecapabilities.com/

O'Meara, J., & MacDonald, D. (2004). Power, prestige and pedagogic identity: A tale of two programs recontextualizing teacher standards. *Asia-Pacific Journal of Teacher Education, 32*(2), 111–127. https://doi.org/10.1080/1359866042000234214

Onweugbuzie, A., Witcher, A., Collins, K., Filer, J., Wiedmaier, C., & Moore, C. (2007). Students' perceptions of characteristics of effective college teachers: A validity study of a teaching evaluation form using a mixed-method analysis. *American Educational Research Journal, 44*(1), 113–160.

O'Shea, A. (2008). *A developmental approach to work- integrated learning*. Unpublished manuscript. Toowoomba, QLD: University of Southern Queensland.

O'Shea, A. (2014). Models of WIL. In S. Ferns (Ed.), *Work integrated learning in the curriculum* (pp. 7–14). Milperra, NSW: HERDSA.

Østergaard, D., Dieckmann, P., & Lippert, A. (2011). Simulation and CRM. *Best Practice & Research Clinical Anaesthesiology, 25*, 239–249.

Osterman, K. F., & Kottkamp, R. B. (2004). *Reflective practice for educators: Improving schooling through professional development*. Newbury Park, CA: Corwin Press, Inc.

Oswald, E. (2017, May 3). 5 Trends that will change the world in 2017. *Digital Trends*. Retrieved from https://www.digitaltrends.com/cool-tech/technology-trends-2017/

Owen, J. M. (2007). *Program evaluation—Forms and approaches* (3rd ed.). New York: The Guildford Press.

Padró, F. F. (1988). *Quality circles and their existence in present-day school administration*. Doctoral dissertation, The University of Arizona.

Padró, F. F. (2018). The doctoral studies paradox: Indigenous cultural paradigms versus western-based research practices. In R. Erwee, M. A. Harmes, M. K. Harmes, P. A. Danaher, & F. F. Padró (Eds.), *Postgraduate education in higher education* (pp. 589–600). Singapore: Springer Nature Singapore.

Padró, F. F., & Green, J. H. (2018). Education administrators in Wonderland: Figuring out how policy-making and regulatory compliance when making decisions. In K. Trimmer, R. Dixon, & Y. Findlay (Eds.), *Education and the law: Considering the legal context of schools* (pp. 141–166). Dordrecht, Netherlands: Springer International Publishing AG.

Padró, F. F., & Hawke, M. F. (2003). A perceptual model of organization behavior. *National Social Sciences Journal, 19*(2), 102–112.

Padró, F. F., Hawke, M. F., & Hawke, L. M. (2016). Assessment and quality: Policy-steering and the making of a *deus ex machina*. In J. Bower & P. L. Thomas (Eds.), *De-testing and de-grading schools: Authentic alternatives to accountability and standardization* (Rev. ed., pp. 33–50). New York: Peter Lang.

Paige, J. B., & Morin, K. H. (2013). Simulation fidelity and cueing: A systematic review of the literature. *Clinical Simulation in Nursing, 9*, 481–489.

Pamela, L. (2011). Technology strategies for teaching and learning in education and the workplace. In *International Conference on E-Learning at the Workplace, ICELW 2011*.

Papathanasiou, I. V., Tsaras, K., & Sarafis, P. (2013). Views and perceptions of nursing students on their clinical learning environment: Teaching and learning. *Nurse Education Today, 34*(1), 57–60. https://doi.org/10.1016/j.nedt.2013.02.007

Parsons, T. (1963). On the concepts of political power. *Proceedings of the American Philosophical Society, 107*(3), 232–262.

Parsons, T. (1981/1951). *The social system*. London: Routledge.

Parsons, T., Bales, R. F., & Shils, E. A. (1953). *Working papers in the theory of action*. New York: Free Press.

Pascale, R. T. (1999). Surfing at the edge of chaos. *Sloan Management Review, 40*(3), 83–94.

Patel, V. L., Arocha, J. F., & Kaufman, D. R. (1999). Expertise and tacit knowledge in medicine. In R. J. Sternberg & J. A. Horvath (Eds.), *Tacit knowledge in professional practice: Researcher and practitioner perspectives* (pp. 75–99). Mahwah, NJ: Lawrence Erlbaum.

Patrick, J. P., & Stanley, E. C. (1998). Teaching and research quality indicators and the shaping of higher education. *Research in Higher Education, 39*(1), 19–41.

Peacock, S., & Murray, S. (2009). Learners' initial expectations and experiences of ePortfolios: A pilot study. *Brookes eJournal of Learning and Teaching, 2*(4).

Pearson, M. (1999). The changing environment for doctoral education in Australia: Implications for quality management, improvement and innovation. *Higher Education Research and Development, 18*(3), 269–287.

Pearson, M., & Kayrooz, C. (2004). Enabling critical reflection on research supervisory practice. *International Journal for Academic Development, 9*(1), 99–116.

Peirce, C. S. (1958). *Values on a universe of chance: Charles S. Peirce: Selected writings* (P.P. Wiener, Ed.). New York: Dover Publications.

Peirce, C. S. (1994). *The collected papers of Charles Sanders Peirce: Electronic Edition* (C. Hartshorne & P. Wiess, Eds, Vols. 1–6, 1935; A. W. Burk, Ed., Vols. 7–8, 1958). Retrieved from https://colorysemiotica.files.wordpress.com/2014/08/peirce-collectedpapers.pdf

Petit, P., Foriers, A., & Rombaut, B. (2008). The introduction of new teaching methods in pharmacy education—II. The starting point. *Pharmacy Education, 8*(1), 19–28.

Pfleger, D., McHattie, L., Diack, H., McCaig, D., & Stewart, D. (2008). Views, attitudes and self-assessed training needs of Scottish community pharmacists to public health practice and competence. *Pharmacy World & Science, 30*(6), 801–809. https://doi.org/10.1007/s11096-008-9228-1

Pharmaceutical Society of Australia. (2014). *Code of ethics for pharmacists*. Retrieved Aprlil 26, 2015, from http://www.psa.org.au/membership/ethics

Pharmacy Board of Australia. (2015). *Revised Registration Standard: Continuing professional development*. Retrieved December 21, 2015, from http://www.pharmacyboard.gov.au/News/2015-10-30-registration-standards.aspx

Pharmacy Board of Australia. (2016). *Obligations of a registered pharmacist*. Retrieved June 3, 2016, from http://www.pharmacyboard.gov.au/Registration.aspx

Pidgeon, M. (2008). *It takes more than good intentions: Institutional accountability and responsibility to Indigenous higher education.* Unpublished doctoral dissertation. Vancouver, BC: University of British Columbia.

Pidgeon, M., Archibald, J.-A., & Hawkey, C. (2014). Relationships matter: Supporting Aboriginal graduate students in British Columbia, Canada. *Canadian Journal of Higher Education, 44*(1), 1–21.

Pidgeon, M., & Hardy Cox, D. G. (2002). Researching with aboriginal peoples: *Practices and principles. Canadian Journal of Native Education, 26*(2), 96–106.

Pijl-Zieber, E. M., & Hagen, B. (2011). Towards culturally relevant nursing education for aboriginal students. *Nurse Education Today, 31*(6), 595–600. https://doi.org/10.1016/j.nedt.2010.10.014

Pincombe, J., McKellar, L., Weise, M., Grinter, E., & Beresford, G. (2010). ePortfolio in Midwifery: "The way of the future". *Women and Birth, 23*(3), 94–102.

Pitsoe, V. J., & Letseka, M. (2018). Heidegger and Althusser on quality management systems in open and distance learning. In L. Kounis (Ed.), *Quality Management Systems: A selective presentation of case-studies showcasing its evolution* (pp. 47–60). London: IntechOpen.

Plaza, C., Draugalis, J., Slack, M., Skrepnek, G., & Sauer, K. (2007). Curriculum mapping in program assessment and evaluation. *American Journal of Pharmaceutical Education, 71*(2), 1–20.

Polanyi, M. (1966). *The tacit dimension.* Garden City, NY: Doubleday & Company.

Pond, W. (2002). Distributed education in the 21st century: Implications for quality assurance. *Online Journal of Distance Learning Administrators, V*(II), 1.

Ponzer, S., Hylin, U., Kusoffsky, A., et al. (2004). Interprofessional training in the context of clinical practice: Goals and students' perceptions on clinical education wards. *Medical Education, 38,* 727–736.

Pool, L. D., & Sewell, P. (2007). They key to employability: Developing a practical model of graduate employability. *Education and Training, 49,* 277–289. https://doi.org/10.1108/004//910710754435

Popkewitz, T. S. (2001). The production of reason and power: Curriculum history and intellectual traditions. In T. S. Popkewitz, B. M. Franklin, & M. A. Pereyra (Eds.), *Cultural history and education: Critical essays on knowledge and schooling* (pp. 151–183). New York: Routledge Falmer.

Popkewitz, T. S. (2007). Alchemies and governing: Or, questions about the questions we ask. *Educational Philosophy and Theory, 39*(1), 64–83.

Porsanger, J. (2004). An essay about Indigenous methodology. *Nordlit, 15, 105–121.* Tromsø: Tromsø University.

Porsanger, J. (2010). *Self-determination and Indigenous research: Capacity building on our own terms*. Paper submitted at the United Nations Department of Economic and Social Affairs International Expert Group Meeting, Indigenous Peoples: Development with Culture and Identity Articles 3 and 32 of the United Nations Declaration on the Rights of Indigenous Peoples, New York, 12–14 January 2010, p. 12.

Powell, S., & Greenberg, N. (2009). EPortfolio: A tool to support best practice in occupational therapy education. *Education Special Interest Section Quarterly, 19*(1), 2–4.

Press, N., & Padró, F. F. (2017, June 27–30). Educating for a profession: Curriculum as transformation and curriculum transformation. In R. G. Walker & S. B. Bedford (Eds.), *Research and development in higher education: Curriculum transformation* (Vol. 40, pp. 313–322). Sydney, Australia: Higher Education Research and Development Society of Australasia (HERDSA).

Press, N. I. (2018). *Educating for a profession: A phenomenological case study of professional practice preparation for the Nursing discipline from a sociocultural perspective*. Unpublished doctoral dissertation. Toowoomba, QLD: University of Southern Queensland.

Price, B. (2010). Disseminating best practice through teaching. *Nursing Standard, 24*(27), 35–41.

Prince, M. J., & Felder, R. M. (2006, April). Inductive teaching and learning methods: Definitions, comparisons, and research bases. *Journal of Engineering Education, 95*(2), 123–138. https://doi.org/10.1002/j.2168-9830.2006.tb00884.x

Professions Australia. (2015). Ethics resource centre; Code of ethics. *Code Principles*. Retrieved April 7, 2015, from http://www.professions.com.au/codeprinciples.html

Project Management Institute. (2013). *A guide to the project management body of knowledge* (5th ed.). Newtown Square, PA: Project Management Institute.

Pumwa, J. (2010, November 12–18). Engineering ethics: A necessary attribute for Papua New Guinea engineers. In *ASME 2010 International Mechanical Engineering Congress and Exposition, Volume 6: Engineering Education and Professional Development* (pp. 223–231). https://doi.org/10.1115/IMECE2010-37023

Pushiter, J. (2016, February 22). *Smartphone ownership and internet usage continues to climb in emerging economies*. Pew Research Center: Global Attitudes & Trends. Retrieved from http://www.pewglobal.org/2016/02/22/internet-access-growing-worldwide-but-remains-higher-in-advanced-economies/

Pyhältö, K., Toom, A., Stubb, J., & Lonka, K. (2012). Challenges of becoming a scholar: A study of doctoral students of becoming a scholar. *ISRN Education, 2012,* 1–12. https://doi.org/10.5402/2012/934941

Pyhältö, K., Vekkaila, J., & Keskinen, J. (2012). Exploring the fit between doctoral students' and supervisors' perceptions of resources and challenges vis-à-vis the doctoral journey. *International Journal of Doctoral Studies, 7,* 395–414.

Pymount, S. (2016). *The effectiveness of the National Student Survey and local institutional surveys as a management tool for setting effective strategies in higher education.* Thesis submitted for Doctor of Business Administration, Nottingham Business School, January 2016.

Quality and Qualifications Ireland. (2014). *Education and Employers: Joining forces to promote quality and innovation across further and higher education and training. A strategic approach to employer engagement.* Retrieved October 14, 2017, from www.qqi.ie

Quality and Qualifications Ireland. (2016). *Quality in an era of diminishing resources' Irish Higher Education 2008–15. An analysis of published institutionally—Organised quality review reports of academic departments, schools and programmes in Irish public higher education institutions.* Retrieved September 15, 2017, from www.qqi.ie

Quality Assurance Agency. (2012). *Chapter B5: Student engagement.* UK Quality Code for Higher Education.

Quinn, S., Gaughran, W., & Burke, S. (2009, June). Environmental sustainability in engineering education—Quo Vadis? *International Journal of Sustainable Engineering, 2*(2), 143–151.

Radio New Zealand. (2014, July 9). 'Critical shortage' of rural doctors in PNG. *Dateline Pacific.* Retrieved from http://www.radionz.co.nz/international/programmes/datelinepacific/audio/20140917/'critical-shortage'-of-rural-doctors-in-png-doctor

Rae, S. B., & Wong, K. L. (2012). *Beyond integrity: A Judeo-Christian approach to business ethics* (3rd ed.). Grand Rapids, MI: Zondervan.

Raes, K. (1997). Teaching professional ethics: A remark on method. *Ethical Perspectives, 4*(2), 243–245.

Rajagopalan, K. (2007). Derrida, deconstruction and education: Ethics of pedagogy and education edited by Peter Pericles Trifonas and Michael A. Peters. *British Journal of Educational Studies, 55*(1), 105–108. https://doi.org/10.1111/j.1467-8527.2007.367_8.x

Rall, M., & Dieckmann, P. (2005). Safety culture and crisis resource management in airway management: General principles to enhance patient safety in critical airway situations. *Best Practice & Research: Clinical Anaesthesiology, 19*(4), 539–557.

Raman, J. (2015). Mobile technology in nursing education: Where do we go from here? A review of the literature. *Nurse Education Today, 35*(5), 663–672 https://doi.org/10.1016/j.nedt.2015.01.018

Ramos, P., & Mota, C. (2014). Perceptions of success and failure factors in information technology projects: A study from Brazilian companies. *Procedia- Social and Behavioral Sciences, 119*, 349–357.

Ramsden, P. (1991). A performance indicator of teaching quality in higher education: The Course Experience Questionnaire. *Studies in Higher Education, 16*(2), 129–150.

Rawls, J. (1970). *A theory of justice.* Cambridge, MA: Belknap Press of Harvard University Press.

Readman, K., & Allen, B. (2013). *Practical planning and assessment.* South Melbourne, VIC: Oxford University Press.

Readman, K., & Ashford, T. (2012). *Connecting with curriculum renewal via 'natural mapping'.* Paper presented at the HERDSA, Hobart.

Reeves, C. A., & Bednar, D. A. (1994). Defining quality: Alternatives and implications. *The Academy of Management Review, Special Issue: "Total Quality", 19*(3), 419–445.

Reeves, S., Lewin, S., Espin, S., & Zwarenstein, M. (2010). *Interprofessional teamwork for health and social care.* Chichester, UK: Wiley- Blackwell.

Reeves, S., Perrier, L., Goldman, J., Freeth, D., & Zwarenstein, M. (2013). Interprofessional education: Effects on professional practice and healthcare outcomes (update). *Cochrane Database of Systematic Reviews, 2013*(3)., Art. No.: CD002213.

Reeves, S., Zwarenstein, M., Goldman, J., Barr, H., Freeth, D., et al. (2010). The effectiveness of interprofessional education: Key findings from a systematic review. *Journal of Interprofessional Care, 24*(3), 230–241.

Reeves, S., Zwarenstein, M., Goldman, J., Barr, H., Freeth, D., Hammick, M., & Koppel, I. (2009). Interprofessional education: Effects on professional practice and health care outcomes (Review). *Cochrane Database of Systematic Reviews, 23*(1), 1–22, CD002213.

Reid-Searl, K., Eaton, A., Vieth, L., & Happell, B. (2011). The educator inside the patient: Students' insights into the use of high fidelity silicone patient simulation. *Journal of Clinical Nursing, 20*(19–20), 2752–2760. https://doi.org/10.1111/j.1365-2702.2011.03795.x

Reidsema, C., Hadgraft, R., Cameron, I., & King, R. (2011). *Change strategies for educational transformation.* Paper presented at the Australasian Association 376 for Engineering Education Conference 2011: Developing engineers for social justice: Community involvement, ethics & sustainability, 5–7 December 2011, Fremantle, Western Australia.

Reis, N., & Villaume, S. (2002). The benefits, tensions and visions of portfolios as a wide scale assessment of teacher education. *Action in Teacher Education, 23*, 10–17.

Resnick, L. (1999). Making America smarter. *Education Week Century Series, 18*(40), 38–40.

Resnik, D. B. (2017). Examining the social benefits principle in research with human participants. *Health Care Analysis*. https://doi.org/10.1007/s10728-016-0326-2

Rhyl, G. (1963). *The concept of mind*. London: Penguin.

Rich, J. (2015). *Employability: Degrees of value*. London: HEPI.

Richardson, J., Grose, J., Doman, M., & Kelsey, J. (2014). The use of evidence-informed sustainability scenarios in the nursing curriculum: Development and evaluation of teaching methods. *Nurse Education Today, 34*, 490–493.

Rienties, B. (2014). Understanding academic resistance towards (online) student evaluation. *Assessment and Evaluation in Higher Education, 39*(8), 987–1001.

Rienties, B., & Toetenel, L. (2016). The impact of learning design on student behaviour, satisfaction and performance: A cross-institutional comparison across 151 modules. *Computers in Human Behavior, 60*, 333–341. https://doi.org/10.1016/j.chb.2016.02.074

Riley, L., Howard-Wagner, D., & Mooney, J. (2015). Kinship online: Engaging 'Cultural praxis' in a teaching and learning framework for cultural competence. *The Australian Journal of Indigenous Education*, 1–15. https://doi.org/10.1017/jie.2015.13

Riley, L., Howard-Wagner, D., Mooney, J., & Kutay, C. (2013). *Embedding aboriginal cultural knowledge in curriculum at university level through aboriginal community engagement* (pp. 251–276). Emerald Group Publishing Limited. https://doi.org/10.1108/S1479-3644(2013)0000014

Roberts, D., & Green, L. (2011). The theatre of high-fidelity simulation education. *Nurse Education Today, 31*(7), 694–698.

Robinson, A. (2010). *Trinity, evolution, and the metaphysical semiotics of C.S. Peirce*. Leiden, The Netherlands: Brill.

Robinson, M. (2015). *From old public administration to the new public service implications for public sector reform in developing countries*. Singapore: UNDP Global Centre for Public Service Excellence Retrieved from http://www.undp.org/content/undp/en/home/librarypage/capacity-building/global-centre-for-public-service-excellence/PS-Reform.html

Roest, H., & Rindfleisch, A. (2010). The influence of quality cues and typicality cues on restaurant purchase intention. *Journal of Retailing and Consumer Services, 17*, 10–18.

Rogers, A. (2014). *The base of the iceberg: Informal learning and its impact on formal and non-formal learning*. Opladen, Germany: Budrich.

Ronfeldt, M., & Grossman, P. (2008). Becoming a professional: Experimenting with possible selves in professional preparation. *Teacher Education Quarterly, 35*, 41–60.

Rosenberg, M. J. (2001). *E-learning: Strategies for delivering knowledge in the digital age*. New York: McGraw-Hill.

Rosenkoetter, M. M., & Milstead, J. A. (2010). A code of ethics for nurse educators: Revised. *Nurse Ethics, 17*(1), 137–139.

Ross, J. G. (2012). Simulation and psychomotor skill acquisition: A review of the literature. *Clinical Simulation in Nursing, 8*(9), e429–e435. https://doi.org/10.1016/j.ecns.2011.04.004

Ruiz, J., Qadri, S., Karides, M., Castillo, C., Milanez, M., & Roos, B. (2009). Fellows' perceptions of a mandatory reflective electronic portfolio in a geriatric medicine fellowship program. *Educational Gerontology, 35*, 634–652.

Rule, A. C. (2006). Editorial: The components of authentic learning. *Journal of Authentic Learning, 3*(1), 1–10.

Russell, C. K., Gregory, D. M., Care, W. D., & Hultin, D. (2007). Recognizing and avoiding intercultural miscommunication in distance education: A study of the experiences of Canadian faculty and Aboriginal nursing students. *Journal of Professional Nursing, 23*(6), 351–336.

Russell, J. S. (2013, June). Shaping the future of the civil engineering profession. *Journal of Construction Engineering and Management, 139*(6), 654–664. https://doi.org/10.1061/(ASCE)CO.1943-7862.0000600. Retrieved from http://ascelibrary.org/doi/10.1061/(ASCE)CO.1943-7862.0000600

Rust, C., Price, M., & O'Donovan, B. (2003). Improving student's learning by developing their understanding of assessment criteria and processes. *Assessment and Evaluation in Higher Education, 28*(2), 147–164. https://doi.org/10.1080/02602930301671

Sadler, D. (1989). Formative assessment and the design of instructional systems. *Instructional Science, 18*(2), 119–144.

Sadler, D. R. (2005). Interpretations of criteria-based assessment and grading in higher education. *Assessment & Evaluation in Higher Education, 30*(2), 175–194. https://doi.org/10.1080/0260293042000264262

Sahi, G., Gupta, M. C., & Patel, P. C. (2017). A measure of throughput orientation: Scale development and nomological validation. *Decision Sciences, 48*(3), 420–453.

Saks, M. (2012). Defining a profession: The role of knowledge and expertise. *Professions and Professionalism, 2*(1). https://doi.org/10.7577/pp.v2i1.151 Retrieved from https://journals.hioa.no/index.php/pp/article/view/151

Saks, M. (2015). Inequalities, marginality and the professions. *Current Sociology Review, 63*(6), 850–868.

Salas, E., Tannenbaum, S. I., Kraiger, K., & Smith-Jentsch, K. A. (2012). The science of training and development in organizations: What matters in practice. *Psychological Science, 13*(2), 74–101. https://doi.org/10.1177/1529 100612436661

Salmon, D., & Kelly, M. (2015). *Using concept mapping to foster adaptive expertise: Enhancing teacher metacognitive learning to improve student academic performance.* New York: Peter Lang.

Samanta, A., & Samanta, J. (2003). Professional issues: Legal standard of care: A shift from the traditional Bolam test. *Clinical Medicine, 3*(5), 443–446.

Sambell, K., McDowell, L., & Montgomery, C. (2013). *Designing authentic assessment for learning in higher education.* Abingdon, Oxon: Routledge.

Sargeant, J., Eva, K., Armson, H., Chesluk, B., Dornan, T., Holmboe, E., & van der Vleuten, C. (2011). Features of assessment learners use to make informed self-assessments of clinical performance. *Medical Education, 45*(6), 636–647.

Sarkisov, P. D. (1988). Professional education. In N. P. Tarasova (Ed.), *Quality of human resources: Education. Encyclopedia of life support systems: Volume 2* (pp. 60–66). Singapore: EOLLS Publishers and United Nations Educational, Scientific and Cultural Organization.

Sarmento, C. (2014). Interculturalism, multiculturalism, and intercultural studies: Questioning definitions and repositioning strategies. *Intercultural Pragmatics, 11*(4), 603–618. https://doi.org/10.1515/ip-2014-0026

Savickas, M. L. (1997). Career adaptability: An integrative construct for life-span, life-space theory. *The Career Development Quarterly, 45*, 247–259. https://doi.org/10.1002/j.2161-0045.1997.tb00469.x

Savin-Baden, M. (2008). *Learning spaces: Creating opportunities for knowledge creation in academic life.* Maidenhead, UK: Open University Press.

Sawyer, T., et al. (2016). More than one way to debrief: A critical review of healthcare simulation debriefing methods. *Journal of Society for Simulation in Healthcare, 11*(3), 209–217.

Schaffer, D. W. (2012). Models of situated action: Computer games and the problem of transfer. In C. Steinkuehler, K. Squire, & S. Barab (Eds.), *Games, learning, and society: Learning and meaning in the digital age* (pp. 403–431). Cambridge: Cambridge University Press.

Schneider, D. M., & Shapiro, W. (1989). Australian Aboriginal kinship: Cultural construction, deconstruction and misconstruction. *Man, 24*(1), 165–168.

Schneider, M., & Stern, E. (2010). The developmental relations between conceptual and procedural knowledge: A multimethod approach. *Developmental Psychology, 46*(1), 178–192.

Schofield, T., O'Brien, R., & Gilroy, J. (2013). Indigenous higher education: Overcoming barriers to participation in research higher degree programs. *Australian Aboriginal Studies, 2,* 13–28.

Scholes, J., Webb, C., Gray, M., Endacott, R., Miller, C., Jasper, M., & McMullan, M. (2004). Making portfolios work in practice. *Journal of Advanced Nursing, 46*(6), 595–603.

Schon, D. (1971). *Beyond the stable state.* New York: W.W. Norton & Co.

Schön, D. A. (1983). *The reflective practitioner: How professionals think in action.* New York: Basic Books.

Schön, D. A. (1987). *Educating the reflective practitioner.* San Francisco, CA: Jossey-Bass.

Schon, D. A. (1987). *Educating the reflective practitioner: Towards a new design for teaching and learning in the professions.* San Francisco, CA: Jossey-Bass.

Schön, D. A. (1988). From technical rationality to reflection in action. In J. Dowie & A. Elstein (Eds.), *Professional judgement.* Cambridge: Cambridge University Press.

Schumpeter, J. A. (2003). *Capitalism, socialism and democracy.* London: Routledge.

Schunk, D. (2003). Self-efficacy for reading and writing: Influence of modeling, goal setting, and self-evaluation. *Reading & Writing Quarterly, 19*(2), 159–172.

Schwarz, S., & Westerheijden, D. F. (2004). Accreditation in the framework of evaluation activities: A comparative study in the European higher education area. In S. Schwarz & D. F. Westerheijden (Eds.), *Accreditation and evaluation in the European higher education area.* Dordrecht, The Netherlands: Kluwer.

Seale, J. (2010). Doing student voice work in higher education: An exploration of the value of participatory methods. *British Educational Research Journal, 36*(6), 995–1015.

Seidl, D. (2004). *Luhmann's theory of autopoietic social systems.* Munich Business Research Paper 2004-2. Munich, Germany: Ludwig-Maximilians-Universität München.

Seipold, J., & Pachler, N. (2011). Evaluating mobile learning practice: Towards a framework for analysis of user-generated contexts with reference to the socio-cultural ecology of mobile learning. *Medienpädagogik, 19*, 1–13.

Sek, Y., Deng, H., McKay, E., & Qian, M. (2015). *Investigating the impact of learners' learning styles on the acceptance of open learner models for information sharing*. Australasian conference on Information Systems, 2015, Adelaide, Australia. Retrieved from https://arxiv.org/ftp/arxiv/papers/1606/1606.00747.pdf

Seltzer, B. (2010). *101 careers in public health*. New York: Springer Publishing Co Inc.

Sen, A. (1993). Capacity and well-being. In M. Nussbaum & A. Sen (Eds.), *The quality of life*. Oxford: Clarendon Press.

Serodio, A., Kopelman, B. I., & Bataglia, P. U. R. (2016). The promotion of medical students' moral development: A comparison between a traditional course on bioethics and a course complemented with the Konstanz method of dilemma discussion. *International Journal of Ethics Education, 1*, 81–89. https://doi.org/10.1007/s40889-016-0009-8

Sharif, S., Gifford, L., Morris, G., & Barber, J. (2007). An investigation of the self-evaluation skills of first year pharmacy students. *Pharmacy Education, 7*(4), 295–302. https://doi.org/10.1080/15602210701725272

Sharifian, F. (2010). Cultural conceptualisations in intercultural communication: A study of Aboriginal and non-Aboriginal Australians. *Journal of Pragmatics, 42*(12), 3367–3376. https://doi.org/10.1016/j.pragma.2010.05.006

Sharma, S., Boet, S., Kitto, S., & Reeves, S. (2011). Interprofessional simulated learning:the need for "sociological fidelity". Editorial. *Journal of Interprofessional Care, 25*, 81–83.

Sharpe R., O'Donovan, B., & Pavlakou, M. (2014). *Using the framework of engagement surveys to evaluate institutional student enhancement initiatives*. Surveys for Enhancement Conference, Birmingham, 4 June 2014.

Shay, S., & Steyn, D. (2016). Enabling knowledge progression in vocational curricula: Design as a case study. In K. Maton, S. Hood, & S. Shay (Eds.), *Knowledge-building: Educational studies in legitimation code theory*. London: Routledge.

Sheehan, T., & Palmer, R. E. (1997). *Edmund Husserl, Psychological and transcendental phenomenology and the confrontation with Heidegger (1927–1931): The Encyclopaedia Britannica Article, the Amsterdam Lectures, 'Phenomenology and Anthropology', and Husserl's Marginal Notes in Being and Time and Kant and the Problem of Metaphysics. Collected Works, Volume 6*. Dordrecht, The Netherlands: Kluwer Academic Publishers.

Shenhar, A. J., et al. (2001). Project success: A multidimensional strategic concept. *Long Range Planning, 34*(6), 699–725.
Shiller, R. (2015, May 22). What to learn in college to stay one step ahead of computers. *The New York Times: The Upshot.* https://www.nytimes.com/2015/05/24/upshot/what-to-learn-in-college-to-stay-one-step-ahead-of-computers.html
Shor, I. (1992). *Empowering education. Critical teaching for social change.* London: University of Chicago Press.
Shulman, L. (2002). Making differences. A table of learning. *Change, 34*(6), 36–44.
Silva, M. C., Sorrell, J. M., & Sorrell, C. D. (1995). From Carper's patterns of knowing to ways of being: An ontological philosophical shift in nursing. *Advances in Nursing Science, 18*(1), 1–13.
Simpson, N. Y., Onumah, J. M., & Oppong-Nkrumah, A. (2016). Ethics education and accounting programmes in Ghana: Does university ownership and affiliation status matter? *International Journal of Ethics Education, 1*, 43–56. https://doi.org/10.1007/s40889-015-0005-4
Singer, J. B. (2007). Contested autonomy: Professional and popular claims on journalistic norms. *Journalism Studies, 8*(1), 79–95. https://doi.org/10.1080/14616700601056866
Slade, C., Murfin, K., & Readman, K. (2013). Evaluating processes and platforms for potential ePortfolio use: The role of the middle agent. *International Journal of ePortfolio, 3*(2), 177–188.
Slay, H. S., & Smith, D. A. (2011, January). Professional identity construction: Using narrative to understand the negotiation of professional and stigmatized cultural identities. *Human Relations, 64*(1), 85–107. https://doi.org/10.1177/0018726710384290
Smith, J., McKnight, A., & Naylor, R. (2000). Graduate employability: Policy and performance in higher education in the UK. *The Economic Journal, 110*(464), 382–411.
Smith, M., Hargroves, K., Desha, C., & Palousis, N. (2007). *Engineering sustainable solutions program: Critical literacies portfolio—Introduction to Sustainable Development for Engineering and Built Environment Professionals.* The Natural Edge Project, Australia. (TNEP).
Snow, C. (2015). Organizing in the age of competition, cooperation, and collaboration. *Journal of Leadership & Organizational Studies, 22*(4), 433–442.
Soja, E. W. (1996). *Thirdspace: Journeys to Los Angeles and other real-and-imagined places.* Malden, MA: Blackwell.

Sonntag, M. (2006). Reflexive pedagogy in the apprenticeship in design. *European Journal of Engineering Education, 31*(1), 109–117.

Sopoaga, F., Crampton, P., Ekeroma, A., Perez, D., Maoate, K., Watson, B., ... Blattner, K. (2015). The role of New Zealand health professional training institutions in capacity building in the Pacific region. *NZMJ, 128*(1420), 6–9.

Sperber, D., & Wilson, D. (1995). *Relevance: Communication and cognition* (2nd ed.). Oxford: Blackwell.

Spinks, N., Silburn, N., & Birchall, D. (2006). *Educating engineers for the 21st century: The industry view*. Henley-on-Thames: Henley Management College.

Stabback, P. (2016). *What makes a quality curriculum?* Geneva, Switzerland: UNESCO IBE.

Stake, R. E. (2005). Qualitative case studies. In N. K. Denzin & Y. S. Lincoln (Eds.), *The Sage handbook of qualitative research* (3rd ed., pp. 443–466). Thousand Oaks, CA: Sage Publications.

Stark, J. S. (1998). Classifying professional preparation programs. *The Journal of Higher Education, 69*(4), 353–383.

Steinbock, A. J. (2001). *Edmund Husserl: Analyses concerning passive and active synthesis: Lectures on transcendental logic* (Transl.). Dordrecht, The Netherlands: Kluwer Academic Publishers.

Steinert, Y., Mann, K., Centeno, A., Dolmans, D., Spencer, J., Gelula, M., & Prideaux, D. (2006). A systematic review of faculty development initiatives designed to improve teaching effectiveness in medical education. BEME Guide No. 8. *Medical Teacher, 28*(6), 497–526.

Stern, N. (2006). *The stern review: The economics of climate change*. Cambridge: Cambridge University Press.

Sterrett, S. E. (2015). Interprofessional learning as a third space: Rethinking health profession students' development and identity through the concepts of Homi Bhabha. *Humanities, 4*, 653–660.

Stretton, A. (2007). A short history of modern project management (2nd ed.). *PM World Today, IX*(X), 1–18.

Stronach, I., Corbin, B., McNamara, O., Stark, S., & Warne, T. (2002). Towards an uncertain politics of professionalism: Teacher and nurse identities in flux. *Journal of Education Policy, 17*(1), 109–138.

Stuart, H. A. (1985). Should concept maps be scored numerically? *The European Journal of Science Education, 7*(1), 73–81.

Stückelberger, C. (2017). The significant role of higher education in developing a global ethical culture. In D. Singh & C. Stückelberger (Eds.), *Ethics in higher education* (pp. 31–52). Education Ethics No. 1. Geneva: Globalethics. net. Retrieved from http://www.globethics.net/publications

Stump, G., & Husman, J. (2014). Engineering student's intelligence beliefs and learning. *Journal of Engineering Education, 103*(3), 369–387.

Sturdy, A., & Wright, C. (2011, November). The active client: The boundary-spanning roles of internal consultants as gatekeepers, brokers and partners of their external counterparts. *Management Learning, 42*(5), 485–503. https://doi.org/10.1177/1350507611401536

Sutherland, J. (2011). *Personalising the ePortfolio experience*. Abstract for presentation at THETA Conference, 3–6 April, Sydney. Retrieved from https://ccaeducause.files.wordpress.com/2012/03/209-775-1-pb.pdf

Swan, D. (1998). The changing university: Fitness of purpose. *Irish Educational Studies, 17*(1), 272–283.

Szilagyi, J. (2008). Curricular progress assessments: The mileMarker. *American Journal of Pharmaceutical Education, 72*(5), 1–101.

Taffs, K. H., & Holt, J. I. (2013). Investigating student use and value of e-learning resources to develop academic writing within the discipline of environmental science. *Journal of Geography in Higher Education, 37*(4), 500–514.

Tait, M. (2011, June). Trust and the public interest in the micropolitics of planning practice. *Journal of Planning Education and Research, 31*(2), 157–171. https://doi.org/10.1177/0739456X11402628

Talbot, M. (2004). Monkey see, monkey do: A critique of the competency model in graduate medical education. *Medical Education, 38*(6), 587–592. https://doi.org/10.1046/j.1365-2923.2004.01794.x

Tan, K. (2013). A framework for assessment for learning: Implications for feedback practices within and beyond the gap. *Hindawi Publishing Corporation: ISRN Education, 2013*, 1–6, Article ID 640609. https://doi.org/10.1155/2013/640609

Tan, P. L., & Pillay, H. (2008). Understanding learning behaviour of Malaysian adult learners: A cross-cultural sensitive framework. *Educational Research for Policy and Practice, 7*(2), 85–97. https://doi.org/10.1007/s10671-007-9039-5

Tanner, C. A. (2004). The meaning of curriculum: Content to be covered or stories to be heard? *Journal of Nursing Education, 43*(1), 383–384.

Tansey, P. J., & Unwin, D. (1969). *Simulation and gaming in education*. London: Methuen Educational.

Task Force on Higher Education and Society. (2000). *Higher education in developing countries: Peril and promise*. Washington, DC: World Bank Retrieved from http://documents.worldbank.org/curated/en/345111467989458740/Higher-education-in-developing-countries-peril-and-promise

Tate, R. B., & Aoki, F. Y. (2012). Rural practice and the personal and educational characteristics of medical students. *Canadian Family Physician, 58*(11), e641–e648.

Taylor, E. W. (2009). Fostering transformative learning. In J. Mezirow, E. W. Taylor, & Associates (Eds.), *Transformative learning in practice: Insights from community, workplace, and higher education* (pp. 3–17). San Francisco, CA: Jossey-Bass.

Taylor, J., O'Hara, L., & Barnes, M. (2014). Health promotion: A critical salutogenic science. *International Journal of Social Work and Human Services Practice, 2*(6), 283–290.

Taylor, K. (2000). Teaching with developmental intention. In J. Mezirow & Associates (Eds.), *Learning as transformation: Critical perspectives on a theory in progress* (pp. 151–180). San Francisco, CA: Jossey-Bass.

ten Cate, T., Snell, L., & Carraccio, C. (2010). Medical competence: The interplay between individual ability and the health care environment. *Medical Teacher, 32*(8), 669–675.

TEQSA. (2015). *TEQSA and quality-assurance.* Retrieved September 28, 2015, from http://www.teqsa.gov.au/regulatory-approach/teqsa-and-quality-assurance

Tertiary Education Quality and Standards Agency. (2015). *TEQSA and quality assurance.* Retrieved from http://www.teqsa.gov.au/regulatory-approach/teqsa-and-quality-assurance

The Teaching Council. (2017). *Striking the balance. Teacher supply in Ireland: Technical Working Group report.* Dublin: Teaching Council of Ireland and Department of Education and Skills.

The Stationery Office. (2009). *Managing successful projects with PRINCE2.* Norwich, UK: The Stationery Office.

Thistlethwaite, J. (2012). Interprofessional education: A review of the context, learning and the research agenda. *Medical Education, 46,* 58–70.

Thistlethwaite, J., & Moran, M. (2010). Learning outcomes for interprofessional education (IPE): Literature reveiew and synthesis. *Journal of Interprofessional Care, 24*(5), 503–513.

Thomas, G. (2016). *How to do your case study* (2nd ed.). London: Sage Publications.

Thomas, H., & Wilson, A. D. (2011). "Physics envy", cognitive legitimacy or practical relevance: Dilemmas in the evolution of management research in the UK. *British Journal of Management, 22*(3), 443–456.

Thompson, W., Nissen, L., & Hayward, K. (2013). Australian pharmacists' understanding of their continuing professional development obligations. *The Australian Journal of Pharmacy, 94*(1123), 58–60.

Thorpe, D. (2013). Reflections on assessment: Comparison of assessment processes for postgraduate engineering management courses. In *24th Annual Conference of the Australasian Association for Engineering Education (AAEE2013)*. December 8–11, 2013, Gold Coast, QLD, Australia.

Thorpe, D. S. (2016). Experiential learning approaches for developing professional skills in postgraduate engineering students. In A. Rahman & V. Ilic (Eds.), *Proceedings of International Conference on Engineering Education and Research 21–24 November 2017 Western Sydney University, Parramatta Campus, Sydney, Australia*. Sydney, NSW: School of Computing, Engineering and Mathematics, Western Sydney University Retrieved from https://www.westernsydney.edu.au/__data/assets/pdf_file/0005/1176746/iCEER2016_Conference_Proceedings_official.pdf

Thurmond, V. & Wambach, K. (2004, June). Towards an understanding of interactions in distance education. *Online Journal of Nursing Informatics (OJNI), 8*(2). [Online]. Retrieved from http://ojni.org/8_2/interactions.htm

Tinto, V. (1993). *Leaving college: Rethinking the causes and cures of student attrition* (2d ed.). Chicago: University of Chicago Press.

Titus, J. J. (2008). Student ratings in a consumerist academy: Leveraging pedagogical control and authority. *Sociological Perspectives, 51*(2), 397–342.

Tosh, D., Light, T., Fleming, K., & Haywood, J. (2005). Engagement with electronic portfolios: Challenges from the student perspective. *Canadian Journal of Learning and Technology / La revue canadienne de l'apprentissage et de la technologie, 31*(3). https://doi.org/10.21432/T23W31

Tosterud, R. (2015a). *Simulation used as a learning approach in nursing education. Students' experiences and validation of evaluation questionnaires.* Doctoral thesis, Karlstad University Studies, 2015: 1.

Tosterud, R. (2015b). Simulering—en hensiktsmessig læringsmetode? [Simulating—A productive learning approach?]. In T. Ødegården, S. Struksnes, & B. Hofmann (Eds.), *Pasientsimulering i helsefag: en praktisk innføring* (pp. 78–87). Oslo: Gyldendal Akademisk.

Tran, D., Tofade, T., Thakkar, N., & Rouse, M. (2014). US and international health professions' requirements for continuing professional development. *American Journal of Pharmaceutical Education, 78*(6), 129. https://doi.org/10.5688/ajpe786129

Transparency International. (2017). *Corruption Perceptions Index 2016*. Retrieved from: https://www.transparency.org/news/feature/corruption_perceptions_index_2016#regional

Trede, F., & McEwen, C. (Eds.). (2016). *Educating the deliberate professional: Preparing for future practices*. New York: Springer.

References

Tremayne, P., Russell, P., & Allman, H. (2014). Service user involvement in nurse education. *Nursing Standard, 28*(22), 37–41.

Trevelyan, J. P. (2014). *The making of an expert engineer.* London: CRC Press/Balkema—Taylor & Francis.

Trigwell, K., & Prosser, M. (1996). Congruence between intention and strategy in university science teachers' approaches to teaching. *Higher Education, 32*(1), 77–87. https://doi.org/10.1007/Bf00139219

Trudgett, M. (2011). Western places, academic spaces and Indigenous faces: Supervising Indigenous Australian postgraduate students. *Teaching in Higher Education, 16*(4), 389–399.

Trudgett, M. (2014). Supervision provided to Indigenous Australian doctoral students: A black and white issue. *Higher Education Research & Development, 33*(5), 1035–1048.

Trudgett, M., Page, S., & Harrison, N. (2016). Brilliant minds: A snapshot of successful Indigenous Australian doctoral students. *The Australian Journal of Indigenous Education, 45*(1), 70–79.

Tversky, A., & Kahneman, D. (1992). Advances in prospect theory: Cumulative representation of uncertainty. *Journal of Risk and Uncertainty, 5*(4), 297–323.

Tzeng, J. (2010). Perceived values and prospective users' acceptance of prospective technology: The case of a career eportfolio system. *Computers & Education, 56*(1), 157–165.

UCAS. (2016). *UK application rates by the January deadline: 2016 cycle.* UCAS Analysis and Research, 4 February 2016. Retrieved from https://www.ucas.com/sites/default/files/jan-16-deadline-application-rates-report.pdf

UN. (2015). *Millennium Development Goals (MDG) Report.* Department of Economic and Social Affairs of the United Nations Secretariat. Retrieved from www.un.org/millenniumgoals/2015_MDG_Report/pdf

UNCED. (1992). *United Nations Conference on Environment and Development. Agenda 21: Program of Action for Sustainable Development.* New York: United Nations.

UNCSD. (2012). *United Nations Conference on Sustainable Development.* Rio+21.

UNEP. (2002). *Johannesburg Earth Summit.* Retrieved from www.unep.org/pdf/annualreport/UNEP2002

UNESCO. (2006). *Framework for the United Nations Decade of Education for Sustainable Development 2005–14: International Implementation Scheme.* ED/DESD/2006/PI/1.

UNESCO. (2016). *Small Island Developing States: UNESCO's Action Plan.* Paris, France: UNESCO Retrieved from unesdoc.unesco.org/images/0024/002 460/246082E.pdf

Universities Australia. (2011). *National best practice framework for Indigenous cultural competency in Australian universities.* Canberra, ACT.

University of Southern Queensland. (2016a). *Master of Engineering Science.* Retrieved from http://www.usq.edu.au/handbook/current/engineering-built-environment/MENS.html

University of Southern Queensland. (2016b). *Master of Engineering Practice.* Retrieved from http://www.usq.edu.au/handbook/current/engineering-built-environment/MEPR.html

University of Southern Queensland. (2016c). *Course Specification, Asset Management in an Engineering Environment, on-campus offer.* Retrieved from http://www.usq.edu.au/course/specification/2016/ENG8104-S1-2016-ONC-TWMBA.html

University of Southern Queensland. (2016d). *Course specification, ENG8103 Management of Technological Risk, on-campus offer.* Retrieved from http://www.usq.edu.au/course/specification/2016/ENG8103-S2-2016-ONC-TWMBA.html

University of Southern Queensland. (2016e). *Course specification, ENG8208 Advanced Engineering Project Management, on-campus offer.* Retrieved from http://www.usq.edu.au/course/specification/2016/ENG8208-S1-2016-ONC-TWMBA.html

University of Southern Queensland. (2017a). *Course specification: ENG8104 Asset Management in an Engineering Environment.* Toowoomba, QLD: Author.

University of Southern Queensland. (2017b). *Course specification: ENG8208 Advanced Engineering Project Management.* Toowoomba, QLD: Author.

University of Southern Queensland. (2017c). *USQ handbook: Engineering and built environment.* Retrieved from https://usq.edu.au/handbook/current/engineering-built-environment/engineering-built-environment.html

University of Technology Sydney. (2017). *Master of Engineering (extension).* Retrieved from https://www.masterstudies.com/Master-of-Engineering-(Extension)/Australia/UTS/

University of the Sunshine Coast. (2013a). *Graduate attributes.* Retrieved from http://www.usc.edu.au/explore/vision/learning-and-teaching/graduate-attributes

University of the Sunshine Coast. (2013b). *Principles informing assessment*. Retrieved from http://www.usc.edu.au/university/governance-and-executive/policies-and-procedures/assessment-courses-and-coursework-programs-academic-policy

UN-WCED. (1987). *UN World Commission on Environment and Development: 'Our Common Future'*. Oxford University Press. ISBN 019282080X.

Usher, K., Lindsay, D., Miller, M., & Miller, A. (2005). Challenges faced by Indigenous nursing students and strategies that aided their progress in the course: A descriptive study. *Contemporary Nurse, 19*(1–2), 17–31.

Uskov, V. (2010). *Advanced web-based education: The next five years and beyond*. Peoria: Bradley University.

Van Bilzen, G. (2015). *The development of aid*. Newcastle Upon Tyne: Cambridge Scholars Publishing.

Van den Akker, J., Gravemeijer, K., McKenney, S., & Nieveen, N. (2006). *Educational design research*. Abingdon, Oxon: Routledge.

Vanderstraeten, R. (2002). Parsons, Luhmann and the theorem of double contingency. *Journal of Classical Sociology, 2*(1), 77–92.

Van der Velden, G., Pool, A. D., Lowe, J. A., Naidoo, R., & Pimentel Botas, P. C. (2013). *Student engagement in learning and teaching quality management: A good practice guide for higher education providers and students' unions*. QAA and University of Bath.

Van der Vleuten, C., & Schuwirth, L. (2005). Assessing professional competence: From methods to programmes. *Medical Education, 39*(3), 309–317.

Van Mannen, M. (1990). *Researching lived experience human science for an action sensitive pedagogy*. Albany, NY: State University of New York Press.

Van Meerkerk, I., Edelenbos, J., & Klijn, E.-H. (2015). Connective management and governance network performance: The mediating role of throughput legitimacy. Findings from survey research on complex water projects in the Netherlands. *Environment and Planning C: Government and Space, 33*(4), 746–764.

Vermunt, J. D., & Verloop, N. (1999). Congruence and friction between learning and teaching. *Learning and Instruction, 9*, 257–280.

Virtual Site. (n.d.) [Online]. Retrieved December 8, 2017, from http://www.leedsbeckett.ac.uk/teaching/vsite/

Von Glasersfeld, E. (1989). Learning as a constructive activity. In P. Murphy & B. Moon (Eds.), *Developments in learning and assessment*. London: Hodder and Stoughton.

Vygotsky, L. S. (1978). *Mind in society: The development of higher psychological processes*. Cambridge, MA: Harvard University Press.

Wächter, B., Kelo, M., Lam, Q. K. H., Effertz, P., Jost, C., & Kottowski, S. (2015). *University quality indicators: A critical assessment*. European Union: Directorate General for Internal Policy: Policy Department B: Structural and Cohesion Policies Culture and Education.

Wagner, R. K., & Sternberg, R. J. (1985). Practical intelligence in real-world pursuits: The role of tacit knowledge. *Journal of Personalily and Social Psychology, 49*(2), 436–458.

Wake, D. (2012). *How nurses talk about ethics*. North Melbourne, VIC: Ausmed Education Pty Ltd Retrieved from http://www.ausmed.com.au/learning-centre/how-nurses-talk-about-ethics-part-1-description

Walker, M. (2010). Critical capability pedagogies and university education. *Educational Philosophy and Theory, 42*(8), 898–917.

Walker, M., & McLean, M. (2009, December 8). *A public good professional capability index for university-based professional education in South Africa*. Presentation to Society for Research in Higher Education, UK. Retrieved from http://www.nottingham.ac.uk/educationresearchprojects/developmentdiscourses/conferencesandpresentations.aspx

Walker, M., & McLean, M. (2013). *Professional education, capabilities and the public good: The role of universities in promoting human development*. London: Routledge.

Walker, M., & McLean, M. (2015). Professionals and public-good capabilities. *Critical Studies in Teaching and Learning (CriSTaL), 3*(2), 60–82 Retrieved from http://eprints.nottingham.ac.uk/32146/1/Prof%20and%20Pub%20good.pdf

Walsh Brennan, A. M., & Cotter, V. T. (2008). Student perceptions of cultural competence content in the curriculum. *Journal of Professional Nursing, 24*(3), 155–160.

Wankel, C., & Law, J. S. (2012). *Streaming media delivery in higher education: Methods and outcomes*. Hershey, PA: Information Reference Section.

Warren, J. N., et al. (2016). A systematic review of the effectiveness of simulation-based education on satisfaction and learning outcomes in nurse practitioner programs. *Nurse Education Today, 46*, 98–108.

Wass, V., Van der Vleuten, C., Shatzer, J., & Jones, R. (2001). Assessment of clinical competence. *The Lancet, 357*(9260), 945–949. https://doi.org/10.1016/S0140-6736(00)04221-5

Watson, L. (2003). *Lifelong learning in Australia*. Canberra: Commonwealth of Australia Retrieved from http://www.forschungsnetzwerk.at/downloadpub/australia_lll_03_13.pdf

Weick, K. E. (1979). *The social psychology of organizing* (2nd ed.). Reading, MA: Addison-Wesley.

Weick, K. E. (1995). *Sensemaking in organizations*. Thousand Oaks, CA: SAGE.

Weidman, J. C., Twale, D. J., & Stein, E. L. (2001). *Socialization of graduate and professional students in higher education. ASHE-ERIC Higher Education Report Volume 28, Number 3*. San Francisco, CA: Jossey-Bass.

Wellard, S. J., & Heggen, K. M. (2010). Are laboratories useful fiction? A comparison of Norwegian and Australian undergraduate nursing skills laboratories. *Nursing & Health Sciences, 12*(1), 39–44. https://doi.org/10.1111/j.1442-2018.2009.00481.x

Wellard, S. J., Solvoll, B.-A., & Heggen, K. M. (2009). Picture of Norwegian clinical learning laboratories for undergraduate nursing students. *Nurse Education in Practice, 9*(4), 228–235 https://doi.org/10.1016/j.nepr.2008.06.005

Wenger, E. (1998). *Communities of practice: Learning meaning and identity*. Cambridge: Cambridge University Press.

Westbroek, H. B., Klaassen, K., Bulte, A., & Pilot, A. (2010). Providing students with a sense of purpose by adapting a professional practice. *International Journal of Science Education, 32*(5), 603–627.

Wetzel, K., & Strudler, N. (2006). Costs and benefits of electronic portfolios in teacher education: Student voices. *Journal of Computing in Teacher Education, 22*(3), 99–108.

WFME [World Foundation for Medical Education]. (2015). Final 2015 Revision of 2012 Basic Medical Education Standards. Retrieved from http://wfme.org/standards/bme

Wheelahan, L. (2007). How competency-based training locks the working class out of powerful knowledge: A modified Bernsteinian analysis. *British Journal of Sociology of Education, 28*(5), 637–651.

Whitchurch, C. (2008). Shifting identities and blurring boundaries: The emergence of third space professionals in UK higher education. *Higher Education Quarterly, 62*(4), 377–396.

White, J. (1995). Patterns of knowing: Review, critique and update. *Advances in Nursing Science, 17*(4), 73–86.

Wiggins, G., & McTighe, J. (1998). *Understanding by design*. Alexandria, VA: Association for Supervision and Curriculum Development.

Williams, J. (2015, August 13). The National Student Survey should be abolished before it does any more harm. *The Guardian*.
Williams, M., & Jordan, K. (2007). The nursing professional portfolio: A pathway to career development. *Journal for Nurses in Staff Development, 23*(3), 125–131.
Wilson, J., Mandich, A., & Magalhães, L. (2015). Concept mapping: A dynamic, individualized and qualitative method for eliciting meaning. *Qualitative Health Research, 26*(8), 1151–1161.
Wingate, R., & Kwint, M. (2006). Imagining the brain cell: The neuron in visual culture. *Nature Reviews Neuroscience, 7*, 745–752.
Winter, C. (2007). Knowledge and the curriculum: Derrida, deconstruction and 'sustainable development'. *London Review of Education, 5*(1), 69–82. https://doi.org/10.1080/14748460701243267
Wisker, G., & Robinson, G. (2014). Examiner practices and culturally inflected doctoral theses. *Discourse: Studies in the Cultural Politics of Education, 35*(2), 190–205.
Wittgenstein, L. (1986). *Philosophical investigations* (G. E. M. Anscombe, Trans.). Oxford: Basil Blackwell.
Wolff, A. C., Pesut, B., & Regan, S. (2010). New graduate nurse practice readiness: Perspectives on the context shaping our understanding and expectations. *Nurse Education Today, 30*(2), 187–191.
Wong, Q. Y.-Y. (2012). An alternative view of quality assurance and enhancement. *Management in Education, 26*(1), 38–42.
Wood, L., Thomas, T., & Rigby, B. (2011). Assessment and standards for graduate outcomes. *Asian Social Science, 7*(4), 12–17.
World Bank. (2011). *PNG health workforce crisis: A call to action*. Washington, DC: World Bank.
World Health Organization. (2010). *Framework for action on interprofessional education and collaboration practice*. Geneva: S & B Graphic Design.
World Health Organization. (2011). *Patient safety curriculum guide: Multi- professional Edition*. Malta. ISBN 9789241501958.
Wu, H.-Y., Lin, Y.-K., & Chang, C.-H. (2011, February). Performance evaluation of extension education centers in universities based on the balanced scorecard. *Evaluation and Program Planning, 34*(1), 37–50. https://doi.org/10.1016/j.evalprogplan.2010.06.001
Yielder, J. (2004). An integrated model of professional expertise and its implications for higher education. *International Journal of Lifelong Education, 23*(1), 60–80.

Yin, R. K. (2012). *Applications of case study research* (3rd ed.). Thousand Oaks, CA: Sage Publications.
Yin, R. K. (2014). *Case study research: Design and methods* (5th ed.). Thousand Oaks, CA: Sage Publications.
Yorke, M. (2005). *Employability in higher education: What it is—What it is not.* York: Higher Education Academy.
Young, M., & Muller, J. (2013). On the powers of powerful knowledge. *Review of Education, 1*(3), 229–250.
Young, M. F. D. (2003). National qualifications frameworks as a global phenomenon: A comparative perspective. *Journal of Education and Work, 16*(3), 223–237.
Zhao, C.-M., Golde, C. M., & McCormick, A. C. (2007). More than a signature: How advisor choice and advisor behaviour affect doctoral student satisfaction. More than a signature: How advisor choice and advisor behaviour affect doctoral student satisfaction. *Journal of Further and Higher Education, 31*(3), 263–281.

Index

A
Adaptive expertise, 74, 79–81, 85
Advanced, 96, 100, 103, 122–124, 139–158
Austerity, 18, 47–64, 209
Australia, 19, 30, 97, 98, 103, 116, 120, 121, 123, 128, 130, 162, 163, 165, 176, 192, 196, 201, 206, 208, 209
Autopoiesis, 14, 15

C
Competency development model (CDM), 170, 172–178
Complexity, 20, 48, 61, 102, 143, 157, 172, 202
Concept mapping, 18, 72–75, 80, 83, 85, 203
Conceptual knowledge, 82
Continuing professional development, 19, 95, 116, 125–127
Corruption, 99, 100
Course Experience Questionnaire (CEQ), 31, 34, 39
Curriculum, 2–4, 16, 18, 20, 51, 62, 75, 76, 103, 104, 164, 166, 168, 170, 172, 178, 184, 201–211

D
Developing countries, 18, 91–109

E
Education, 2, 30, 50, 71, 91–109, 116, 148, 162, 184, 201

Embedding, 164, 204, 208
Employer engagement, 61–63
Engineering, 7, 19, 20, 51, 56, 57, 62, 96, 100, 116, 118–125, 127–131, 139–158, 161–180, 183–198, 202, 204, 206–208
ePortfolio, 19, 170–171, 177, 207
Ethical education, 101, 106, 118
Evaluation, 18, 29, 31, 33–35, 37, 38, 40–42, 50, 51, 128, 140, 146, 152–154, 168, 170, 176, 177, 186, 209, 210
Extension learning, 19, 116, 117, 119–123, 125–131, 208

Globalisation, 141, 189
Government regulation, 48–51, 98
Graduate employability, 48, 52–54
Graduate outcomes, 20, 32, 37

Higher education, 2, 4–6, 8, 18–20, 29–31, 34, 41, 42, 47–54, 56, 61–64, 92, 94–96, 98, 99, 105, 108, 116, 131, 201–203, 205, 209, 210
Higher Education management, 18, 29–42

Immanent, 10–11, 16
Institutional benchmarking, 39

Integrity, 7, 11–12, 91, 92, 99, 105, 107
Intentional, 8–10

Marketization, 30, 31
Marketization of higher education, 30
Measurement, 53, 127

National Student Survey (NSS), 29, 30, 33, 34, 36–40
National Survey of Student Engagement (NSSE), 31, 36, 37, 39

Papua New Guinea (PNG), 19, 92, 97–100, 207
Participative research methods, 41, 42
Pedagogic frailty, 79–81, 204
Perceptual, 8, 10–11
Performance, 2, 4–7, 9, 11, 12, 16, 18, 30, 36, 49, 53, 56, 58, 63, 124, 128, 140–142, 144, 163, 172, 174, 176, 209
Political and economic contexts, 20, 183–198
Postgraduate, 19, 116, 122, 123, 125, 128, 129, 140, 146, 151, 152
Postgraduate education, 116, 120, 201

Powerful knowledge, 79, 84
Practice, 2–4, 11, 12, 15–20, 30, 35, 40, 42, 49, 50, 55, 57, 61, 72, 74, 76, 77, 79–85, 91–109, 116–118, 120, 122–126, 128–131, 139–141, 143, 145, 146, 148–150, 154, 164, 166, 167, 169–172, 174–177, 179, 188–190, 202–204, 206–210
Procedural knowledge, 82
Professional education, 2–5, 15–20, 30, 34, 35, 37, 38, 40, 53, 71–85, 91–96, 99, 101, 102, 106–108, 117, 128–131, 203, 207, 210
Professional ethics, 97, 99, 101
Professions, 1–20, 51, 53, 55–57, 63, 91, 93–96, 99, 100, 102, 107, 108, 115–118, 122, 123, 125, 127, 130, 131, 158, 163, 165, 186, 188, 193, 201–203, 205–210
Project management, 19, 122, 124, 139–158, 204

Q

Quality, 1–20, 29–31, 34–36, 38, 40, 47–64, 91–109, 115–131, 139, 141, 143, 149, 156, 157, 161–180, 186, 193, 201–211
Quality assurance (QA), 7, 18, 20, 40, 48–50, 52–61, 63, 64, 98, 108, 163–164, 201
Quality of purpose, 3–5

R

Reflective practice, 19, 74, 105, 106, 124, 166, 169–171, 174, 175, 177, 207
Reliability, 29, 37, 140, 141, 144
Resilience, 104, 107, 127, 191, 195
Risk, 38, 101, 123, 127, 140, 143–146, 148, 151, 153, 154, 157, 209, 210

S

Sample, 39
Sampling methods, 33–34
Scaffolding, 167–168, 171, 177
Semantic density (SD), 76, 77, 79
Semantic gravity (SG), 76, 77, 79
Semantic plane, 77–79, 85
Social, 4, 15, 20, 53, 56, 59, 72, 73, 93, 95, 97, 98, 100, 103, 105, 107, 108, 115, 118, 120, 126, 129, 162, 183–198, 202, 205–207, 210
Stakeholder, 5, 8, 13–14, 16, 18, 52, 103, 121, 124, 140, 142, 144–146, 148, 152, 156, 203, 204, 208–210
Student evaluations of teaching, 31, 38, 40, 154
Student experience, 18, 29–42, 51, 55, 178
Student representatives, 40, 41
Student satisfaction, 4, 34, 35, 42, 55, 209, 210
Success, 14, 16, 19, 37, 53, 81, 140–147, 150, 151, 154, 157, 172

Surveys, 18, 29–42, 49, 50, 55, 61, 154, 155, 186, 209, 210
Sustainability, 8, 20, 58, 105, 116, 119, 124, 129, 130, 140, 142, 144, 145, 148, 153, 183–188, 190–192, 203, 206, 208
Sustainable engineering education, 19, 183–198
System of profound knowledge (SPK), 1, 9

Temporality, 12–13
Throughput, 6–8, 16
Training, 19, 62, 91, 102, 103, 108, 119, 125–129, 142, 162, 166, 190, 201
Transformation, 2, 3, 6–8, 16, 85, 202–210

Universities, 10, 16, 18, 19, 29–37, 39, 41, 42, 47–64, 72, 80, 92, 95, 98, 100, 101, 103–105, 107, 116, 120, 121, 123, 126, 127, 148, 158, 162, 163, 166, 186, 189, 202–210

Validity, 29, 37, 41
Venezuela, 19, 116, 120, 125, 126, 128, 130, 208

Whole of course engineering curriculum, 20, 161–180